Equivocal Death

Equivocal Death: Investigating Suicide, Accidental, and other Questionable Deaths refocuses the attention of first responders and investigative personnel to the concept of treating every death as a homicide, until sufficient evidence is discovered to validate another manner of death and eliminate the possibility of a staged homicide.

All death investigations should include a well-documented and examined crime scene and a thorough preliminary investigation. It is a well-established, unwritten "rule" when conducting death investigations to initially treat every death as a possible homicide. This includes the examination of the body, the recovery scene, the autopsy, collection of forensic evidence, and subsequent laboratory analysis. Police and investigators are often confronted with a death scene that they cannot initially determine the manner of death; these instances are known as *equivocal death*.

Coverage focuses on the basics of death investigation and the *how to's* rather than dwelling on extraneous and unnecessary detail. By example, it is generally more important for the detective or CSI to understand how to properly pick up forensic evidence at the scene, and how the resulting analysis relates to their investigation, rather than the mechanics of how the evidence is extracted and analyzed at the lab. For suicide and equivocal deaths, it is likewise important that detectives also understand the importance of such things as a victimology assessment, risk factors, and/or antemortem behaviors of the victim – that may provide clues that would be consistent with someone contemplating suicide. The book also features several aspects of criminal investigation that are not found in similar books, including coverage of victimology, crime scene staging, the notion of psychology autopsy, and how to identify those risk factors or behaviors that are consistent with suicide, including motive, intent, and ability.

Equivocal Death: Investigating Suicide, Accidental, and other Questionable Deaths serves as an essential reference for the detective, crime scene investigators, coroners and medical examiners, medicolegal investigators, and prosecutors actively involved in ~of cases.

Equivocal Death
Investigating Suicide, Accidental, and other Questionable Deaths

Arthur S. Chancellor

CRC Press is an imprint of the
Taylor & Francis Group, an **informa** business

Front cover image: Arthur S. Chancellor

First edition published 2025
by CRC Press
2385 NW Executive Center Drive, Suite 320, Boca Raton FL 33431

and by CRC Press
4 Park Square, Milton Park, Abingdon, Oxon, OX14 4RN

CRC Press is an imprint of Taylor & Francis Group, LLC

© 2025 Arthur S. Chancellor

Reasonable efforts have been made to publish reliable data and information, but the author and publisher cannot assume responsibility for the validity of all materials or the consequences of their use. The authors and publishers have attempted to trace the copyright holders of all material reproduced in this publication and apologize to copyright holders if permission to publish in this form has not been obtained. If any copyright material has not been acknowledged please write and let us know so we may rectify in any future reprint.

Except as permitted under U.S. Copyright Law, no part of this book may be reprinted, reproduced, transmitted, or utilized in any form by any electronic, mechanical, or other means, now known or hereafter invented, including photocopying, microfilming, and recording, or in any information storage or retrieval system, without written permission from the publishers.

For permission to photocopy or use material electronically from this work, access www.copyright.com or contact the Copyright Clearance Center, Inc. (CCC), 222 Rosewood Drive, Danvers, MA 01923, 978-750-8400. For works that are not available on CCC please contact mpkbookspermissions@tandf.co.uk

Trademark notice: Product or corporate names may be trademarks or registered trademarks and are used only for identification and explanation without intent to infringe.

ISBN: 978-1-032-44779-7 (hbk)
ISBN: 978-1-032-44773-5 (pbk)
ISBN: 978-1-003-37386-5 (ebk)

DOI: 10.4324/9781003373865

Typeset in Minion
by Newgen Publishing UK

I want to dedicate this book to Tara, one of the first cases that I consulted on after I retired. It is one of the most frustrating cases I have ever worked on. As described multiple times in the text, the police made an instantaneous decision upon arrival at her scene that she had committed suicide. The police only completed a A three-page police report, requested no forensic exams and no forensic autopsy was conducted. There were no interviews conducted, no toxicology, and no motive or risk factors were ever established for her suicide. The police responded, took ten photos of the scene, but collected no evidence, and conducted no further investigation. Then they provided erroneous information to the family about the scene and their findings on multiple occasions, and when challenged, the police became extremely uncooperative. Efforts to get the police to reopen the case, even when they were presented with a detailed event analysis and forensic evidence that countered their finding, the police declined to do anything. It was while working on this case that I made a personal commitment to Tara that I would write this book to help detectives understand these events and hopefully prevent any other family from going through what Tara's family has gone through for over eight years now. I hope I have succeed. Tara this is for you.

Contents

Preface	**xiii**
Acknowledgments	**xvii**
About the Author	**xix**

1 Introduction to Death Investigations — 1

Detective's Role in Death Investigations	2
Why Treat Every Death Case as a Homicide?	3
Extent of the Problem	7
Cause and Manner of Death	9
Equivocal Deaths	10
Suicide Investigations	11
Stages of Grief	17
Denial	17
Anger	18
Bargaining	18
Depression	19
Acceptance	19
Establishing and Maintaining a Working Relationship with the Family	19
Chapter Summary	22

2 The Initial Response and Preliminary Investigation for Suicides — 24

Preliminary Investigation	24
The 911 Call	25
Scene Documentation	25
Physical Evidence	26
Informational or Testimonial	26
Behavioral	27
Reactions to Reported Suicides	27
Antemortem Activities of the Victim	28
Explanation of Events	32
Changes in the Explanation of Events	33
Precipitating Event	36

viii

Contents

Suicide Notes	37
Who Would Benefit from the Death?	37
Chapter Summary	38

3 Staged Crime Scenes — 39

Introduction to Crime Scene Staging	39
Ad Hoc Staged Scenes	40
Premeditated Staged Scenes	41
Motives Behind Staging	43
Suicides that Are Staged to Resemble Homicides	44
Tertiary or Incidental Scene Alterations	54
Chapter Summary	56

4 The Crime Scene — 59

Responding to Reported Deaths	59
The First Responders Role	64
Arrival of Detectives	66
The CSI Response	69
Burned Bridges	71
Scene Documentation – Photography	73
Written Notes	74
Crime Scene from the Detective's Perspective	74
Time of Death	75
Release of the Body	76
Search Beyond the Scene	77
Completion of Crime Scene Examination	77
Chapter Summation	78

5 Forensic Autopsy — 79

The Need for Autopsy	79
Working with the Medical Examiner (ME)	80
The Autopsy	81
Cause of Death vs. Manner of Death	83
Time of Death and Postmortem Interval	84
Identify and Document All Injuries	86
Gunshot Injuries	87
Location of Injury	87
Distance between Firearm and Injury	89
Correlating the Weapon with the Injury	91
Sharp Force Injuries	93
Incised Wounds	95
Stab Wounds	96

Contents   ix

Location of Injury	97
Shape of Wounds	97
Wound Orientation	98
Correlate an Injury to Objects Producing the Injury	100
Hanging	101
Hanging Injuries	101
Accidental Hanging	102
Drug Overdose	103
Toxicology	104
Chapter Summation	104

6   Victimology   107

Victimology Concept	107
Victimology Assessment	109
Factual Information	109
Subjective Criteria	110
Teenagers	113
Subjective Criteria for Teens	114
Adolescents	117
Risk Factors	119
Gathering Victimology Information	120
Employment	121
Investigative Uses of Victimology	122
Domestic Issues	125
Assessing Risk	126
High-Risk Victims	126
Moderate or Medium Risk	127
Low Risk	127
Chapter Summary	128

7   The Latent Investigation   131

After the Preliminary	131
The Latent Investigation	133
Evidence	134
Theory of the Crime	135
Scientific Method	136
Investigative Plan	137
Homicide Investigative Considerations	139
Suicide Investigative Considerations	140
Motive	140
Intent	141
Complex Suicides	142

Ability	144
Precipitating Event	146
Suicide Notes	147
Recent Changes to Wills or Insurance	147
General Suicide Investigative Concepts	148
Suicides Staged to Resemble Homicides	150
Psychological Autopsy	152
Outlines for Psychological Autopsy	154
Value to the Investigation	155
Court Acceptance	156
Chapter Summary	156

8 Notes or Last Communication — 159

Suicide Notes Are Important but Are Not Always Present	160
General Categories of Suicide Notes	160
The Format of the Note	162
Social Media and Bystander Apathy	164
Live Streaming of a Suicide	165
Interpreting Suicide Notes	166
Suicide Notes and Equivocal Deaths	168
Suicide Note Investigation	169
Suicide Note Authenticity	172
Suicide Note Investigative Considerations	175
Chapter Summation	176

9 Atypical or Special Suicides — 179

Introduction	179
Sacred Suicides	179
Military Suicides	180
Suicides as a Dramatic Performance	181
Suicide by Cop (SbC)	184
Primary Indicators of Suicidal Intent	185
Secondary Indicators of Suicidal Intent	185
Evidence of Irrational Thought	186
Minimal Evidence of Suicidal Intentions	186
Murder-Suicide	187
Mercy	191
Justice	192
Duty	194
Heroic Glory	194
Chapter Summary	195

Contents   xi

10 Accidental Deaths 197

Introduction to Accidental Deaths	197
Responding to Accidental Deaths	197
Preliminary Investigation of Accidental Deaths	199
Vehicle Accidents	200
Accidental Falls	203
Accidental Fires	208
Drowning	213
Firearm Accidental Deaths	216
Chapter Summary	219

11 Accidental Death Latent Investigation 221

Introduction	221
Victimology and Accidental Deaths	221
Limiting Physical Abilities	222
Antemortem Behaviors and Events	222
Multiple "Accidents"	231
Chapter Summary	235

12 Common Investigative Mistakes 236

Complacency and Routine Cases	236
Assuming a Suicide Posture	237
Improper Scene Documentation	237
Failing to Believe or Listen to the Family	237
Failure to Request or Conduct an Autopsy	238
Failure to Obtain Toxicological Samples	238
Failure to Look for also and Validate Risk Factors	239
Failure to Conduct Victimology Assessment	239
Interviews with Next of Kin and Family	239
Failure to Interview Significant Witnesses	240
Failure to Seek Corroborating Evidence	240
Developing Tunnel Vision	241
Failure to Consider Motive, Intent, and Ability (MIA) When Considering Suicide	241
Conducting an Incomplete Investigation	241
Failure to Properly Document Police Activity	242
Failure to Follow Logical Leads	243
Investigation Stopped Too Early	245
Failure to Fully Exploit Digital Evidence	245
Overdependence on Forensic Evidence	245
Misunderstanding Forensic Analysis	246

xii Contents

Failure to Send Evidence to the Lab 247
Lack of Supervisory Oversight 248
Chapter Summary 249

Appendix: Homicide Staged as a Suicide 251
Summary 261
Index 263

Preface

This book is about an investigation of equivocal deaths that generally revolve around accidental, suicide, and homicide. This a vital book because in most textbooks related to death investigations, suicide is usually covered in only a few pages, and in books on crime scenes, a suicide scene seems to be lacking. Accidental deaths are seldom covered at all. One reason is because neither suicide nor an accidental death is a criminal act. Therefore, there's not going to be an arrest or a trial. Police often look at suicide or accidental deaths as routine happenings, and any such investigation is a waste of manpower and resources.

Unfortunately, most detectives are not aware that suicide and accidental deaths are two of the top four themes used to stage a scene to misdirect a police investigation. The goal of the staging effort is to get past the first responder, and if successful, there will probably be no further investigation. Because of the typical police response to these events, one has to wonder how many homicides were not discovered and how many offenders got away with murder.

The real genesis for this textbook is my consulting with multiple families unhappy with the police investigation into their family member's death. Having worked dozens of suicide cases personally and then supervised and approved over 100 others throughout my career, I truly believed when I started consulting, my review was going to be an exercise of translating the police investigation and their findings to help the families understand the investigation.

As a consultant, I've had the chance to review suicide cases from several different jurisdictions across the United States and even several in the United Kingdom, and I am sad to conclude that the police are woefully inadequate in conducting suicide investigations, dealing with families of the deceased, and most lack any detailed knowledge of the suicide event and what leads a person to commit suicide. This may seem like a harsh indictment of our law enforcement, but I have seen the same mistakes made by different police agencies, regardless of agency size or where the event took place. Family members also report similar complaints, including the police did not listen to them, the police were not interested in any information or evidence they might have, and the police did not provide them with basic details of the investigation. The police investigations I've reviewed universally failed to identify any antemortem behaviors or risk factors that would be consistent with suicide. Perhaps the most upsetting was the typical police response to family's questions about their loved one's death is to refuse to cooperate, decline to speak further to the family, or provide the family any information, including a copy of their final police reports.

After a few cases, it was also easy to see the same pattern of how police responded to scenes, how they conducted their investigations, and how they treated the families. I also saw how the families learn there is no recourse open to them if the police decline to further investigate. No matter the other information or evidence families have presented to the police, if the police decide, the case is closed. Then it's closed, and there is no other state agency for them to appeal that decision.

The idea for this book was to address certain common-sense procedures and provide detectives guidelines when responding to the scene, establishing early contact with the family, turning the family into cooperating witnesses, and what steps to take during the initial stages of the investigation. The purpose is to hopefully counter what can only be described as *police complacency and extremely poor public relations.*

Many of these guidelines are really based on responding to homicide cases, because even if reported as a suicide or an accidental death, all deaths should be initially looked at as homicides until they can be proven otherwise. In keeping with this general concept, Chapter 1 covers the initial response and the duties of the first responder and detective to the scene. Just as important is some guidance on the importance of interacting with the family at this highly emotional time. This first interaction with the family can set the tone for the entire investigation and either start building trust and confidence in the police or mistrust and hard feelings toward the police.

Chapter 2 stresses the importance of the preliminary investigation, those initial steps during the first 48–72 hours, when there are so many critical tasks that need to be accomplished.

Chapter 3 details the concept of crime scene staging and provides the rationale why every death should be looked at as a homicide to prevent someone from altering the scene and getting away with a murder.

Chapter 4 details the basics of a crime scene examination from the detective's perspective. Again, most of the guidance is similar to a homicide scene, but this ensures there are no short cuts that could impact the investigation at a later date. There is a concept that is very valuable in these cases: *It's better to have the evidence and not need it, than to need the evidence and not have it.*

Chapter 5 details the importance of conducting a forensic *autopsy* and toxicology analysis even when the *cause of death* appears to be evident. There

Preface

are other factors and information that may be useful during the investigation. Even if nothing useful is gained after the examination, at least you know there was nothing there and no one can second guess the investigation.

Chapter 6 details the importance and necessity of conducting a *Victimology assessment*. This is one of the most important aspects of any violent crime investigation but one of the most ignored or improperly completed. No one commits suicide suddenly or without a reason, and a Victimology assessment will help identify the presence of any of the risk factors or suicidal behaviors that would be consistent with suicide. However, the absence of such risk factors and suicidal behaviors is a red flag that demands additional investigation.

Chapter 7 details the investigative steps taken after the crime scene, autopsy, and preliminary investigation are completed. The investigation now turns to completing the other important investigative leads that are related to both homicide and suicide investigations, including coming up with the theory of the crime or what happened during the event. The scientific method is presented as a useful tool to complete an organized and methodical review of each theory of what happened.

Chapter 8 discussed the presence and importance of the suicide note, or the last communication of the deceased.

Chapter 9 outlines atypical or unusual suicides that occur infrequently but will generate media attention and require additional investigation. Such events include *suicide as a dramatic event, suicide by cop*, and *murder/suicide*. This chapter addresses an unusual finding in the research that it is *suicide* that is first accepted and planned, then another event, such as a murder, is planned in conjunction with suicide.

Chapters 10 and 11 address the importance of investigating accidental deaths. Since there are more accidental deaths than homicides, police are more likely to be called to these scenes more than a homicide. It is important to remember that accidental deaths are also among the top four themes used to stage a homicide by making it appear to be the result of an accident. Therefore, it is imperative that these scenes and events are also looked at with a critical eye to make sure they are actually accidental.

Chapter 12 addresses some of the more common investigative errors that result from poor training or a lack of experience and are repeated by detectives across the United States.

There are numerous texts on the whole subject of suicide written from various sociological and psychological perspectives dedicated to understanding the reasons behind acts of self-destruction. I have wanted to write this text for a long time after my business partner Grant Graham and I wrote an early text *Crime Scene Staging*: Investigating Suspect Misdirection of the Crime Scene and first researched the concept of staging and saw how staged suicides were so common. I also have personally reopened a closed suicide investigation and was able to prove that it was a murder as documented in the Appendix of this text. Resulting in a conviction of the offender. During that case, I realized how little I really knew about the subject of suicide and started studying the event to make sure I would not miss something in the future. That's what this text is about. Helping detectives understand the entire event of suicide and being able to recognize when something is missing. This text is written for detectives and in their language. It is designed to provide ideas and investigative tips for confirming the death is the result of suicide or developing evidence that the death is inconsistent with suicide. There is a sad fact that if the detective fails to recognize the signs at the scene or fails to identify the motive or reasons behind the suicide, they may unintentionally help someone get away with murder.

Detectives this is for you – go and solve your cases.

A. Chancellor

Acknowledgments

I want to express my deepest thoughts to Mark Listewnik from Taylor and Francis Publishing for all of his assistance through this process. Especially being patient through this year as I had multiple issues that caused some delay. But he was always there, and it is much appreciated.

Also, a special thank you to Stephanie Davies from the United Kingdom, who wrote Chapter 8 of this text on Last Communications. Stephanie is a good friend and an exceptional crime scene analyst. I appreciate her assistance greatly.

About the Author

Arthur S. "Steve" Chancellor began his law enforcement career in 1973 when he enlisted in the US Army as a Military Policeman. He remained in the MPs until 1981, when he was accepted into the US Army Criminal Investigation Division (CID) program as a Special Agent. As a CID Special Agent, Steve worked on felony crimes at various military posts across the United States and overseas. He later commanded three different CID units and in 2001 retired as a Chief Warrant Officer Four as the Operations Officer for a CID battalion where he was responsible for the supervision of 5 different CID units and covered an 11-state area of responsibility. Once retired, Steve was employed by the Mississippi State Crime Lab as a senior crime scene analyst and conducted the examination of over 200 violent crime scenes across the state of Mississippi. In 2004, Steve was transferred from the crime lab to the Mississippi Bureau of Investigation (MBI) as the first director of the MBI Cold Case Unit, responsible for assisting police agencies across the state working on unresolved homicides. While working at the crime lab and MBI, Steve helped develop several different training courses for the Mississippi State Police Academy covering topics that included basic and advanced crime scenes, death investigations, and adult sex crimes. Steve was also involved in the development and as an instructor of the Certified Investigator Program (CIP) at the MS State Police Academy. Steve has a master's degree and undergrad degrees in criminal justice, is a graduate of the FBI National Academy (Session 185), and has been a college adjunct instructor for Austin Peay State University, Clarksville, Tennessee; the University of Mississippi, Oxford, Mississippi; and Clayton State University, Morrow, Georgia. He is a fellow of the American Academy of Forensic Science and a member of the International Association for Identification (IAI), the International Homicide Investigators Association (IHIA), the North Carolina Homicide Investigators Association, and the Southeastern Homicide Investigators Association. Steve is also the coauthor of the books *Staged Crime Scenes: Investigating Suspect Misdirection of the Crime Scene Death Investigations: 1st and 2nd editions*, co-authored Homicide: Guidelines for Conducting Homicide Investigations, by Detectives for Detectives, and the author of *Investigating Sexual Assault Cases*. Steve has also developed and instructed courses on staged crime scenes, adult sex crimes, death investigation, and basic and advanced crime scene examination.

Introduction to Death Investigations

It is almost universally accepted by law enforcement professionals that *death* is the most serious of all crimes or events that detectives are called to investigate. Traditionally, detectives responsible for death investigations are part of a *homicide unit* within the detective division of a police department. Because of the seriousness of the event, those assigned are generally the most experienced and best trained detectives within the department. Most detectives first gain their investigative experience by working on lower-level crimes for several years before they are ever selected to move up to investigating homicides. The logic and tradition that the best detectives should be working the most serious of cases, has been around for a hundred years and continues today.

The modern detective has usually received extensive training and can rely on crime scene investigators to conduct detailed processing of the crime scene and forensic experts to examine and analyze the evidence collected. The forensic technology and capabilities available to the modern detective have greatly increased in recent decades and were unheard of even 50 years ago. Most detectives have completed on the job training as well as attended various training courses, so they have probably been exposed to the latest theories of crime solving. Many years ago, it was not uncommon for the detective to also process the crime scene and collect any physical evidence, in addition to his other investigative duties. Most agencies today have developed their own specialized crime scene unit that is able to process even the most complicated scenes, allowing the detective to concentrate on conducting the investigation.

With the most experienced detectives and all the modern forensic equipment and laboratory support, how is it that detectives still make mistakes in death investigations? A simplistic answer is because they are human, and all humans make mistakes. That is a true statement of course, but some of the reasons mistakes are made are often because of the individual detective's overall experience level and over reliance on forensic evidence to solve their case. As an example, when a modern detective responds to a new crime scene and there is forensic evidence present or an eyewitness to the crime is available, they know exactly what to do and how to respond. The

DOI: 10.4324/9781003373865-1

problem for most modern detectives, if they go to a scene, and there is no forensic evidence and there is no eyewitness, they're often stuck. They do not always know how to proceed with the investigation because they have never learned or have forgotten the basics of criminal investigations. This is one of the primary challenges for the modern detective: that they have become so dependent and "spoiled" by forensics that they are often lost when there isn't any forensic evidence.

Approaching these types of investigative difficulties can initially seem to be a daunting task, with at times seemingly no place to start or gain momentum in the case. Approaching this investigative dilemma and obtaining fruitful information and evidence is of course the goal of your investigative efforts and is the essence of this text.

Detective's Role in Death Investigations

It is the goal of all detectives to respond to reported crimes and then determine the facts of the incident based on the totality of evidence and any unique event circumstances, then identify who was involved. Involvement would include victims, witnesses, and potential offenders. This same goal is obviously true for those involved in death investigation. One of the main goals for detectives working death cases is determining whether the death is the result of a criminal or a non-criminal act.

Some deaths are certainly criminal in nature, such as those that take place during another criminal event such as robbery, a domestic violence incident, or a sexual offense. These are typically straightforward homicides and criminal offenses and are easily identified as such by witnesses, the crime scene, or other factors. Other deaths may require additional inquiry to determine if they are homicides or other non-criminal deaths. For example, looking at three different death scenarios: drowning in a lake while swimming, falling off a ladder while making home repairs, or someone being crushed by a vehicle that was improperly backing up at the workplace. In these examples, considering the circumstances, the drowning and falling off a ladder are likely the result of "accidental deaths" where there is no criminality, and there will probably be limited follow-up investigation. However, being killed by someone who was *improperly* backing up a vehicle, the death might be "accidental and unintended," but the investigation might determine that the death was the result of *negligence* or *negligent homicide*, and thus the "accident" is criminal in nature.

Introduction to Death Investigations

Why Treat Every Death Case as a Homicide?

There is a long-standing basic investigative concept in death investigations *that all deaths should be considered as homicides until proven otherwise*. This concept is found in nearly every professional text and taught in nearly every death investigation training course. The concept is to ensure that the investigation and crime scene examination are conducted in the same thorough manner as one would conduct for a homicide. This concept is supposed to preclude detectives from arriving at a scene with a "biased" mindset that the death is not suspicious and may not require additional investigation. With this mindset, they may miss evidence that points to the death being the result of a homicide. Therefore, in every case, the detectives are expected to respond with an open mind. They should listen to what has been reported and examine the scene, but they should always delay forming a final opinion until the evidence and other information is corroborated through their investigation.

Under this general concept, the responding detectives should always conduct a thorough preliminary investigation, including witness interviews, crime scene examination, collection of evidence and if necessary, laboratory analysis of the evidence. The rationale for this concept is to avoid someone *staging or altering* the scene to appear as if some other event took place and thus get away with a murder. A proper investigation will hopefully ensure someone does not get away with murder. Yet, despite all the training and countless professional writings, this does not always happen.

This is especially true in cases of reported suicide or accidental death. What frequently happens in these incidents the police dispatcher or radio operator receives a call for police assistance because of a reported death. The dispatcher then directs a patrol to "check out" the complaint. The first police responders arrive at the scene, and based on their quick observations and perhaps a quick witness interview, they are satisfied that the death is a suicide or is the result of an accident. This information is reported back to the dispatcher. Depending on the agency, if the initial responders are satisfied it is a suicide or accidental death, detectives might not even show up at the scene. If they do, many times, they have already heard the report and arrive at the scene with a *preconceived* idea of what happened, and many times they only perform a perfunctory preliminary investigation.

Geberth (2013), a leading expert in death investigation, specifically identifies this problem of responding to a death scene with a *preconceived* idea or an assumption because the police tend to find what they are expecting to find. Geberth states this problem succinctly:

4   Equivocal Death

If the case is reported as a "**Suicide**," the police officers who respond as well as the investigators *automatically* (emphasis added) tend to treat the call as a suicide. It is a critical error in thinking to handle the call based on the initial report. The immediate problem is that psychologically one is assuming the death to be a suicide case, when in fact this is a basic death investigation, which could very well turn out to be a homicide...

Geberth then continues,

Any preconceived theories or notions are dangerous in professional death investigation. In addition to errors of assuming a "suicide" or natural death, other preconceived notions may include deaths, which appear to be drug related and/or domestic violence. One must keep an open mind and not be influenced either by the initial reports or the presentation in the crime scene.

During research for this text and in multiple case consultations, the *preconceived response,* as described by Geberth, was found to exist with both smaller and larger police departments across the United States. What was surprising was a similar response to these events, which also take place in different countries around the world. Unfortunately this seems to be a common police response to reported suicides.

This *preconceived response* is also often present when the county coroner arrives at the scene and is briefed by police. Many times, after the police briefing and a quick view of the scene, they are satisfied and decide, without further investigation, that the death is consistent with suicide or accidental means. Then, despite any state requirements, they decide on their own that a forensic autopsy is unnecessary. Instead of being properly examined, the remains are released back to the family to make funeral arrangements, and in many cases, they are cremated.

After the coroner's decision on the manner of death, it is likely no further investigation is going to take place. Because once the manner of death is determined to be suicide, the police often consider further investigation as unnecessary. Therefore, no further scene examination or collection of evidence takes place. The resulting "*investigation*" becomes a short two- or three-page police report documenting their arrival, the coroner's collection of the remains, their determination as to the manner of death, and the police departure from the scene.

The problem of course is not everything is always as it appears. If the scene had been *altered or staged* by someone to appear as a suicide or accident, and the police simply accept an explanation from a witness without

Introduction to Death Investigations

corroborating the explanation, then quite possibly someone could get away with murder. If treating every death as a homicide is such a standard rule, then why aren't detectives following through? For many detectives, it comes from the feeling of being overworked or having too many other open cases they need to work on. Suicide cases therefore take a lower priority and interest. Also, because as tragic as they may be, suicide is not a case that will ever be prosecuted. So, the detective might feel that their time is better spent trying to resolve other actual criminal cases rather than working on a case with no "suspect" to prosecute. An example of this thought process can be found in Case Study 1.1.

CASE STUDY 1.1

A middle-aged school child came home from school and found his mother collapsed on the floor in her bedroom. She was cold and stiff to the touch. He called 911 and EMTs and a Deputy Sheriff quickly arrived at the scene. The coroner arrived shortly thereafter, and having received a call from the victim's boyfriend explaining the decedent's medical conditions, he determined the manner of death was from *"natural causes,"* based on her medical conditions as explained by her boyfriend. The boyfriend explained that the woman had Multiple Sclerosis and was known to have seizures, and this was the likely cause of death. There was no autopsy conducted, and the woman was buried. Three years later, the boyfriend was being investigated for the homicide of his wife when detectives learned information relating to the death of his former girlfriend. It was also discovered that the boyfriend had received $80,000 from a life insurance policy taken out on the girlfriend. The deceased's body was eventually exhumed, and an autopsy was performed. Her cause of death was determined to be manual strangulation, and her manner of death was homicide. The boyfriend was later charged with the murder, but for many reasons, including no preliminary investigation was ever conducted and witnesses were never interviewed, he was acquitted in court. There was strong circumstantial evidence based on the autopsy, the insurance policy, and the boyfriend's call to the coroner. But no evidence linking the boyfriend to the actual death scene could be established in court because it was never gathered during the preliminary investigation.

Although Case Study 1.1 shows how events can be altered or *staged to divert attention away from the true facts,* there are always potential problems when there is an incomplete preliminary investigation or a rush to judgment to classify the death as suicide or other manner of death. The first is the potential for evidence being missed and someone getting away with murder, which clearly happened in Case Study 1.1. As also noted, with an incomplete preliminary investigation comes the difficulty of working the case if new evidence ever comes forth establishing the victim was murdered. With an incomplete preliminary investigation, the chance of successfully recovering from an incomplete investigation is significantly reduced.

The sad reality is that staging a homicide to resemble a suicide or an accidental death takes place far more often than some detectives or coroners believe. What is not well known to many detectives is that suicide and accidental deaths are two of the most common themes for staged scenes that are used to cover up a homicide and misdirect police away from the true facts of the case (Chancellor & Graham 2017). Thus, it is critical to follow the adage to *treat every death as a homicide until you can prove otherwise* (Geberth 2013).

Even when the police are "correct" in their initial assessment that the death was the result of suicide, another potential problem may come from surviving family members that do not accept the suicide determination. Without a thorough and documented investigation, the police are often unable to validate their investigative findings to the satisfaction of the family. This leads down a common path found during the research for this book. The family challenges the incomplete police investigation, but they receive no satisfaction from their inquiries to the police, so they hire private investigators, or they attempt to engage the media. This is followed up with accusations made toward the detective, their supervisors, or the agency, ranging from incompetence to corruption. Many times, the result is the agency resting with their investigative findings and then refusing to further engage with the family, hoping they will eventually go away. However, this does not happen all the time.

The above description of "routine cases" and the events described in Case Study 1.1 probably take place across the world many times a day. To the police and coroner, they have probably seen suicide and natural death events many times, so there is often no cause for concern on their part. If everything "appears" to be right, the "routine case" is quickly closed. Until someone comes forward with new information or evidence that raises concerns as to what might have really happened. Unfortunately, now police are confronted with a potential homicide, but the victim's body has been buried or cremated, and there is little if any crime scene evidence. Sometimes the scene is not even properly photographed or otherwise documented.

One factor to remember is that nothing in a death investigation is absolute. There are often other possible explanations for the same event; we must look for them and eliminate them as a possibility. No one should make such

Introduction to Death Investigations

Homicides	16,425	Staged	1,371
Robberies	267,988	Staged	22,277
Rapes	139,815	Staged	11,647
Burglaries	998,474	Staged	83,373
Suicides*	47,511	Staged	3,967

Figure 1.1 These figures are 2019 UCR data compared to estimates based on the 8.35% rape of staged scene found in Schlesinger's et al. (2014) homicide study. (Chancellor & Graham 2017.)

a final determination of what happened in a vacuum without full knowledge and consideration of any other potential factor.

Extent of the Problem

What are the chances that a homicide could be staged to resemble some other event such as a suicide or accidental death? Is there a statistical basis to be concerned that this might happen? Although there is a myriad of statistical information collected by the federal or state governments on different aspects of reported crimes across the country, no one collects information in relation to potentially *staged scenes*. Therefore, there is no state or national database or any way to collect or report such information.

There has been one study completed by Schlesinger et al. (2014) that involved the review of 946 homicides supplied by the FBI Behavioral Science Unit. The analysis of these cases noted that out of the 946 cases reviewed, a total of 79, or 8.35% were found to be staged or altered to misdirect the subsequent criminal investigation. If this 8.35% rate of staging is extrapolated and compared to the US national crime statistics, we can get a picture of the potential problem. In Figure 1.1, the 2019 crime statistics were annotated and then each crime type was multiplied by 8.35%, resulting in the number of potential staged scenes in each category. As noted by Chancellor and Graham (2017), such extrapolations are not necessarily accurate, but they do provide a rough estimate of the number of potential staged events. Unfortunately, there is no method or database that collects specific information on staged events. Therefore, the 8.35% was applied to get a general idea (albeit not statistically accurate) of how often these types of crimes might be staged.

Figure 1.2 This figure depicts an elderly woman found in a garage in the back of her house, staged to resemble a suicide. (see Case Study 1.2).

According to the above extrapolated statistics, an estimated 1,371 homicides and 3,967 suicides were potentially staged during the 2019 year. That is a total of 5,338 death investigations that should have required additional police investigation to determine the facts. It is unknown how many of these cases resulted in additional investigation or how many reported suicides were actually staged events. But it is certainly likely that many of these cases, for different reasons, were never properly investigated. It's therefore unknown how many offenders were able to commit a murder that was then undetected. Because *suicide and accidental deaths* are among the top four themes used to stage a homicide (Chancellor & Graham 2017), these reported deaths should always be looked at initially with a critical eye. An example is found within Case Study 1.2 (Figure 1.1)

Introduction to Death Investigations

CASE STUDY 1.2

An elderly woman was found in her garage hanging with a rope around her neck and tied onto the overhead rafters that were 10′ above the ground. The scene was reported as a "suicide"; however, police responded, and in a brief viewing of the scene, there was no ladder or other means in the garage or in the immediate area to allow her access to secure the rope to the rafters. Police further discovered through interviews of friends that the victim's hands were so arthritic, she would also be physically unable to tie the rope to the rafter. In this case, the woman did not have the physical ability to complete the act depicted at the scene. Her death was later determined to be a homicide, and after she was killed, she was placed into the garage to stage the scene as a suicide.

This case study will be referenced several times throughout the text, as there are several important aspects to discuss in this particular case.

Other factors and information related to Staged Crime Scenes are found in Chapter 3.

Cause and Manner of Death

The term *"cause of death"* is basically the medical reason for the death, e.g., disease, accidental fall, or, in the case of violent crimes, asphyxiation, gunshot wound, blunt force trauma, or stab wound. This is determined by the coroner and/or Medical Examiner (ME), usually following the forensic autopsy. The term *"manner of death"* is a medicolegal term provided by the coroner or ME, based on the evidence and all the facts and circumstances surrounding the death. A medicolegal term refers both to medicine and the law.

While there are a multitude of *"causes of death,"* there are only five *"manners of death."* These are:

1. Natural
2. Accidental
3. Suicide
4. Homicide
5. Undetermined

In most instances, the cause and manner of death can be discerned by the scene and witness statements. For instance, police are called to the scene of a death wherein the resident calls 911 and reports that someone broke into their house, and they shot the person in self-defense. The police arrive and find evidence of forced entry on the front door, and there is the body of a stranger inside the house. In this case, the offender was also wearing a mask or gloves and maybe was carrying a weapon. A quick criminal history check of the victim notes they have a past arrest record for residential burglary, and the residents of the home have a clean record. This limited evidence is certainly consistent with the initial report. There still needs to be some follow-up investigation and corroboration of evidence and statements, but based on this simple scenario, this is not a complicated case. It is also an example of many cases where the police arrive at the scene and there is a witness, and sufficient forensic or other evidence available that enables them to quickly resolve any questions they may have. Unfortunately, this is not always the case, and sometimes it is just not clear what happened or there are multiple possibilities.

Equivocal Deaths

Out of the thousands of deaths that occur each year in the United States, only roughly 1% are the result of homicide. Another 2–3% are suicides, and the rest are either natural, accidental, or undetermined. An *undetermined* manner of death is based on the inability to accurately determine the *cause of death* or the circumstances surrounding the death, based on a lack of medical findings or an incomplete police investigation. The best example of an undetermined death is skeletal remains that are found, but there is no evidence of trauma to the bones or other evidence to determine the cause of death. It might be impossible to determine the *cause of death*; thus, the *manner of death* is initially listed as undetermined. Deaths wherein the initial manner of death is questionable are also known as *equivocal*.

An *equivocal* death is basically uncertainty as to the manner of death even after the initial viewing or examination of the scene, the deceased, and other evidence. To be more specific, the responding authorities (police and coroner) cannot readily determine exactly what happened because there are multiple possibilities. In some cases, this uncertainty may extend even after an autopsy has been completed. In those instances, the manner of death may be initially listed by the coroner or ME as *undetermined pending investigation* or sometimes just "*pending.*" In both terms, it just means a decision as to the manner of death has not yet been reached. During the initial stages of the investigation, undetermined or "pending" would be the proper determination.

Introduction to Death Investigations 11

An *equivocal* case by its uncertainty demands additional investigation. In many of these equivocal deaths, the main question is determining if the death is the result of suicide, accidental, or homicide. One of the problems in conducting a suspected suicide investigation is that most detectives are not always adequately trained in conducting these investigations and do not understand what leads a person to self-destructive behaviors. Instead, they tend to focus on what they do understand, such as wounds, injuries, ballistics, forensics, and scene examinations. But conducting a suicide investigation is so much more.

Suicide Investigations

Webster's dictionary defines suicide as "the act or an instance of taking one's own life voluntarily and intentionally." In the German language it is defined as *selbstmord*, or murder of oneself. Joiner (2011) notes that suicide is one of the only acts that is almost universally condemned by all the major religions and cultures and in earlier times, a stigma was attached to those who died by suicide. For example, earlier Christian beliefs noted that the souls of those who committed suicide would not find a place in heaven.

BOX 1.1   RISK FACTORS. LISTS SOME OF THE RISK FACTORS OR POTENTIAL MOTIVES THAT COULD LEAD SOMEONE TO CONTEMPLATE SUICIDE.

- Personal or romantic relationship issues (divorce or separation).
- Experiencing domestic violence or child abuse.
- Experiencing bullying (particularly for teens and children).
- Experiencing sexual abuse or sexual assault.
- Alcohol or substance abuse.
- Their current or long-term physical health.
- Experiencing chronic pain.
- Employment status (loss of job).
- Money or financial problems (i.e., bankruptcy).
- Legal issues particularly pending prosecutions or recent convictions of a criminal act.
- Engaged in alternate lifestyle (i.e., lesbian, gay, or bisexual).
- Those with disabilities.
- Veterans with PTSD issues.

Suicide is one of the leading causes of death in the United States, and there are more suicides reported annually than homicides. According to the Center for Disease Control (CDC) (2021), there were 24,576 reported homicides and 45,979 reported suicides in 2021. Although some ethnic and age groups may tend to have a higher risk for suicide, it occurs within all races, genders, and age groups. There are some groups that tend to experience suicide rates higher than others, including those experiencing serious untreatable medical conditions, those experiencing excruciating pain, veterans, and the elderly who have lost life partners. Other groups may experience higher rates because of their lifestyles, such as younger people who identify as lesbian, gay, or bisexual. They tend to have higher rates of suicidal thoughts and behavior compared to their peers who identify as heterosexual.

There are many factors that may cause someone to commit suicide, but the victim's mental health condition is often identified as the motivational basis for the act. The reality, of course, is that many people who have committed suicide were never diagnosed with any type of mental health condition. There are many other issues in the victim's life that could be motivating factors. A short list of these issues is found in Box 1.1.

As noted in Box 1.1, there are many factors that can potentially increase the risk for suicide. However, a good family background, maturity, and a viable support structure, coupled with easy access to family or health care, can often mitigate or limit thoughts of suicide. This is one of the reasons for conducting a detailed victimology assessment in cases of suicide, as noted in Chapter 6.

Figure 1.3 outlines other important statistics relating to suicide that many detectives are often unaware. This includes those admitted to the hospital or who received medical intervention following a suicide attempt and those who have previously contemplated suicide.

Statistically, detectives are far more likely to encounter an attempted or completed suicide than a homicide, but most of their training on death investigation and professional literature only addresses limited aspects of investigating a suicide. If addressed at all, suicide training is limited to focusing on wounds, injuries, ballistics, some forensics, and generally only minor mentions of the importance of aspects of *victimology* or *risk factors*.

In addition to motivational factors for suicide, there are also risk factors that may lead to suicide and should be considered as part of the victimology assessment that should be conducted as part of every death investigation. The victimology assessment is described in detail in Chapter 6. The victim's state of mental health, specifically depression, is often identified as the main risk factor for suicide. As mentioned earlier, many people who have committed suicide have never been diagnosed with any type of mental health condition,

Introduction to Death Investigations

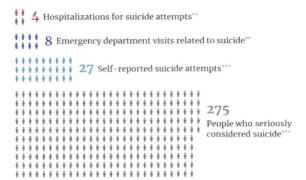

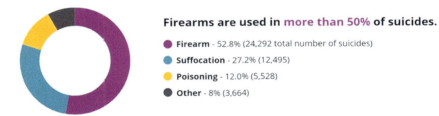

Figure 1.3 These figures (a and b) depict statistical data reflecting attempted suicides or those that have considered suicide in their recent past. (Source: CDC WISQARS and 2020 SAMHSA's National Survey on Drug Use and Health.)

and there are also thousands of persons diagnosed with depression who do not commit suicide. So, the aspects of mental health are but one factor that must be considered, but, as stated previously, there are often many other issues in the victim's life that are contributing factors.

However, a good family background, maturity, and a viable support structure, coupled with easy access to family or health care, can often mitigate or limit some thoughts of suicide. This is one of the reasons for conducting a detailed victimology assessment, particularly in a suicide investigation.

Not understanding the concepts of risk factors, the deceased's background, and what was going on in their lives immediately prior to their death is a critical failing in investigating these cases. Because many times these reported "suicide" incidents are far from the open and shut or "routine" cases that many detectives have allowed themselves to believe. Vernon Geberth (1996) sums up this reality very succinctly stating:

14   Equivocal Death

...Suicide cases can cause more problems for detectives than homicide investigations.

There is probably no truer statement in criminal investigations. Because to correctly investigate a suspected suicide, the detective must do many things that are not always required in other death investigations. Such as identify the reason or motive for the suicide. This is based on the reality that no one wakes up one morning and just decides to kill themselves. There is a process or other factors that lead to this final decision. Police should also determine if the victim had the physical ability and the specific intent to cause harm to themselves. This is especially problematic when the victim left no note to explain their action or chose an unusual method to cause their death, such as setting themselves on fire, stabbing themselves multiple times, or using a chainsaw.

Perhaps the best example of suicide cases causing more difficulties than homicides is found in Case Study 1.3, which was the suicide of Vince Foster, a member of President Clinton's White House Staff, in 1993.

CASE STUDY 1.3

On July 20, 1993, the body of Vince Foster, a White House employee and close personal friend of Bill and Hillary Clinton, was found in Ft. Mercy Park, just off the George Washington Parkway. He died from an apparently self-inflicted gunshot wound to the mouth. A pistol was found in his hand, and the autopsy and subsequent investigation determined that Foster had committed suicide. Although police found no evidence of foul play, Foster's connection to the Clintons fueled tabloids that speculated his death was potentially a homicide, and the Clintons were likely involved. There were also different allegations made during the investigation to include that the body had been moved and rearranged by someone to resemble a suicide. Because of the various allegations and his connection to the White House, numerous police agencies, including the Special Prosecutor Kenneth Star (The Whitewater Investigation), were involved in the investigation. The final determination from all investigations established that Foster owned the handgun that was found and was used to cause his injuries, and confirmed that the body had not been moved from its position prior to its discovery by police. The conclusion by all police agencies was that Foster had committed suicide. However, this did not silence many Clinton critics.

The previous case study is an example of how so called "routine cases" suddenly find themselves on the front page of major newspapers

Introduction to Death Investigations 15

and on the nightly news. It is a fact that every police department in the United States is only one phone call away from the next *Vince Foster case*.

Detectives will also have to deal with some widely accepted suicide myths and false beliefs about the act of suicide. These long-standing myths or beliefs will often influence how the investigation is going to be perceived by the family or the public and may lead to challenges to their findings, particularly when they are going through the various stages of grief. Box 1.2 identifies some of these commonly accepted suicide myths.

Box 1.2 shows some of the more common suicide myths that affect both the police and society when thinking about suicide.

Because of these myths, cultural beliefs, and the shock to family members, the assigned detective must be able to communicate with the surviving family more often than they might do with a homicide victim's family. This increased communication demand is based on the surviving family member's questions and their insistence on receiving answers. One of the main issues often raised is the suspicion the victim did not take their own life but was murdered. Police often associate this belief or reaction with the "denial" *stage of grief* as noted by Kübler-Ross (1969). However, there are many times when

---

BOX 1.2 SUICIDE MYTHS.

- People who talk about suicide are just seeking attention.
- People who attempt suicide and survive will not attempt suicide again.
- Young people never think about suicide because they have their entire life ahead of them.
- Anyone who tries to kill oneself is crazy, irrational, or insane.
- There is little correlation between alcohol or drug abuse and suicide.
- Suicide only affects individuals with a mental health condition.
- Suicide is hereditary.
- Breakups in relationships are so frequent; they do not cause suicides.
- The military will report the death of a service member as suicide and not homicide to protect a Commander.

the family can identify a specific suspect they believe was involved in the death. Their suspicion is usually based on prior interactions with the suspect or other information provided to them antemortem by the deceased. The frustration grows when they perceive the police are not paying attention to them and decline to even consider the information or potential evidence the family might have on the event.

The correct answer to these issues is to establish good communication with the family and answer their questions as they arise. Many times, this takes a thick skin because families can be very hostile if they don't readily accept the death as a suicide. When such communication is missing or if the police are not forthcoming with answers, they seek out their own answers through others. For instance, because their neighbor or friend might be a patrol officer or deputy sheriff, they might ask questions about forensics evidence and the crime lab, or they may ask their family dentist a question about the autopsy report. In both examples, the questions are probably out of their normal expertise or knowledge, but they try to be helpful, so they provide their opinion. Unfortunately, they are seldom trained in these specialized topics, so their answers are usually incorrect and sometimes conflict with information provided by the police. This immediately sparks conflict with the police and leads to the family mistrusting the police investigation.

This situation is only aggravated when the family does not readily accept the suicide determination, and only a token police investigation was conducted. When questioned, detectives might respond with inaccurate or conflicting details about the death or the scene, often because they did not take the time to conduct a thorough investigation. Even worse, they make offhanded remarks such as "the deceased drank alcohol and took some pills before they took their own life." However, that family noted there was never any evidence of alcohol consumption at the scene, and no toxicology on the deceased's blood was conducted. These comments are examples of the police seeming to "lose their patience" with the family and deciding just to tell them something to make them go away. It's even worse when they decide to cut off any further contact with the family. Many times, this only throws gasoline on a smoldering fire, leading the family to go to the media, employing a private investigator, and in some instances initiating lawsuits.

From the police perspective, any investigation of a suicide is traditionally limited to ensuring that the death was the result of an intentional self-infliction by the victim and not the result of a criminal act or an omission of another. For family members, they need to know the facts and evidence to enable them to reach a point of acceptance and move on with their lives. Trying to understand or accept suicide is extremely difficult because no one wants to believe that their relative has taken their own life. There is also a

Introduction to Death Investigations

social stigma that may be attached to the family, which can sometimes cause great harm to the survivors and their subsequent lives. Suicides certainly are emotionally difficult, but they can also be costly if the victim was the breadwinner of the family and now the source of income is lost or if there was an insurance clause that prevents the family from collecting on any insurance policy.

Suicides are often highly emotional events and detectives must be able to express empathy, sympathy, understanding, and maintain their professionalism while sometimes facing a wide range of emotions as the family begins to deal with what Kübler-Ross (1969) describes as the *stages of grief*.

Stages of Grief

Kübler-Ross (1969) identifies five stages of grief that people go through when confronted with the death of someone they know. The emotions and reactions are likely to be intensified if the deceased is a family member. Suicides might cause even a stronger reaction because in homicides, many times it is just a question of someone being in the wrong place at the wrong time, and the family is at least able to place the blame on some other person. For suicides, it is different because this is an intentional self-destructive act, so there is likely to be a lot more questions asked of themselves and others to understand what could have driven this person to end their life.

How a person responds to the death depends on the individual, their age, maturity level, and other life experiences. Therefore, it is important to note that not everyone will go through these same stages in the order in which it is written. Some may skip or not go through a certain stage, and others may take longer to work through one stage than another. There is also no specific time span when a person can move from one stage to another and reach final acceptance. These stages may take days, weeks, or even years before final acceptance, and it is also possible to return to one of the stages. The response is generally related to the individual and their relationship with the victim. For instance, parents, spouses, children, or siblings of the deceased may take longer to recover than close personal friends.

Denial

Denial is one of the first stages of the grieving process. This is basically an inability or even refusal to accept or believe their loved one is deceased. Especially when it comes as a total shock, such as with a crime of violence or a suicide. Denial is not just an attempt to pretend that the loss does not exist;

it can sometimes psychologically protect people during the initial stages until they can cope with the loss. This is described as entering a "temporary cocoon" or "balloon" that acts as a shield to protect them from the initial pain or shock. Some emotions or actions expressed during this stage include avoidance, confusion, numbness, or even self-blame.

Anger

Anger is the next stage and tends to be one of the first emotions felt when we begin to relate to the loss. Anger gives some an emotional outlet to verbally express their feelings with less fear of judgment or rejection. In some cases, expressing anger may be more acceptable than admitting they are scared. Anger can take on many forms, including directed at the deceased, particularly if they were doing something at the time of their death they were warned against or asked not to do. Sometimes it is because their death is causing a great problem within the family, such as loss of income or other interfamilial issues.

At this stage, they have gone through the denial stage and have at least realized the death has occurred. This is when the family begins to ask serious, often pointed questions to the police, and because of their anger, they can become quite demanding in their questioning. Especially if they are not getting answers or feel the case is not being correctly pursued. This is a problem that might continuously confront detectives involved in any suspected suicide investigation. Some of the emotions expressed during this stage include frustration, anxiety, irritation, embarrassment, and shame.

Bargaining

In this stage, there are efforts to negotiate or strike a deal with God, fate, or some other higher power to mitigate or somehow miraculously reverse what has already happened. Many times, guilt accompanies this stage, as the surviving family might hold themselves responsible for the actions of the deceased. This is often expressed as: "If only I had done more, paid attention more, or reached out, or if I had called them that night, none of this would happen." During this stage, people tend to focus on their personal faults, regrets, or previous interactions with the deceased and what they might have done to help them. Bargaining is a way to temporarily hang on to hope until they finally accept what has happened. Some emotions expressed during this stage include guilt, shame, self-punishment, and fervent prayer.

Depression

Eventually there is recognition of what has happened, and the denial, anger, and bargaining are replaced by depression. This is the result of their episodic grief caused by a particular incident and should not be confused with normal clinical depression. The signs of depression tend to appear once a sense of finality is realized. In these incidents, depression is marked by feelings of sadness, helplessness, and fearfulness of what the future is going to hold or what has been lost. Some of the emotions expressed during this stage include feeling overwhelmed, sadness, lack of energy, numbness, and hopelessness.

Acceptance

This is supposed to be the final stage of the grieving process. This stage appears when people begin to realize that the loss is real and that they must accept that fact. It is important to note that an acceptance of the loss does not mean the grief is over. Rather, they have reached the point where they are just accepting the situation and begin to rebuild their lives. Acceptance is the point where the thoughts and behaviors become more about the people left behind and not just about the deceased. Although sadness and regret can still be present, instances of denial, bargaining, and anger are less likely. Depression, however, may linger for a longer period, depending upon the individual. Once reaching the acceptance phase, they begin to understand there is a new beginning on the horizon. Emotions expressed are now more about their future options. Some of their actions begin to include recognizing the need to move on and developing a new life plan.

Establishing and Maintaining a Working Relationship with the Family

In every death investigation, it is imperative to establish and maintain a good working relationship with the deceased's family. There are instances when the family had no real recent contact with the deceased, so this coordination may have to be made with their "life partner" or close personal friends. For simplification, the term "family" in this section will encompass those persons with the closest relationship with the deceased. Establishing this relationship is crucial because generally it's the family that is going to be able to provide information as to the deceased's background, their last known activity or whereabouts, the identity of their friends and associates, and what was going on in their lives before their death. This information is absolutely a critical step in homicide investigations, but it is also just as important for suicide investigations. Unfortunately, when confronted with a "routine suicide or accidental death" often the only real contact with the family may be limited to a death notification. With no further attempt to obtain any information about the deceased.

The rationale and best example for taking the time to talk to the family during the preliminary death investigation is found back in Case Study 1.1. In that incident, the parents of the deceased were never interviewed or even talked to by anyone other than the coroner when he made the death notification. When, years later, the body was exhumed and autopsied, the family was finally interviewed for some background on the victim. The parents only then told the police that contrary to the boyfriends' allegations, their daughter had never suffered seizures in her entire life, and they were not aware the boyfriend had made this claim. They were also not aware of any life insurance policy taken out by the boyfriend. When the coroner determined her death to be from natural causes, they assumed it was based on her history of Multiple Sclerosis. They were not aware of the boyfriend's call to the coroner claiming their daughter suffered from seizures.

At some time, the police should be prepared to sit down and try to answer the families' questions. As noted previously, often the family wants to talk with the police as they are in the *anger stage* of the grieving process. Police must be prepared for the families' responses and direct questions. At this stage of the investigation, the family is not concerned with the detective's other cases or normal police procedures. They are focused on their relative's death because that is the most important thing in their lives at the time. This is also the time when families are likely to present information that they believe the death is more consistent with a homicide rather than a suicide.

During these briefings with the family, there are likely to be questions about a note or any last communication left by the victim. Such communications should be shared with the family if they exist unless there is a specific investigative reason not to share. This needs to be shared with the family so they understand any need to withhold such communications. In those cases where any last communication is hurtful or accusatory toward members of the family, then the suggestion is to explain this to the family and perhaps limit who is to initially receive the information and let the family decide to completely release the contents of the communication or not.

It is in these conversations with the family that the detective must have thick skin because some questions might be presented in a somewhat confrontational or accusatory manner. Again, this is usually in the anger stage of the process, and such language is one of the manifestations. The detective must also be able to almost assume the roles of a counselor or instructor

Introduction to Death Investigations

to answer the questions. The key is to listen to the family's concerns and questions and answer them truthfully as best as possible. The detective needs to pay attention to what they are saying to the family. In one instance, while talking to the parents of a female deceased of a suspected suicide, the detective stated, *"at least she wasn't raped."* It is unclear if the statement was made to "comfort" the parents or was just a random thought. But the comment was not well received and it certainly did not comfort the family. Such statements, personal opinions, and offhanded comments are totally unprofessional and should never be made to the family. Another example of such comments is found in Case Study 1.4.

CASE STUDY 1.4

The family was questioning the suspected suicide of their daughter as it took them completely by surprise. The family had spoken to the victim only hours before and the conversation was about a planned trip home for a visit, the tickets were already purchased; she had started changing her summer clothing for fall clothing, and potentially buying a house. There were no indications of any suicidal behaviors and no elevated risk factors. The police then made an offhanded remark to theorize that perhaps she was taking a nap when her cell phone rang, and she mistakenly picked up a gun instead of the phone and shot herself. The family was dumbfounded by the comment and immediately concluded the detective was *stupid* even to suggest that possibility. This directly led to developing mistrust of the agency to handle the investigation.

It is unclear if the detective in Case Study 1.4 was serious about his suggestion, but regardless, the family lost all confidence in him, and any other briefing he provided was immediately challenged by the family.

In the early stages of the investigation, when the case is still being looked at as a homicide, there may be evidence or factors the police do not want to discuss. This is normal in all investigations when there is certain information never released outside the agency. When this is explained to the family generally, they will accept that decision and allow the investigation to progress, but eventually they are going to come back and ask again.

For many families, this tragic event might be their first contact with the police ever. So it is going to be important to be able to explain police procedures as well as aspects of forensic evidence and forensic analysis. Remember, the American public is flooded with TV programs about homicide investigation, forensic evidence, and various police tactics. Unfortunately, many of the TV programs are not accurate as to forensic capabilities, so this may need to be explained to the family.

One of the recommendations made to detectives is to try to initiate contact with the family and arrange a time to speak with them either in person, by telephone, or in some cases even through a tele-video conference. Set up a time, ask them to prepare any questions, and if they choose to gather the entire family to discuss the case. Then conduct the interview and answer their questions truthfully as best you can. It is important if the detective does not know for sure what the answer to a question is, they need to say so. They should avoid guessing or supposing because these guesses are often taken as facts. If later these "facts" are proven incorrect, the confidence in the detective can be lost very quickly. The best answer is to say, "*I don't know or am not sure, but I will find out and get back with you.*" I don't know or I'm not sure are better answers than providing erroneous information. There tend to be more questions generated after this initial meeting, so the detective should arrange a time to call back in a few days or a week and repeat the question-and-answer session.

At the same time, the detective asks the family not to continuously call them to ask more questions that they should save them for their appointed time. Explaining that when multiple calls come in from different family members, asking the same questions, they can be time-consuming and distracting. If the detective promises to answer all questions at a specific time and then makes the appointment, the other calls for an update are greatly reduced. Further, if the family does not feel they are being abandoned and their questions are being answered, the anger stage tends to dissipate quicker, and this will help the family move through the grieving process until they reach final acceptance of the death.

The other most important reason for talking with the family is to determine if they have evidence supporting their allegations that the victim was murdered. This is obviously something police need to hear and pay attention to. The importance of talking with the family is covered in greater detail in Chapters 6 and 8.

Chapter Summary

There is really no such thing as a routine death investigation, and every death should be treated as a homicide until proven otherwise. Not doing so is a common mistake with many detectives who assume the death is suicide and therefore do not conduct any follow-up investigation. Statistically, a detective is more likely to be presented with a suicide death rather than a homicide, but it is incumbent upon every detective and agency to take the time and

Introduction to Death Investigations

"prove" the death was a suicide and not just assume it to be so. The detective and agency have a duty not just to the families of the deceased but to the community to make sure the death is not the result of a homicide that has been staged to resemble a suicide.

It is also important to realize that there will be incidents, like Case Study 1.3, that will never be resolved to the ultimate satisfaction of all concerned. Even when the police have conducted a thorough investigation and collected overwhelming evidence establishing the suicide, there will be families or others that refuse to accept the suicide determination. The best defense for the agency is a thorough and well-documented investigation and establishing early contact with the family to answer their questions or concerns.

Bibliography

Adcock, J. M., & Chancellor, A. S. (2016). *Death Investigation* (2nd ed.). Amazon Press.

Center for Disease Control and Prevention (CDC). (2020). *Web based Injury Query and Reporting System (WISQARS)*. www.cdc.gov/injury/wisqars/index.html

Center for Disease Control and Prevention (CDC). (2021a). *Homicide Statistics*. www.cdc.gov/ncsh/fastats/homicide

Center for Disease Control and Prevention (CDC). (2021b). *Suicide Data and Statistics*. Suicide Data and Statistics | Suicide Prevention | CDC

Center for Disease Control and Prevention (CDC). (2022). *Disparities in Suicide*. Health Disparities in Suicide | Suicide Prevention | CDC

Chancellor, A. S., & Graham, G. D. (2017). *Crime Scene Staging Investigation of Suspect Misdirection of the Crime Scene*. Springfield, IL: Charles C. Thomas.

Geberth, V. J. (1996). *Practical Homicide Investigation* (p. 359). Boca Raton, FL: CRC Press.

Geberth, V. J. (2013). The Seven Major Mistakes in Suicide Investigation. *Law and Order Magazine*, 61(1), 54–56.

Joiner, T. (2011). *Myths about Suicide*. Cambridge, MA: Harvard University Press.

Kübler-Ross, E. (1969). *On Death and Dying*. New York, NY: Macmillan Publishing Company.

Pew Research Center. (n.d.). www.pewresearch.org/fact-tank/2021/10/27/what-we-know-about-the-increase-in-u-s-murders-in-2020/

Schlesinger, L. B., Gardenier, A., Jarvis, J., & Sheehan-Cook, J. (2014). Crime Scene Staging in Homicide. *Journal of Police Criminal Psychology*, 29, 44–51.

The Initial Response and Preliminary Investigation for Suicides

2

Preliminary Investigation

The preliminary investigation or prelim is basically the initial response and investigative steps taken during any investigation. It is during the preliminary investigation and the initial response to the scene that the concept previously discussed in Chapter 1 of "*treat every death as a homicide until you can prove otherwise*," is applied. Thus, it should be the standard response from any police agency to send detectives to every reported death. Unfortunately, this does not always happen and frequently it is the uniform first responder that will make the decision that the death is the result of suicide, and therefore no follow-up investigation is required. Theoretically the detective has more training and experience than the typical patrol officer and is therefore in a better position to observe and understand the scene, so they should respond to make any investigative decisions, but because of agency policy this might not always occur.

Responding to a scene is a critical concept because the prelim, also referred to as the first 48 hours, is so important to all criminal investigations that mistakes made during this stage are often difficult to overcome. Conducting the preliminary investigation is scene and event specific, meaning there isn't any absolute guide on conducting an initial investigation, because every event is different. But generally, the preliminary investigation consists of responding to the scene, conducting the crime scene examination, scene documentation, collection of evidence, canvass interviews, and the interview of key witnesses. The main idea behind the preliminary investigation is to accomplish as much as possible within the first hours of the report.

Death investigations should proceed under the concept that the chances of solving a homicide are cut in half if police are unable to develop investigative leads or identify any potential suspects within the first 48–72 hours.

24   DOI: 10.4324/9781003373865-2

The Initial Response and Preliminary Investigation for Suicides   25

Because some witnesses might leave the area, others decide or are convinced not to cooperate, evidence is destroyed, and offenders have a chance to create an alibi. Therefore, immediate action is needed during the critical 48–72 hours of the preliminary investigation.

Based on the initial observations of the scene and initial interviews, additional investigative leads such as identifying additional witnesses, persons of interest, or the collection of other types of evidence at other locations will probably be generated. Because each scene and event are different, there is no exact time frame for conducting a preliminary investigation but again the concept of the first 48–72 hours is critical. Because the preliminary investigation is based on the specific circumstances of each event, some prelims can be completed within hours, and others may take several days because of additional leads that are generated and need to be immediately accomplished.

The 911 Call

The investigative process for all crimes begins with the first notification to the police, most often this notification comes from the 911 emergency notification system. Therefore, one of the critical steps in all violent crime investigations includes obtaining a copy of the initial 911 call reporting the incident. The 911 calls for all reported death incidents have proved to be a significant investigative step. As noted by Harpster and Adams (2017) and Miller et al (2020) there are some key features found within 911 calls that make them potentially valuable as evidence in all death investigations. These key features include voice modulation, hesitation or pauses, or providing extraneous or unrelated information. Analyzing the call could give indications that the caller is being truthful or deceptive while reporting the death. These indications of deception are found both in reported homicides as well as reported suicides (Miller et al 2020). Therefore, collection of the 911 call should be an automatic investigative step regardless of the reported death.

A transcript of the call might be helpful, but a transcript does not pick up voice modulation, stuttering or hesitation, or potential background sounds which may prove to be important that are going to be found on the actual recording.

Scene Documentation

All death investigations should be documented in the same way every time. As noted repeatedly, all deaths should be treated initially as a homicide until another manner of death can be positively determined. A thorough crime scene investigation includes a detailed report of all observations, lists of all evidence collected, and scene photography. As noted by Geberth (2013) everything at the scene should be considered as potential evidence. This of course does not always happen because of the immediate determination that the death is a suicide and thus no need to conduct a crime scene, or only a limited crime scene examination is requested or performed. There are multiple examples of "suicides" later determined to be homicides that require additional investigative effort, but because there was just a brief and incomplete documentation of the scene it is nearly impossible to reconstruct what happened. If the case is ever reopened with a good crime scene examination, there is usually sufficient documentation that can be used to determine what really happened. Chapter 4 covers a more detailed approach to crime scene examinations and forensic evidence.

When evaluating death scenes, detectives, and CSI personnel should be looking for the three major components of a preliminary investigation which includes *physical evidence, the informational pieces, and the behavioral aspects* (Adcock & Chancellor 2016).

Physical Evidence

This includes primarily any weapon or whatever means caused the death. If the investigation is a reported or suspected suicide, then the instrument or means to cause the death must be at the scene. If the means to cause the death is missing, then this is an inconsistency for suicide. Also was there any inconsistent movement of the victim or alterations within the scene. Other aspects of physical and forensic evidence should also include the typical evidence found in other death investigations including possible bloodstain pattern analysis, DNA, latent prints, toxicology, and trace evidence.

Informational or Testimonial

This includes the interviews of all witnesses, and possibly written documents such as personal letters or correspondence, social media, personal or business records, prior police reports, suicide notes, 911 calls, canvass interviews, or any other relevant documentation. This also includes cell phone analysis. This is especially important in these modern times as most of our normal activity is now documented either in social media or on our cell phones.

Behavioral

This includes the actions of the deceased or others, before, during, or after the event. It is especially important to note any behavioral efforts at the death scene such as preparation for the event, any alteration of the scene, or unusual postmortem disturbance of the scene or the victim.

The requirements for the preliminary investigation into all reported deaths are generally the same, but there are some important differences which will be detailed later in this chapter.

Reactions to Reported Suicides

Unfortunately, detectives do not always take the time to evaluate the scene before they begin to make assumptions of what happened. Geberth (2013) describes some common errors when responding to reported suicide events. He identified these efforts as the *Seven Mistakes in Suicide Investigation*. These common mistakes are:

1. Assuming the case is a suicide based on the initial report.
2. Assuming a "*Suicide position*" at the crime scene (taking short cuts or failing to follow standard investigative steps once they believe it is a suicide).
3. Not initially handling the "suicide" as a homicide investigation.
4. Failure to conduct a victimology.
5. Failure to properly document any note.
6. Failure to follow the three basic considerations to establish the death is a suicide. These considerations are:
   a. The presence of a weapon or means of death at the scene.
   b. Injuries or wounds could have been inflicted by the deceased.
   c. The existence of motive or intent to take their own life.
7. Failure to take each factor to its ultimate conclusion.

Geberth (2013) notes that detectives arriving at a reported suicide with a *predisposition* the death is a *suicide*, tend to find and accept all evidence that is consistent with suicide. Because they are expecting and are conditioned to find such evidence. Unfortunately, because of their mind set and assumptions, they may not consider or accept evidence that points *away* from suicide. This is an example of *cognitive bias* or commonly referred to as *tunnel vision*. Once detectives develop *tunnel vision*, they often become steadfastly unwilling to accept any evidence or information or consider any other possibility that goes against their initial concept regarding the death.

Detectives need to avoid the concept of any death investigation being just a *routine case*. Because in all death cases, we are still concerned with establishing the "*who, what, when, where, and how*," questions relating to the death. But for suicides, there is a special requirement to try and determine the "*why*" or *identify the* "*motive*" for suicide. This is going to cause more of an effort to find out even more about the victim and their background than might be necessary for many homicide cases.

In approaching all death scenes, detectives should be initially looking at the death as a potential homicide. Therefore, one of the first steps in the homicide investigative process is to try and determine the type or category of homicide that is present. In many instances the category of homicide and thus the *motive* for the death, can be discerned by a quick overview of the scene or from witness statements. There are four categories of homicide according to Douglas et al. (2006). These are:

1. **Criminal Enterprise:** Homicides that take place during another crime (i.e., armed robbery or residential burglary).
2. **Personal Cause:** Homicides resulting from a personal conflict between the victim and offender.
3. **Sexual:** Homicides that take place within the context of a sexual assault or rape.
4. **Group Cause:** Homicides that are motivated by a political ideology or religious beliefs.

All homicides will fall within one of these four categories and once the category of homicide can be determined then the search for an offender can often be narrowed. When the category of homicide cannot be readily determined or there are multiple possibilities to explain the death, this is an example of an **equivocal** death and suicide may be one of those possibilities. One important factor to remember, homicides that are staged to resemble suicide, often originate from some type of *personal conflict or personal cause*.

Antemortem Activities of the Victim

For all death investigations during the preliminary investigation, the deceased's antemortem activity is important but there are there are some significant differences between suicide and homicide death investigations. For homicides, the victim's antemortem activity is typically centered on the

The Initial Response and Preliminary Investigation for Suicides   29

victim's last activities, movements, and potential contacts. This effort is also focused on trying to narrow the time frame of their death. This might include determining the last time they were seen alive, where were they were last at or where had they gone, what were they doing at the time, and who were they with. This effort is also to attempt to identify potential witnesses, suspects, or persons of interest based on the category of homicide behind the crime, and the deceases last activity.

Learning the last known activity of the deceased, is an immediate need, to get an understanding of any recent events in their life and generate investigative leads. Efforts to determine their activities in homicide cases are initially focused on the activities immediately preceding their death.

For reported or suspected suicide cases, the deceased's antemortem activities are also critical, but may have to be expanded from the previous day's activity to weeks and even months prior to their death. Joiner (2011) notes that contrary to a suicide myth, *suicides do not happen suddenly or without warning*. Generally, there are verbal or behavioral clues expressed by the deceased prior to the actual event. In real suicide cases, there are often significant changes in the victim's personality, their outlook on life, and their interaction with family and friends. The problem is that many of these verbal indicators or behaviors were not recognized or were misinterpreted by those close to them. Box 2.1 are examples of some typical verbal or behavioral indicators that are consistent with those contemplating suicide.

When conducting interviews of family and friends during the preliminary stage, detectives should be listening for any verbal or behavioral indicators as indicated in Box 2.1. The more verbal and behavioral indicators that are found, the more consistent the event is likely a suicide. Some of the indicators might be "long term" meaning they have been occurring for a length of time before death, in some cases were noticed weeks or even months before their death. Such long-term actions may include increased consumption of alcohol or drug abuse, withdrawing from normal activities, saying goodbye to friends or extended family, giving away their personal property. Other behaviors may have been noticed only shortly before the event such as changes in sleeping habit, changes in personal hygiene or living conditions, or collecting the means to commit suicide such as the purchase of a weapon. Verbal behavior as noted in Box 2.1, can often be subtle and at the time they were said may not have been associated by others as contemplating suicide.

These types of questions concerning the victim, their background, and recent activities are automatic in cases of homicide, yet they are seldom if ever asked or followed up on in cases of suspected suicide. Detectives often

BOX 2.1 VERBAL AND BEHAVIORAL INDICATORS OF THOSE CONTEMPLATING SUICIDE.

- Talking about suicide – making statements such as "I'm going to kill myself," "I wish I were dead," or "I wish I hadn't been born" "You would be better off without me."
- Collecting the means to end their life, obtaining a gun and ammunition or stockpiling pills.
- Researching suicide online.
- Withdrawing from social contact and wanting to be left alone.
- Experiencing mood swings, such as being emotionally high one day and deeply discouraged the next.
- Preoccupied with death, dying or violence.
- Feeling trapped or hopeless about a situation.
- Increasing use of alcohol or drugs.
- Changing normal routine, including eating or sleeping patterns.
- Change in personal hygiene and dress.
- Doing risky or self-destructive things, such as using drugs or driving recklessly.
- Giving away belongings or getting affairs in order when there is no other logical explanation for doing this.
- Saying goodbye to people as if they won't be seen again.
- Sudden and extreme changes in eating habits/losing or gaining weight.
- Withdrawal from friends/family or other major behavioral changes.
- Dropping out of group activities.
- Personality changes such as nervousness, outbursts of anger, impulsive or reckless behavior, or apathy about appearance or health.
- Frequent irritability or unexplained crying.
- Lingering expressions of unworthiness or failure.
- Lack of interest in the future.
- A sudden lifting of spirits, when there have been other indicators, may point to a decision to end the pain of life through suicide.
- The recent suicide, or death by other means, of a friend or relative.

The Initial Response and Preliminary Investigation for Suicides 31

make one of two common mistakes concerning the antemortem verbal or behavioral aspects of a potential suicide.

1. Either they never interview the family or attempt to look for any these indicators and thereby establishing evidence that the death was consistent with suicide.
2. If they do ask or collect such information, it is generally obtained from a single source, such as a spouse, but there is seldom any attempt to confirm with others such as parents, siblings, close personal friends, or with juveniles, their teachers, or classmates.

Because suicide is a *death investigation*, such background information should be confirmed or corroborated in the same manner as homicide cases. If the background information, the physical and forensic evidence is all consistent with a suicide, then there are no other real issues. The need for clarification and confirmation of the background information was previously indicated in a previous Case Study 1.1, but is also found in Case Study 2.1.

CASE STUDY 2.1

Police were called to a reported suicide in a motel room at a vacation spot. The 35-year-old "boyfriend," stated that he and his girlfriend, the 21-year-old deceased female, came to the hotel for a brief vacation. While there they got into an argument, and he threated to end their relationship and then stormed out of the room to "cool off." He returned an hour later and found his girlfriend hanging in the bathroom by her belt on the bathtub shower rod. The boyfriend told responding police he felt bad because she clearly was upset over the potential break up and before he left, she told him "*She couldn't live without him,*" and "*You'll be sorry.*" The boyfriend believed his threat to break up caused his girlfriend to commit suicide. However, when the police spoke to the parents of the deceased, another explanation of the event was provided. The parents stated their daughter went to the hotel, not to stay for a vacation, but to break up with the boyfriend. This was based on his previous abusive and controlling behavior toward her. According to the parents she finally realized she had made a mistake by getting involved with him and wanted to get away. The family also noted that the deceased was neither highly emotional or impulsive and she had made plans for later that same evening to meet the family and discuss the results of the breakup and her plans to change her life's direction.

Case Study 1.1, and the previous Case Study 1.2, are both examples of "*routine cases*" that were certainly more than routine. Both case studies highlight the importance of confirming facts as reported and inquire about the deceased's background or what was going on in their lives preceding their death, using multiple sources.

Explanation of Events

During the preliminary investigation of any death, there are some standard investigative steps. This includes a detailed interview of the person that found the body or discovered the crime, and then the persons that are closest to the deceased. One of the first steps in any death investigation is the elimination of the person that reported the crime or found the body, from being involved in the death. Studies by Miller et al (2020), Harpster and Adams (2017), and Chancellor and Graham (2017) are clear that in many instances, persons involved in causing the death of the deceased, were the ones that make the 911 call to report the death.

Those immediate interviews would include the spouse, and those having an intimate relationship with the deceased. In the case of deceased children, those questioned should include the parents, caregivers, and other relatives. Depending on the event, this might also include close friends or coworkers. Detectives should also look for confirmation from other witnesses that are unlikely to be suspects if the death is later determined to be a homicide.

There are a couple of reasons for these immediate interviews such as obtaining information as to what happened, if they were witnesses to the event, or the circumstances surrounding the discovery of the body. Of critical importance during these initial interviews is to also establish the whereabouts or alibi for each witness during the time before the death, including the person that found the body or reported the crime. If a person can be confirmed to be in another location at the time of the death, then they can theoretically be eliminated as a potential suspect. Establishing their whereabouts is important because as noted by Chancellor and Graham (2017) person(s) most likely to be *considered as a suspect* are the ones most likely to attempt to misdirect the police. It is easy to eliminate most witnesses who happened to discover the crime or just made the 911 call. It is always easier to eliminate those persons who report the crime, as soon as possible; then try to eliminate them if they ever become a suspect.

The Initial Response and Preliminary Investigation for Suicides   33

Changes in the Explanation of Events

The following case study is a much more extreme example of changes in a suspect's explanation of events. Once it became clear the initial version of events was not being accepted by the police, the woman simply changed tact; and initiated an entirely different narrative as to what happened. Not all suspects are able to pivot in midstream and change their story completely, but some have that talent and can be very believable.

CASE STUDY 2.2

In the early morning hours a wife made a hysterical 911 call reporting an unknown man, dressed in black clothing, had broken into her house, shot her husband, hit her in the head, and then fled the scene. Police officers quickly arrived and found the husband in bed with a single gunshot wound to the right temple and the wife with a blunt forced injury to the forehead. During their crime scene examination police noted fresh pry marks on the door, but they were inconsistent with someone trying to force entry into the house. The police department's K-9 officer was dispatched to the scene but found no indication of an intruder inside the house or that anyone had fled the scene. The house was also located in a gated community and security cameras at the entrance did not identify any traffic entering or departing the scene. The wife was examined and found to have a small contusion on her forehead but did not seem consistent with her report. The investigation quickly turned toward the wife; but when confronted with all of these inconsistencies she changed her story. She admitted staging the scene and reporting a false home invasion because her husband had actually committed suicide. She explained that she had been in the living room when she heard a noise in the upstairs bedroom. She went upstairs to investigate and discovered her husband had shot himself. She then cleaned up evidence in the bedroom, made the pry marks on the front door, and then struck herself in the head with a blunt object all in an attempt to provide evidence of a home invasion. She explained that she was only trying to protect her young daughter from ever finding out her father had committed suicide. The medical examiner later determined the gun that killed the husband was fired at a distance of between 12 and 18 inches away from his head and therefore would be inconsistent with a self-inflicted wound. The wife was later arrested for murder.

Chancellor and Graham (2017) provide the following case study of another staged scene wherein the offender placed a pistol in the victim's hand following their murder, to make the murder appear as a suicide.

CASE STUDY 2.3

A 28-year-old female was found shot to death in her car in a church parking lot about a block from her home. When officers arrived at the scene, they observed the female sitting in her vehicle, with a bullet wound above her left ear, and a small caliber pistol found in her right hand. Also found at the scene was an unsigned computer "*note*" that stated: "*I can't do this anymore, my life was a lie, may God have mercy.*" The scene was clearly presented as a suicide. However, when the police questioned the deceased's family, they told the police the deceased did not own a gun and had given no indication of any problems in her life. The only real personal issue involving the victim was a dispute over lateness or nonpayment of child support with her former boyfriend. The boyfriend was located, but during his initial police interview denied he had even seen the victim for over a year. After two hours with the police, the boyfriend changed his story and admitted he had agreed to meet the victim and talk about the child support issue. He admitted meeting her in the church parking lot but only for a few minutes. While there, he said he wrote her a check for back child support and then departed. When he left the scene, she was still alive and sitting in her car. The police had already found the check inside her purse during the examination of the vehicle. The police interrogation continued and a short while later, the boyfriend changed his story again and admitted that while they were talking, they started to argue, and the victim produced a pistol and they had fought over it, and she was accidentally shot. Instead of trying to revive the victim, the boyfriend said he returned to his own vehicle where his own young daughter was waiting and drove away. Along the way he tossed his shirt with the girlfriend's blood on it into a trash can and then returned home and took a shower. He was just finishing the shower when the police arrived to talk with him. The boyfriend was eventually arrested and charged with first degree murder. He later pled guilty and was sentenced to 30 years.

This death was clearly a premeditated homicide, evidenced by the preprinted computer suicide note and the placement of the weapon in her hand. But, as in many staged scenes, the offender makes a mistake by placing

The Initial Response and Preliminary Investigation for Suicides 35

the pistol used to kill her not in her left hand to correspond with the entrance wound, but into her right hand which was immediately recognized as an inconsistency.

Case Study 2.3 highlights the importance of scene observations and follow-up interviews concerning the recent activities and what was happening in the deceased life prior to their death.

Other aspects to consider when considering the deceased's intent to end their life is the mechanism that was used to end their life. For instance, a firearm tends to be more lethal than other means such as poison, intentional drug overdose, or mixing drugs and alcohol. Another indication of the intent to end their life is found when the victim used multiple means to do so. These events are known as *complex suicides* and if present, is consistent with the intend to end their own life. Case Studies 2.4 and 2.5 are examples of *complex suicides*.

CASE STUDY 2.4

A man was found in his garage hanging by a rope tied to the rafters. The garage was filled with car exhaust from his running vehicle. At autopsy multiple undigested capsules and pills were found in his stomach and toxicology revealed a high blood alcohol level. In this case the man combined alcohol and prescription medicine, carbon monoxide from his car engine, and then hanged himself.

CASE STUDY 2.5

A man was found in his laundry room in a large sink filled with water. He was found with his head and upper torso underneath the water and his legs positioned above the sink. It appeared that he placed water into the sink and then lowered himself into the water as if to drown. The water was bloody from several deep cuts to both wrists and other parts of his body. From the scene the man had cut himself at another part of the house, then went to the laundry room and got into the sink full of water.

Clearly in Case Studies 2.4 and 2.5, the victims used multiple means to ensure their deaths. Using multiple means is a clear indication of their intent to end their life.

Other general facts and circumstances relating to the intent of the victim to end their life may be established by identifying other risk factors that they are dealing with in their life. This includes their current life situation, past experiences, relationships, work habits, social environment, and mental issues.

Gathering background information on the deceased from family and friends can sometimes be problematic because of the initial disbelief and denial of the person taking their own life. Suicidal intentions aren't always obvious to family and friends, especially if the deceased tried to conceal such thoughts. However, the outward signals and behaviors as noted in Box 2-1, if present, are consistent with someone thinking of suicide. One key factor to determine is if there are any recent or sudden significant changes in the victim's personality, outlook on life, or interaction with family and friends. Sometimes these changes can be traced back to a *precipitating event*.

Precipitating Event

A precipitating event is an antemortem event occurring shortly before the homicide or suicidal act that may be interpreted as *"the last straw"* or what may have contributed to the victim's final decision to follow through with their suicide. In a homicide, the precipitating event may be something that

---

BOX 2.2 THESE ARE THE HIGH-RISK FACTORS THAT SHOULD BE CONSIDERED WHEN APPROACHING A POTENTIAL SUICIDE INVESTIGATION.

- Age of the victim.
- Marital/relationship status of victim, experiencing separation, divorce, or loss of partner?
- Overall health: any recent changes, problems, or diagnosis?
- Experiencing long term pain?
- Socioeconomic living conditions.
- History of alcohol or drug abuse.
- Prior suicide attempts?
- Are there any financial problems?
- Are there any employment problems, layoffs, terminations, loss of pay, or responsibility?
- Recent arrests or legal actions?
- Are there any pending court actions?

The Initial Response and Preliminary Investigation for Suicides　　37

angered or upset the offender that led to violence against their victim. These precipitating events often, but not always, takes place within the preceding 96 hours of their death. For suspected suicides, an example of a precipitating event might include a recent severe life stressor such as loss of employment, loss of a significant other, or other traumatic event.

Box 2.2 highlights some of these significant risk factors that could contribute to thoughts of suicide or become that final *precipitating event*. Efforts should be made to identify, document, and confirm any of these risk factors that were present at the time of their death.

The importance of examining the deceased's background to identify such factors will be apparent when following their background check and canvass of family and friends, and whether the deceased experienced any of these risk factors. The absence of risk factors with a suspected suicide is inconsistent and highly suspicious. Such incidents require additional investigation.

Suicide Notes

Another element which may or may not be present at a suicide death scene is a *suicide note*. The suicide note is considered as the last communication by the deceased to family and friends. If found, they can be extremely important to understand the mindset of the deceased prior to death. However, notes are only found in about 20% of the time and the presence or absence of a note does not necessarily prove or disprove a suicide took place (Adcock & Chancellor 2017; Joiner 2011). There have been instances where a suicide note was found at the scene that was actually written by the victim but at an earlier time in their life and was used by the offender as evidence to stage the scene of the murder. If notes are found, then they should be evaluated as evidence and if appropriate, sent to the crime laboratory for DNA, fingerprint, and handwriting analysis. Notes written on a computer or printed by a printer, as noted in Case Study 2.4 should be questioned, since there is no way to really verify if it was the victim that wrote the note. What has become popular in recent times are "*suicide notes*" or the last communication of the victim is recorded as an audio or video file on a phone or other digital device. This of course is very valuable evidence. Additional detailed information on suicide notes is found in Chapter 9.

Who Would Benefit from the Death?

As part of any death or murder investigation consideration must be given to whom would benefit from the death of the victim. The most common benefit is monetary based on insurance or inheritance. Other more intrinsic benefits could also include freedom from a failing or unsuccessful marriage without a divorce action, removal of the victim from a business partnership, revenge based on some personal slight or other action by the victim. As stated, many times before in this text, there are as many motives as there are offenders. Generally, it is not difficult to determine who would most benefit from the death. As with any death investigation, this is an important investigative step as this would be a potential motive for murder.

Chapter Summary

The key to all death investigations is a good preliminary effort and the first 48–72 hours are critical to obtain evidence and conduct key interviews. Every death should be considered as a homicide, even those that are initially reported as suicide or those instances when the initial scene observation appears to be consistent with suicide.

This concept is extremely important because suicide is among the top four themes used to misdirect a police investigation away from the true facts. When the scene is staged, the offender is counting on the police to accept their version of events and prepare a cursory report and close their investigation. When this happens, the offender gets away with their criminal act.

The preliminary investigation into suicide cases should focus on identifying the *why* or the motive behind the act. If the why cannot be easily discerned, then additional investigation is warranted.

References

Adcock, J. M. & Chancellor, A. S. (2016). *Death Investigation* (2nd ed.). Amazon Publishing.

Chancellor, A.S. & Graham, G.D. (2017) Crime Scene Staging, Investigating Suspect Misdirection of the Crime Scene, Charles C. Thomas, Springfield, IL.

Douglas, J. E., Burgess, A. W., Burgess, A. G., & Ressler, R. L. (2006). *Crime Classification Manual* (2nd ed.). New York, NY: Lexington Books Inc.

Geberth, V. J. (2013). The Seven Mistakes in Suicide Investigation. *Law and Order Magazine*, 61(1), 54–567.

Harpster, T., & Adams S. H. (2017). *Analyzing 911 Homicide Calls: Practical Aspects and Applications*. Boca Raton, FL: CRC Press.

Joiner, T. (2011). *Myths about Suicide*. Cambridge, MA: First Harvard Press.

Miller, M. A., Merola, M. A., Opanashuk, L., Robins, C. J., Chancellor, A. S., & Craun, S. W. (2020). "911 What's Your Emergency?": Deception in 911 Homicide and Suicide Staged as Homicide Calls. *Homicide Studies*, 25, 108876792094824. https://doi.org/10.1177/1088767920948242

Staged Crime Scenes

3

Introduction to Crime Scene Staging

One of the cautions of conducting a death investigation is the real possibility that the facts and circumstances presented to the first responding officers were altered from what really happened to resemble some other fact or circumstance. The alterations of the scene and false information provided by witnesses are examples of the concept of *crime scene staging*. Altering the scene is basically an effort for offenders to distance themselves from a crime, by misdirecting the police investigation away from the true facts and hopefully shifting the blame or responsibility onto something or someone else.

Most law enforcement practitioners are familiar with the general concept of staged crime scenes, wherein the offender has added, removed, or changed the location of evidence or the victim. This effort is done with criminal intent to misdirect a police investigation. During these events, an offender is essentially attempting to create a false reality by making the scene resemble some other set of facts or circumstances. In most professional literature, whenever the topic of staging is discussed, case studies of a homicide staged to resemble either a suicide or accidental death are often used as examples of crime scene staging. As noted previously, Chancellor and Graham (2017) identified suicide as one of the top four themes used to misdirect a police investigation and cover up a homicide.

Suicide as a theme is popular because it doesn't take a lot of preparation or require a lot of scene alteration to make the claim. As noted previously, if an altered scene appears to be consistent with the reported death, it is very likely that the explanation will be accepted. If the first responder accepts the version of events offered by the witness, it is likely no additional investigation will take place. Therefore, the offender's general intent when staging any scene is to get through the initial police response. If they are successful, there is a good chance there will not be an investigation, and they will get away with murder.

According to Chancellor and Graham (2017) staging or crime scene alteration can be categorized based on the behavior and intent of the offender. They have identified two distinct categories of crime scene staging, *identified*

DOI: 10.4324/9781003373865-3

39

as primary or secondary staging. They have also identified other crime scene alterations as being *Tertiary or MO Related Behaviors.* Efforts to misdirect a police investigation is generally understood as the main motive behind most scene alterations and is categorized as *primary staging.*

The focus on this chapter is in the *primary category* of staging wherein the offender is attempting to *misdirect* the police investigation. Within primary staging there are two subcategories known as *ad hoc and premeditated.*

Ad Hoc Staged Scenes

The term *ad hoc* is generally defined as: impromptu, unplanned, and without apparent forethought or prompting. These staging events refer to scene alterations that take place after some other unplanned event has taken place. The best example are those deaths that take place during a domestic violence incident, and now the offender must come up with an explanation for the authorities. The scene alteration is an active effort to divert attention away from themselves and what really happened, to some unknown person or event, and thereby avoid any responsibility for their actions. In these cases, staging is seen as necessary because the offender realizes that they are going to be the most likely suspect if the death was the result of a criminal act. Most *ad hoc* type events are based on a need for the offender's *self-preservation*; that is the offender is attempting to cover up another criminal event by creating another explanation for the event or death. Chancellor and Graham (2017) note that in *ad hoc* events, the scene alteration and the explanation of the event tends to point away from them and onto some unknown person, action, or event.

Because the scene alteration takes place after another incident has already occurred, it is generally easier to sort out and identify because the offender is forced to base their explanation and alterations on whatever material happens to be present at the scene. Since offenders attempting to stage the scene are not real victims, they must rely on what they have seen on TV, read in a magazine or book, or seen in the movies. Ultimately the scene alteration boils down to what *they think* would convince the police that their version of events is true. They also must depend on their ability to convincingly relate a rational and believable story.

Because the explanation of events is not planned out in any great detail, inconsistencies are usually much easier for investigators to recognize and uncover. One of the key features of this type of staged scene is the nature of the description of events and the *"evidence"* left behind or presented to the investigators at the scene. This is why often when the victim has suffered

Staged Crime Scenes

blunt force trauma during the initial event, the scene is staged to resemble some type of fall such as falling downstairs. For those victims that may have been strangled during the previous event, they may be staged to resemble a hanging, suffocation, or drowning event.

Premeditated Staged Scenes

The second subtype of primary stage scene is referred to as *premeditated*. These are events wherein the offender has *planned* the crime, i.e., homicide, beforehand often meticulously. Premeditation offers the suspect the opportunity to plan, conduct research, preposition evidence, practice or conduct a trial run if needed, and even come up with a believable story and often be able to provide an alibi. The important difference between *ad hoc* and *premeditated* staged scenes is the amount and type of physical evidence that is often provided to establish what is being portrayed. Premeditated scenes therefore tend to be more complex and well thought out and often include physical and sometimes even forensic evidence. Whereas *ad hoc* staging explanation of events and evidence tends to point *away* from the actual act, and onto other "unknown factors;" premeditated primary staging tends to have clear evidence an explanation that focuses the police "*onto the act*" or the event being portrayed. Basically, the offender wants the police to concentrate on the event being portrayed, thus the need for physical and forensic evidence.

Even in premeditated incidents, offenders will make mistakes because they are not fully aware of what happens during these events for instance, a very common mistake in staging a scene to resemble a suicide is the placement of the weapon in the victim's hand as depicted in Figure 3.1. Placing the weapon into the victim's hand postmortem is supposed to make it appear that the weapon was in the victim's hand when they were shot. Placement of the weapon, in the victim's hand is one of the easiest things to add or change to the scene to make it seem consistent with the reported death. But note in Figure 3.1, the offender made a mistake because all four fingers are around the pistol butt. The question is, if the victim was holding the weapon in this manner, how could they pull the trigger? This is the type of simple mistake made by the offender in their attempt to stage or alter the scene.

Garavaglia and Talkington (1999) completed a study of suicide deaths involving the use of firearms. In their review of 498 suicides by firearms, they found the gun remained in the deceased's hand in only 24% of the total cases and only 25% of the time when handguns were used. In 69% of the time the gun was found on, or immediately near the body. In the remaining 7% of cases, the gun was found a little further away from the victim. They

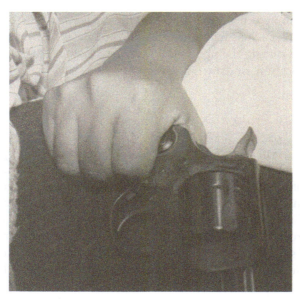

Figure 3.1 This is a reenactment demonstrating how the first responder found the weapon in the victim's hand. Note, it is in an unlikely position to have pulled the trigger.

did find the gun had a greater chance of remaining in the deceased's hand if the person was lying down or in a sitting position when the gunshot wound was received. Variables such as gender, wound location, or caliber of handgun were not significant in predicting whether the gun stayed in the hand after a suicidal gunshot wound. Therefore, it is more likely to find the weapon on or adjacent to the victim, rather than in their hand following a self-inflicted wound, but laymen staging a suicide are not aware of this fact and frequently insist on putting the weapon in the deceased hand as evidence of their suicide. This aspect of the weapon location is covered in greater detail in Chapter 4.

Many times, the offender attempting to misdirect the police investigation may play a major role in the staged event by being the person who finds the body or reports the crime to the police. In other incidents they may arrange for others to find the body while they are away establishing an alibi. Thus, as noted in Chapter 2, it's of great importance to eliminate the person that finds the body or reports the crime first. In many instances another person may have found the body, but they did so because of a request to *"check"* on the victim by the offender. An example would be an offender who asks the police to do a welfare check on someone because there has been no contact

Staged Crime Scenes

with them for some time. The police then respond to the scene and discover the deceased victim had committed suicide. By arranging for someone else to find the body the offender is attempting to establish an alibi as to their location as the event is discovered.

In both subcategories of primary staging, the offender will often state how shocked they are over the suicide, because they know of nothing in the preceding weeks to indicate the victim was even contemplating ending their life. This is especially prevalent in domestic situations where the spouse or significant other has allegedly taken their own life. The surviving spouse/partner insists there were no recent arguments or fights, no current relationship issues, no overwhelming financial problems, or any medical issues. Basically, they tend to deny the presence of any risk factors that are present in most suicides. There seems to be an overwhelming need for the offender who stages a scene, particularly a domestic partner, to *paint themselves in the most positive manner*, by pointing out how responsible they were; how strong the relationship was, or express frustration at the event taking place when they were not around to prevent the act.

These efforts to portray the event as a total surprise are actually harmful to the offender because they are denying any of the motives that would cause someone to take their own life. This presents a clear *dichotomy*, wherein the person closest to the victim reports none of the common risk factors being present prior to the death; yet the presence of the various risk factors is consistent and expected in real suicides. As previously noted, no one just wakes up and decides to end their life, so such dichotomies should be considered as inconsistent with suicide, and further clarification is needed.

Motives Behind Staging

Understanding motive will help in identifying the offender involved in the scene alterations. Hazelwood and Napier (2004) note that in staged scenes there are always two motives present that must be considered. The first is the *original motive* behind the crime and the second is the *staging motive* or what the offender is trying to portray. For those events staged to resemble a suicide, the original crime is murder, and the original motive typically focuses on:

1. **Greed or Monetary:** Where the motive is some financial gain from the victim's death. Typically, this involves collecting life insurance or other monetary benefit from the victim's death.
2. **Anger/Revenge**: Where the homicide is motivated by some deep personal conflict, relationship, or domestic issues. Many times, the

homicide is planned with the intent to stage the scene as a suicide to avoid suspicion onto the offender.

3. **Cover Up Criminal Conduct or Self-Preservation**: In these circumstances, the offender attempts to alter the scene to explain away their own participation in another criminal act, such as domestic homicide. The staging effort is an attempt to avoid being held responsible for their actions. Another example is a fatal traffic accident where a deceased passenger is removed from their position in the vehicle and placed into the driver seat and the actual driver attempts to assume the position of a passenger; thereby, placing the blame of the traffic accident on the deceased and not themselves, the actual driver.

As noted by Chancellor and Graham (2017) there are as many motives for committing a criminal act or staging a scene as there are criminals. Motives for suicide are covered more extensively in Chapter 8.

Suicides that Are Staged to Resemble Homicides

In staging events surrounding suicides, there is also another real possibility that might confront police. This is an *actual suicide* which is staged to resemble a homicide. This of course is a twist, but the intent is still to *misdirect a police investigation*, only this time the intent is to portray the death as a homicide to police. Chancellor and Graham (2017) described these incidents as a victim attempting to shift responsibility for their deaths onto someone else rather than onto themselves. They want to be remembered as a *victim of a crime*, and thus blameless for their death, opposed to someone that took their own life. These events can also include efforts to implicate a particular person for their death, to cause that person some problems or to some unknown person. There are some that may stage their deaths as homicides because of a suicide clause in their life insurance policy. If they simply committed suicide, their families might not receive the proceeds for their life insurance.

These events are typically premeditated and some instances there is extensive research into various ways to stage their death as a murder. As such there tends to be evidence at the scene that appears to be consistent with homicide.

Chancellor and Graham (2017) provide Case Studies 3.1, 3.2, and 3.3 as examples of victims who have committed suicide but staged their death to resemble a homicide.

Staged Crime Scenes

45

CASE STUDY 3.1

A 25-year-old man was found in the early morning hours, dead inside his car parked on a city street a short distance from his own house. Responding police initially looked at the scene as a possible homicide based on the initial observations at the scene. The victim's legs were bound by duct tape, his mouth had a cloth stuffed inside and was covered with duct tape, and his entire head was covered with plastic and secured with duct tape. Preliminary investigation on the victim's background however discovered the victim had become upset when a female he had met on-line refused to meet him in person and was trying to break off any contact with him. The police contacted the woman who provided them the last email she had received from the victim where he had stated words to the effect of "If you don't receive a "good morning message from me in the morning you can read about me in the newspaper." Also attached to the email was a photo of a stuffed animal he said he had bought for her as a present. The police noted the same stuffed animal was found in the front seat of the victim's vehicle when they found his body. At autopsy the Medical Examiner (ME) noted no signs of physical trauma and the man's wallet, and cash were found in his trousers and personal jewelry such as ring and gold necklace was also present. The ME determined the cause of death was asphyxia and most likely caused by the plastic wrapped around his head. He also found approximately 100 undigested sleeping pills in his stomach.

During their preliminary investigation, the police were initially confused as to the cause of death and were unable to identify any clear motive for the victim's murder. Based on the autopsy and scene examination they began to look at the death as a possible suicide. The autopsy finding of undigested sleeping pills in his stomach and the other pills found inside the car are examples of a complex suicide wherein the victim will use multiple means to ensure their death. Police also learned the victim was emotionally crushed when the woman he had established an online relationship, declined to meet him in person. It was clear from his online communication he had become enamored with her and believed they were establishing a serious romantic relationship. The woman was clearly not interested in such a relationship and had lied to him, writing that she was moving to another city some distance away to break off their communication. This is a good example of the victim

46   Equivocal Death

wanting to inflict guilt onto the woman through his very public death but did
not want it to appear that he had committed suicide.

CASE STUDY 3.2

A male census worker was found hanging from a tree near a cemetery
in a national forest. He was naked, his hands loosely bound with duct
tape, his identification badge taped to his neck, the word "FED" was
scrawled across his chest. His pickup truck was found parked nearby,
the tailgate was down, and police considered the victim may have been
transported to this location in the bed of the truck. Police and witnesses
initially theorized the man may have been murdered by antigovernment
adherents upset by some action of the federal government and perhaps publicly displayed his body to gain attention to their cause. Police
noted, however, that although he was hanging from the rope, he was
not actually off the ground, in fact his feet were on the ground and all
he needed to do was to stand up and relieve the pressure. Analyzing the
word "FED" written across his chest, the police concluded the letters
were written from the bottom to the top, which is inconsistent with
someone facing the victim and writing on his chest, but totally consistent with the victim looking down as he wrote the word. The police
also found no evidence of a struggle at the scene, there was no other
trauma to the victim's body, and laboratory analysis revealed only the
victim's DNA was on the gag in his mouth. The police also discovered
the victim had recently taken out two separate life insurance plans just
before his death, but each policy had a clause that would not pay for
suicide. Additionally, if the victim was killed on his job, his family could
receive an additional $10,000 death gratuity from the US Government.
Based on the totality of circumstances, the police concluded the victim
had staged the scene to resemble a *"lynching,"* but had committed suicide. Police believe that staging his death as a homicide was a way to
avoid the *suicide clause* in the recently purchased insurance policies.

CASE STUDY 3.3

A base employee arrived at a US Army Reserve Center and found the
body of the Commander, a Major General in the army reserve, hanging
from a rope in a stairwell of the headquarters. His hands were bound

Staged Crime Scenes

behind his back with a military web belt and although there were no signs of physical trauma, the employee reported seeing blood coming from his nose and mouth. Police responders found the general dressed in civilian clothes, his jacket folded neatly on the second-floor landing, with his wallet and his glasses on top of the jacket as if carefully placed there. Police also found a typewritten note pinned to his shirt that read:

> Convicted, sentenced, and executed for crimes by the U.S. Army against the people of the world.

During a search of his office, the police also found a handwritten note on a writing tablet that read:

> It is about 1145 hours and I started out of the building and caught a glimpse of some people in the building who moved toward the back of the bldg. I don't know who they are or what they are doing. They were apparently startled. I came back here to call the MP's, however I cannot get any of the telephones to work. Just as a precaution I am placing my office keys in my shoe. I will call the MP's as soon as I can get to a phone.

The autopsy concluded the cause of death was asphyxiation from hanging; but the ME found no evidence of trauma and the blood found on his face was likely the result of pulmonary edema a common finding in asphyxia deaths. The ME also found no defensive wounds or any signs the General had put up any resistance throughout the incident.

The crime scene examination and subsequent investigation could find no evidence of anyone else having been in the building. The phone system was operational and there was no evidence that it had been shut down or tampered with. Additionally, the note pinned to his chest was typed on the electric typewriter found in his office. The handwritten note was written in his own handwriting, but the contents did not really make sense. If he had surprised someone suspicious coming into the building, then why would anyone take the time to write this all down instead of escaping to safety? Also, was there a need to explain in a note where he was hiding his office key? This last statement seems too inconsistent if he were really concerned for his personal safety.

The theme of the previous case study seems to resemble a terrorist act wherein the general was somehow targeted by terrorists for punishment or

48   Equivocal Death

in retribution for some political act of the US Government. The idea to stage the scene in this manner may have originated with the circumstances of the kidnapping of Brigadier General James Dozier by the Red Brigade that had taken place in Italy in 1982.

A background investigation discovered the victim was being investigated by the federal government for fraud and tax problems, and his family business was failing. His suicide appears to be a way to avoid any embarrassment by his arrest and possible conviction, and if his death was accepted as a homicide, he would die a hero not a criminal.

The following case study is an well publicized event that hit national news just a few years ago.

CASE STUDY 3.4

In the morning hours of September 1, 2015, in Fox Lake Illinois, Charles Gliniewicz a police lieutenant with the Fox Lake Police Department, radioed his dispatched that he was pursuing three men, he described as two white and one black, for some unknown offense. He reported his location as in the rear of an abandoned cement plant. After the initial radio call, the dispatcher was unable to establish further contact with him. Other Police officers responding to the area discovered his body about 50 yards from his vehicle. The scene appeared as if a struggle had taken place as his head was scraped and bruised and his radio, taser, and pepper spray were found scattered around him and his weapon was also found nearby. Gliniewicz had been shot, apparently by his own weapon twice. One bullet struck his mobile phone and ballistic vest, and another pierced his upper chest. Massive efforts to locate any suspects were undertaken but were unsuccessful. A homicide task force was created because it was the murder of a police officer who well respected in the community. Gliniewicz was known to the community by his nickname "G.I. Joe," and because of his work with the youth in the city through the police explorer scouts. His popularity combined with his position as a law enforcement officer added to the pressure to find his killers. But, as the police began the investigation, they began to discover some information that made them reassess the event. They soon discovered Gliniewicz was being questioned by members of the city council about the explorer scout program and the expenditure of funds, resulting in an audit of the police explorer scouts. This was clearly going to be a problem because the police discovered he had embezzled thousands of dollars from the youth program. These thefts amounted to a five-figure sum and had taken place over a seven-year time frame. Further they were able to determine that Gliniewicz used the money on such things as home mortgage payments, vacations, first class air fares, gym membership, and pornography he obtained through adult websites. Further infractions involving Gliniewicz were also uncovered including threatening a dispatcher with a firearm, allegations of sexual harassment of other employees, alcohol use on duty, and numerous suspensions based on his personal conduct. Reviewing his emails and text messages police recovered over 6,500 deleted text messages and over 40,000 emails many detailed his criminal activities and comments to others about his desire to "take out" the village administrator who was demanding the audit of the Explorer program. The Task Force that was formed during the initial stages of the investigation eventually determined that his death was not the result of a homicide but a carefully staged suicide.

In the previous case study, the victim, a well responded police officer, was about to be found out as a thief and was likely going to be fired and probably prosecuted. He was not willing to face the possibility of his loss of status and chances of ending up in prison, so he chose to end his life, but he wanted to "go out as a hero and not a criminal." Although he avoided embarrassment and potential punishment for his actions, this did not happen to his wife and family. His wife was later indicted on four counts of disbursing charitable funds without authority and for personal benefit, and two counts of money laundering. Authorities later seized five bank accounts believed to be derived from embezzled funds. His wife later pleaded guilty to some offenses. Military investigators later found out his son, an active duty soldier, participated in a fraudulent marriage to Gliniewicz's girlfriend, so she could receive medical and other benefits from the military.

The events described in the preceding case studies do not happen often, but they do happen are additional examples of crime scene staging to misdirect a police investigation. There is another type of staging that is uniquely found in cases of real suicides, and it also involves the altering or rearranging of the scene, however, the scene is not altered with the intent to misdirect a police investigation, it is altered or staged by the victim in almost a ritualistic manner. Such activity is an example of what Chancellor and Graham (2017) identify as *secondary staging*.

Secondary Staging

According to Chancellor and Graham (2017) *secondary staging* basically refers to a second type of scene staging wherein offender scene alterations are unrelated to efforts to misdirect a police investigation. Rather the alterations are made for more personal reasons that are important to the offender. Douglas et al (2007) describe this effort as *personation* of a scene, wherein the offender inserts their *personality* into the scene. Such alterations may include aspects of the offender's fantasy that may include murder, body posing, postmortem mutilation, or depersonalization when involving a sexual offense. In other cases, it is something the offender needed to do at the scene for their own personal reasons. Most aspects of secondary staging are found in relation to sex offenses or sexual homicides.

However, there are also examples of the victim staging or rearranging the scene in a symbolic manner in suicide cases, probably to help them go through with their planned suicide. The rearranging of the scene for this purpose is not designed to misdirect the police investigation but should be seen as consistent evidence that the death was the result of suicide. Case Studies 3.5 and 3.6 are examples (Figure 3.2).

Figure 3.2 This figure depicts deceased surrounded by photographs of his family and other personal items. His favorite music was being played by a cassette recorder also present.

Staged Crime Scenes

CASE STUDY 3.5

Police were called to a motel after management found a deceased person in one of their rooms. When police arrived, they discovered a fully clothed man, lying in bed, with his hands crossed over his chest as if he were sleeping, except he had a plastic bag over his head. On the other bed was several small and one large photo album opened to what appeared to be family pictures. The other smaller albums also contained photos of what turned out to be the man's family. Next to the photos album was the man's wallet, check book, and car keys. On the end table between the beds was a note, an empty pill vial of sedatives, and the book *Final Exit,* about assisted suicide. There were no signs of trauma, and the motel room was locked from the inside with a chain lock. At autopsy the pathologist found several undigested tablets of the sedative in his stomach and toxicology noted the presence of a large amount of the drugs in his body.

CASE STUDY 3.6

A wife returned home to find her estranged husband sitting on the living room floor, leaning back against the sofa. He had a gunshot wound to his right temple and a pistol was found on the floor next to him. Surrounding him were photos of his family and wife, and some of his children's stuff toys. A cassette deck was playing music which his wife identified was "their" favorite artist. There were also several empty bottles of beer near the victim. On the small table next to the sofa was the deceased's wallet, checkbook, keys, and a few other personal effects and several notes in sealed envelopes. The wife explained that they were in the process of divorce and that she had moved out of the house several weeks prior. She had only returned to the house to obtain some additional personal effects because she thought her husband was at work and would not be there. The wife reported that her husband had called her the previous night and begged her to return and reconcile, but he sounded drunk, and she didn't want to talk to him when he was drinking.

In Case Studies 3.5 and 3.6, each victim had taken the time and effort to place photos and other special items near them where they could be viewed before they finally took their own life. Each victim laid out their personal effects, wallet, car keys, and checkbooks, where they could be easily found, and both left a note. Arranging the photographs and personal effects at the scene is an example of *secondary staging* because these items were added to the scene but were not needed to complete the act. Chancellor and Graham (2017) describe the arrangement of these items as being placed symbolically at the scene. It was clearly important to the victims, perhaps to view as they worked up the courage for the final step of ending their life. This type of scene addition should be looked at as part of the victim's plan to end their life and if present at the scene, it would be consistent with a suicide.

This type of scene alteration does not take place often and when it does, responding police do not always recognize the victim's effort to arrange the scene is an example of staging. These additions to the scene are obviously important to the victim and unlike other staging efforts to misdirect an investigation, these scene alterations are consistent with suicide.

One of the more famous examples of this type of secondary staging was the mass suicide of members of the Heaven's Gate religious cult in March 1997. Details are found within Case Study 3.7.

CASE STUDY 3.7

On March 26, 1997, the San Diego Sheriff's Office found the bodies of 39 members of the Heaven's Gate religious cult. The mass suicide was confirmed when police found several video tapes recorded by the cult leader Marshall Applewhite, wherein he noted his belief that mass suicide was "the only way to evacuate this Earth." He also provided an explanation of their beliefs that after their deaths, their souls would be collected by a spacecraft that was following behind the Hale–Bopp comet which would be passing by earth at the time of their deaths. This spacecraft or UFO would take their souls to another "level of existence above human." The group further exposed beliefs that human bodies were merely vessels, or "vehicles," which could be "abandoned" when they were ready to ascend to the next level. Their deaths were necessary so their souls could board the spacecraft as the comet was passing earth. As part of their preparations for a ritualistic suicide, each member videotaped their farewell message. To end their life, members voluntarily consumed apply sauce or pudding mixed with phenobarbital and drank vodka. They then secured plastic bags around their heads and basically went to sleep. The combination of drugs, alcohol, and plastic

Staged Crime Scenes

bag covering their heads, led to an asphyxia death. The staging aspect is seen with how the victims were found. Each of the victims had shaved their heads and were identically dressed in black shirts, sweatpants, and Nike sports shoes. They all wore an armband patch reading "Heaven's Gate Away Team." Each also had a five-dollar bill and three quarters in their pocket. Lester (2015) notes that the uniformity of dress symbolized their membership and concurrence of the group's action. The suicides were not completed all at once but rather in groups of around 15. After each member died, the remaining members would remove the plastic bag from the person's head and then arranged the body, so it lay neatly and comfortably in its own bed, their faces and upper bodies were then covered by a square purple cloth. Police surmise that they died in three separate groups over the course of three successive days. The 39 victims included 21 women and 18 males, ranging in ages between of 26 and 72.

Case Studies 3.5, 3.6, and 3.7 are examples of what Lester (2015) describes suicide as being a *staged performance* wherein suicidal individuals may create a dramatic event by the choices they make for their suicidal act. This can be seen in the clothes they may choose to wear, the location they pick for their death, the method they use to kill themselves, and what communications they may leave for others. This seems to imply that suicide is often much more of a deliberative event rather than just an impulsive spur of the moment reaction to something.

Other examples of "staged performances" are those "suicides" wherein the victim arranges it to be viewed by others. The following are examples of this effort.

1. There are numerous cases wherein the victim commits a public suicide by self-emulation as a form of political protest. Perhaps the most famous was Thích Quảng Đức, a Vietnamese Mahayana Buddhist monk, who died by suicide on June 11, 1963. Đức, sat in the middle of a busy street in Saigon, Viet Nam. Another monk doused him with gasoline and then he struck a match and was immediately engulfed in flames. He explained in a letter that his death was a protest against the persecution of Buddhists by South Vietnam's Roman Catholic government. His death became so well-known because it was photographed by an AP reporter.

2. A soldier deployed to combat zones, had received a "Dear John Letter" from his wife asking for a divorce. The solder managed to contact the wife over the internet and when using a computer video

application, took his life, which was observed by his wife. The purpose was to inflict pain onto his wife for "causing his death."

3. A man found out his wife was involved in an extra marital affair with their neighbor. The victim asked the neighbor to come over to his house to discuss the situation. In front of his wife and neighbor he produced a pistol and took his own life in front of the other two people. A note found later explained his personal devastation over the affair but absolved the neighbor from any involvement in what happened. He blamed his death on his "cheating wife."

4. Another well publicized "public suicide" took place in July 1974, when Christine Chubbuck, a local television news anchor took her own life on camera, after first stating: "In keeping with Channel 40's policy of bringing you the latest in blood and guns and in living color, you are going to see another first—attempted suicide." She then produced a pistol and shot herself in the head while still on camera.

5. On January 22, 1987, Robert Dwyer, the then Pennsylvania state treasurer, called for a public press conference just hours before he was to be sentenced after being convicted of bribery. Dwyer began speaking to reporters and live television crews about his situation, including his innocence and distrust of the justice system. Dwyer then pulled a .357 Magnum from an envelope. From the video recording taken of the incident, it was clear he wanted to make a final statement, but when several persons tried to approach him, probably to obtain the pistol, Dwyer suddenly placed the barrel of the gun into his mouth and shot himself without making a final statement.

As noted in previous case studies and other examples, some victims will take the time and effort to "stage" their suicides. But such staging is not designed to misdirect the investigation and such efforts should be seen as evidence *consistent* with suicide.

Tertiary or Incidental Scene Alterations

There are additional examples of scene alteration, that commonly take place, but these alterations are not made by an offender or the victim and have no criminal intent. Most of these alterations are made by others such as family and friends of the victim. Douglas and Munn (1992) and Chancellor and Graham (2017) note that these alterations occur to protect the victim or the

Staged Crime Scenes

victim's family, and often take place in cases of autoerotic misadventures, or suicides. The alterations are normally performed without a lot of forethought by the person who finds the body and the intent is to avoid embarrassment to the rest of the family or to restore some dignity to the victim. Examples could include a husband covering or redressing his wife's body or in the case of an autoerotic fatality, someone may cut the noose, or the device suspending and, in some cases, may attempt to remove female clothing that many times the victims are wearing.

Douglas and Munn (1992) described these scene alterations as examples of staging because they have altered the scene. However, Geberth (2006) and Chancellor and Graham (2017) do not describe these actions as staging, because they are not made by the offender and there is no criminal intent associated with the alterations. Chancellor and Graham (2017) categorize these scene alterations as *tertiary or incidental scene alterations*. Tertiary simply refers to a 3rd type of scene alterations.

An example of this type of scene alteration is found in Case Study 3.8.

CASE STUDY 3.8

A family physician went to the residence of one of his patients and found the 25-year-old female deceased in the master bedroom. She was found in bed and had apparently overdosed on several medications and alcohol and had left a note explaining her actions for her parents. The doctor immediately collected the medications and the note and hid them before he called the police and report the death. The police arrived and began their investigation and quickly determined that the victim did not die because of a criminal act and autopsy confirmed there was no trauma on her body, and she did not die from natural causes. However, toxicology results revealed excessive amounts of drugs in her system. The police then turned to the physician who finally admitted that he had cleaned up the scene, including taking the suicide note to protect the family. The physician later plead guilty to obstruction of justice.

Efforts to protect the family by rearranging the scene or the victim can be confusing to responding to police but can be understandable. If there was no criminal intent to misdirect an investigation, then these actions are not examples of "staging." However, in those situations where the victim or scene is altered with the intent to change the manner of death from suicide to another manner, with the intent to obtain some reward such as insurance settlement, then the scene was altered with criminal intent. Because there was criminal intent, this would be an example of staging.

Therefore, it is always critical to determine the motive or reasons behind any scene alteration.

Chapter Summary

The concept of crime scene staging is really a relevant term; meaning, there are no absolutes as to what constitutes a staged crime scene and there is no limit to what efforts an offender may take to alter the scene. It literally depends upon the offender and the crime they are attempting to portray. Much depends on the amount of *"false evidence"* that is available for them to use, and the general intelligence or willingness of the offender to produce the false evidence.

Suicide is one of the more common themes used to stage a homicide and misdirect a police investigation. Because suicide is such a common occurrence in our society, police are almost desensitized to the event and are often ready to accept the premise of self-destruction without a great deal of investigation. The various case studies in this chapter highlight the philosophy that *every death should be initially viewed as a homicide until the facts and circumstances can be established*. The offender attempting to stage a homicide to look like a suicide is counting on the complacency of the police to only take a minimum look at the scene and accept their version of events to get away with their criminal act.

As the case studies noted, the true facts of the event may be uncovered by that critical look at the scene, conducting a basic victimology assessment, identifying any precipitating act, and eliminating as a suspect anyone who may benefit from the death of the victim.

Bibliography

Chancellor, A. S., & Graham, G. D. (2017). *Crime Scene Staging: Clues to Suspect Misdirection at the Crime Scene.* Springfield, IL: Charles C. Thomas.

Douglas, J. E., & Munn, C. (1992). Violent Crime Scene Analysis: Modus Operandi, Signature, and Staging. *FBI Law Enforcement Bulletin,* 61(2), 1–9.

Douglas, J. E., Burgess, A. W., Burgess, A. G., & Ressler, R. K. (2007). *Crime Classification Manuel, A Standard System for Investigating and Classifying Violent Crimes* (2nd ed., p. 34). San Francisco, CA: Jossy-Bass Publishers.

Ferguson, C., & Petherick, W. (2016). Getting Away with Murder: An Examination of Detectives Homicides Staged as Suicides. *Homicide Studies,* 20(1), 3–24.

Garavaglia, J. C., & Talkington B. (1999). Weapon Location Following Suicidal Gunshot Wounds. *American Journal of Forensic Medicine and Pathology*, 20(1), 1–5. https://doi.org/10.1097/00000433-199903000-00001. PMID: 10208326.

Geberth, V. J. (2006). *Practical Homicide Investigation, Tactics, Procedures, and Forensic Techniques* (4th ed.). Boca Raton, FL: CRC Press.

Hazelwood, R. R., & Napier, M. R. (2004). Crime Scene Staging and Its Detection. *International Journal of Offender Therapy and Comparative Criminology*, 48, 744.

Lester, D. (2015). Suicide as a Staged Performance. *Comprehensive Psychology*, 4, Article 18.

McNamara, J. J., McDonald, S., & Lawrence, J. M. (2012). Characteristics of False Allegations of Adult Crime. *Journal of Forensic Science*, 57(3).

The Crime Scene

4

Responding to Reported Deaths

Only a small proportion of deaths that occur in the United States every year actually require any additional investigation because most deaths can be attributed to old age, disease, some other natural occurrence such as weather (tornados, floods, lightening, or exposure) or are clearly accidental. As noted previously, there are actually more reported suicides and accidental deaths than there are homicides, so the police are much more likely to respond to a reported accidental death or a suicide.

However, many times the only thing separating a criminal from being held responsible for their actions is a good scene examination and subsequent follow-up investigation. This is the basis for Geberth's (2015) insistence that all *deaths should be approached as if they were homicides until the true facts can be pieced together*. Therefore, a crime scene examination should be an automatic request for every death case.

This is an important concept because as noted by Chancellor and Graham (2017) those offenders who try to stage a crime scene or otherwise misdirect a police investigation understand to be successful in their crime, they often only have to get through the initial police response. If the police suspicions are not aroused by their initial viewing of the scene, then it is likely their crime will never be investigated. Offenders are counting on their ability to alter the scene, police complacency, or the general lack of training by patrol officers to get away with murder.

As repeated throughout this text, it is imperative that regardless of the initial report, all deaths should be considered as potential homicides and first responders should not be arriving at the scene of a reported "suicide" with an expectation of what they will find, because first impressions do not always prove to be accurate. As noted in Chapter 2, if the police arrive at the scene with a *predisposition* that they are responding to a suicide, their subsequent actions tend to mirror their predispositions as noted in Case Study 4.1.

DOI: 10.4324/9781003373865-4

59

CASE STUDY 4.1

The fire department of a major US City received a call of an injured person and responded. Upon arrival they discovered a 22-year-old male college student in his bedroom bleeding from the mouth, nose, and ears. His roommates volunteered their belief that he must have somehow taken a fall and hit his head. The EMTs noted a small 0.22 caliber survival rifle laying nearby and based on the amount of blood emitting from his mouth, the EMT suspected he may have been shot intraorally. Based on the bleeding, they were never able to make a positive determination at the scene. An ambulance arrived and the young man as transported to a local hospital and later succumbed to his injury. The fire department had also called the city police and reported the possible shooting. It's important to note that the following actions of the responding officer were captured on his own body. As the patrolman arrived at the scene he was met by the fireman and other two roommates outside the residence. The patrol officer was briefed and went inside the residence, followed by the other two roommates and the fireman. They all made their way to the bedroom where the young man was shot and at one time there were four people inside the bedroom that was a potential crime scene. With the other three people remaining in the room, the officer then began walking around the room picking up various personal items from the floor, looking at the various objects them and setting them back down. He picked one item from a pile of clothing and personal effects looked at it and put it back down onto the pile. That object then slid off the pile of clothes and into a pool of blood on the floor. The officer made no attempt to remove the item from the blood. He also picked up the small caliber rifle from the floor, made sure the weapon was not loaded, and then put it back down on the floor. But not in the same position as he found it. He continued looking around the room and eventually, he observed an expended shell casing and picked it up, looked at it and returned it to the general location where it was found. A few minutes later he picked the rifle up again, placed it on the dresser, and took several photos of the weapon. He then placed the gun onto a stack of boxes a few feet away from where he initially found it on the floor. By picking up and setting down these items he was basically creating post event artifacts including moving the location of the weapon. In all death case the location or position of a weapon is a critical piece of evidence. From his actions it is clear that the officer was responding to what he believed was a suicide and there was little concern to protect the scene separate witnesses or keep scene integrity.

The Crime Scene 61

Case Study 4.1 is an unfortunate but common example of initial police responses to what they believe is a suicide or accidental death. When responding to such incidents, even experienced police officers seem to completely forget their training and basic responsibilities as the first responder. But there is no excuse for any uniformed police officer to ever pick up or move anything in the scene regardless of the crime but especially in a death investigation. Patrol officers are typically not trained to examine the scenes; but even so, they should not be moving anything until the scene has been correctly documented. What is so tragic about the above case study, information was later developed that indicated the manner of death was possibly homicide. However, because of the failures and mistakes of the first responder, the police were in a difficult position to really conduct a further investigation.

Closely related to Case Study 4.1 is Case Study 4.2, which is another common occurrence in initial police response to "suicide" cases.

CASE STUDY 4.2

In the early evening, Officers were called to an apartment by a woman who reported after a domestic violence incident, her boyfriend believed he would be going back to jail and produced a pistol. He shot several times toward her and then turned the gun on himself. He had been sitting on a chair in the living room but after shooting himself in the head, he fell to the floor. Police arrived at the scene, observed the man on the floor, and checked him for signs of life. After determining he was dead, the police then observed a pistol on the floor next to the man. Almost automatically, an officer picked up the pistol, unloaded it, and then "tossed it" onto the sofa located a few feet away. They also determined there was a child still in the back bedroom, so they covered the man's body with a bed covering, picked the child up and took him outside (see Figure 4.1). Upon CSI's arrival the initial responding officers initially insisted they had only checked for signs of life and did not otherwise enter the residence. However, CSI quickly observed the body was covered, the pistol was not near the body, and there were bloody footprints in the carpeted hallway (see Figure 4.2). The officers finally admitted to covering the body, to avoid letting the child see the man as he was removed from the residence. They also admitted to unloading and moving the pistol as a safety measure, and they must have stepped into the blood in the living room as they recovered the child. It was not clear why the officers initially denied entering the scene.

Figure 4.1 Responding officers placed the bed spread over the man's body, unloaded the pistol, and then tossed it onto the sofa (see arrow). They then initially denied altering the scene. With the pistol so far away from the body, it changed the initial perception of the event.

Luckily in Case Study 4.2, the scene alteration did not really change the outcome of the investigation. Based on the totality of evidence and information the death was correctly determined to be the result of suicide. Both Case Studies 4.1 and 4.2 illustrate one of the most common first responder mistakes in all instances of violent crimes. That is the overwhelming need for police to render a weapon found at the scene "safe." It's not clear why this is such a universal mistake made by first responders, but it happens at great frequency.

The Crime Scene 63

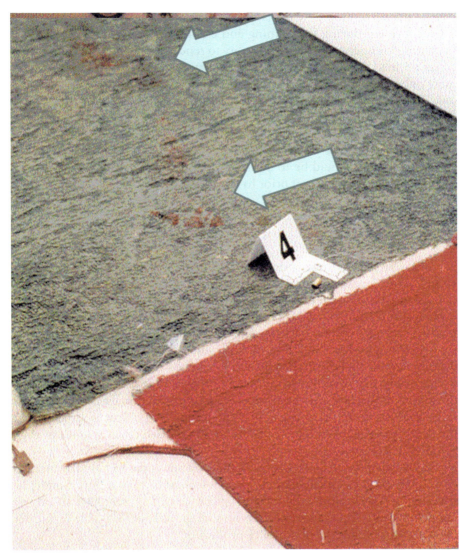

Figure 4.2 Arrows indicate bloody footwear impression found on the hallway carpet. The officer's initial denial of entering the residence changed the initial perception of the scene.

As a follow up to Case Study 4.2, the situation and errors identified in the case study were used in a training session with the same department. One of the main teaching points was there was no need to render a weapon safe if the victim is deceased and there is no one else around. The weapon is not going to discharge by itself and moving the weapon could potentially change the perception of what happened. The officer involved in Case Study 4.2 was present during the training and emotionally responded to the class by stating his opinion as to the necessity to render all weapons safe at a crime scene no matter the situation. He then stormed out of the training session quite offended by his actions being questioned or the mistake being pointed out. This is clearly a problem not just with suicides as noted in the above case studies but in many other crimes of violence and needs to be corrected throughout all law enforcement.

Therefore, one of the detective's first steps upon arrival at any violent crime scene, should be to address if the responding officers or anyone touched or moved a weapon prior to their arrival.

The First Responders Role

So, what are the first responders' actual duties in a violent crime or death scene? Most departments rely on their uniform personnel to make an initial assessment as to the basic facts of the death and the need for additional investigation. Unfortunately, as noted in the previous case studies, not all uniformed police officers have the experience and training necessary to make such on the spot determinations and this often results in some questionable deaths never being fully investigated or erroneous conclusions made because of the lack of investigative effort. Many of these procedural errors start with the initial responding officer that makes a snap evaluation based on a limited scene evaluation. In many agencies if the responding officer is satisfied that the death was the result of an accident or suicide detectives might not even respond to the scene.

Sadly, when the true facts of a death may not come to light for months or even years, until an offender commits a second or even a third homicide, covering up their criminality by staging the scene to resemble a suicide or accidental death. The tragedy of course is that the offender was able to murder other victims because of poor police procedure.

The investigation of all crimes begins with receiving the information from the complainant, responding to the scene, and in most cases conducting a crime scene examination. The crime scene examination is considered to be the bedrock or foundation for all criminal investigations and Gardner (2005) states its importance very clearly, "*Crime scene processing is an inherent task and duty associated with most criminal investigations, for rarely does one encounter a crime without some kind of crime scene.*"

The initial police response to every reported crime is typically the uniformed patrol officer that answers the initial complaint. The uniformed first responder has several specific important duties and responsibilities, in

The Crime Scene

65

violent crimes that need to be accomplished often following an emotional or chaotic event. Therefore, it is imperative that the first responder quickly assesses the scene and then takes charge because there are a lot of things that need to take place in a short period of time. The first responder is expected to rapidly accomplish the following tasks:

1. Get a briefing from the complainant.
2. Arrest the suspect if present.
3. Assess the victim, secure medical assistance (ambulance) if possible.
4. Secure and define the scene (crime scene tape if needed).
5. Separate witnesses.
6. Identify and protect any fragile evidence.
7. Contact detectives as soon as possible.
8. Document activity in their notes for their later report.

There is no real set order for the first responder to accomplish these tasks and a lot will depend on the individual circumstances of the event. For example, if the event has just occurred, upon arrival the office may be confronting witnesses experiencing fear or shock from having observed or discovered a violent act. If the event has taken place sometime before, and the victim was just found, then other emotions might be in play, all of which the first responder may be confronted.

Usually, the most important task for responders is to first assess the victim, check for signs of life, and determine if the victim requires medical attention. Once the victim is confirmed to be deceased, the responding officer should consider the immediate area surrounding the body, or room where the body was found, as a potential crime scene. Therefore, the responder's attention should next be focused on scene protection. This means securing the area by moving other witnesses out of the area to prevent anyone from accidentally or purposely damaging, altering, or destroying anything within the scene.

The next goal is to identify any potential witnesses and if present, to separate them to keep them from comparing their stories with each other. This is often difficult in situations that take place within the family home or involve members of the same family. Remember especially in cases of suspected suicide and accidental deaths, these are often emotional events, and the family are likely to experience shock, denial, and disbelief. The first responder must simply do the best they can under the circumstances to maintain control of the situation until detectives can respond to the scene.

A first responder is generally not trained and should not be expected to conduct any type of crime scene examination. Other than ensuring there is no one else injured or anyone else in the area of the body, or to possibly protect fragile evidence, there is no need for the first responder to walk around

66 Equivocal Death

or remain in the scene. There is also no need to touch or move anything, especially as noted previously, any weapons that may be at the scene. The location or position of the weapon is one of the most critical pieces of evidence when conducting a death investigation. Therefore, moving or changing the location of the weapon can result in the misinterpretation of the scene by oncoming detectives.

For all crimes, especially crimes of violence, the crime scene(s) is perhaps the one only time and location we'll ever know for certain, that both the victim and the offender were together at one location. Therefore, the crime scene is the most logical place for evidence of the crime that can link a suspect, a victim, and a location to each other. A scene examination can also confirm or refute any allegation or complaint.

Arrival of Detectives

Upon arrival of detectives to a death scene, there are several important factors that need to be quickly addressed and confirmed. First to get a briefing by the first responding officers or complainant as to what was initially found. In those cases where the death is believed to be or reported to be a suicide, the detective should view the scene and compare it to the information received about the event, without automatically assuming it is a suicide.

When initially viewing any death scene as a potential suicide detectives should be asking themselves:

1. Could the injury or cause of death have been self-inflicted by the victim?
2. Is the instrument used to cause death present at the scene?
3. Where is the instrument located?
4. Was the victim or scene altered after the death of the victim?
5. Is there unexplained evidence at the scene? (i.e. bloodstains a distance away from the body)
6. Are there any unexplained injuries?
7. Is the lividity and rigor mortis consistent with the deceased's position?

These are just a few of the basic questions that a detective should be asking themselves and observing upon initially viewing the scene. If the questions cannot be answered or seem to be inconsistent, more investigation is probably needed.

Of particular importance when handguns are used to self-inflict injuries is the location of the weapon. As noted previously, offenders seeking to

The Crime Scene

stage a homicide to look like a suicide, typically believe they have to place the weapon in the victim's hand to be consistent (see Figure 3.1.) However, finding the weapon in the victim's hand is possible, but actually infrequent. Figures 4.3, 4.4, and 4.5 are scene are photos of handguns that were found in or near the hands of deceased suicide victims.

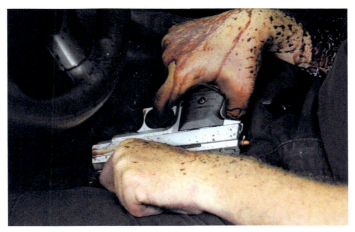

Figure 4.3 This figure depicts a handgun found still in the victim's hand after a self-inflicted wound to the head. The bloodstains on his right hand and on the handgun are a consistent finding of a gunshot wound to the head of the victim. Finding the weapon in the hand of the deceased does happen, but it is rare.

Figure 4.4 This figure depicts the handgun that fell out of the victim's hand as his body fell to the ground after he shot himself. This is a common finding at suicide scenes. The gun is near the hand but is not grasped.

Figure 4.5 The deceased was in a sitting position and shot themselves in the head with a pistol. The hand dropped and the weapon fell out of his grasp. This is a common finding in such scenes.

Note that in Figures 4.4 and 4.5, the guns are found near the hands, but they are not still gripped by the hand.

Figure 4.6 depicts the location of a weapon at the scene of another suicide. In this case, the deceased was sitting on the edge of his bed when he shot himself; he immediately dropped the pistol and fell onto the floor. He landed with his foot near the pistol. This is more common than finding the gun in the deceased's hand, and is also consistent with suicide, as it is only necessary for the weapon to be in the immediate area of the victim.

Even when the initial responding officer believes the scene is consistent with suicide, there is still a need for a proper crime scene examination. Unfortunately, this is when some departments draw the line as to the proper use of their resources. As noted previously, there is often a general belief that since suicide is not a criminal act, there is no need to "waste" resources investigating these incidents. However, as noted throughout this text, there are repeated examples of why it is necessary to confirm or refute the claim of suicide, and the crime scene examination is critically important to do so. But for many agencies this remains problematic.

In death investigations, including homicides, suicides, or accidental, there is no such thing as a "typical or routine" scene. Although there are some standard procedures and protocols for scene examinations, each reported death should be treated as an individual event with its own set of circumstances and dynamics. Therefore, the crime scene protocols should be adjusted to those circumstances. Detectives typically view the death scene

The Crime Scene

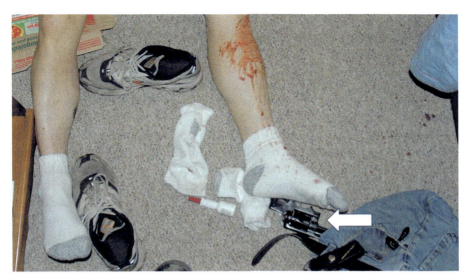

Figure 4.6 This figure depicts weapon found at the scene of a suicide that is not close to the deceased's hand. The weapons' location is still consistent with suicide because the weapon was found at the scene near the deceased. The white arrow is pointing toward the gun.

from a different perspective than crime scene technicians. Whereas the crime scene technicians are concerned with physical and forensic evidence such as fingerprints, blood spatters, DNA, and properly documenting the scene. The detective is concerned with identifying the victim, determining the cause of death, and if the death was the result of a criminal act.

For the remainder of this chapter, it is assumed that the death was reported as a suicide and the best practices for conducting the scene examination are covered. It is also assumed that the detectives have obtained the legal authority to conduct the examination either through consent or through a crime scene search warrant.

The CSI Response

Depending upon the size of the department there may be specially trained personnel that normally conduct violence crime scene examinations. In other agencies it may be detectives specifically detailed to perform scene examinations, or even uniformed officers may be specially trained to work scenes as an additional duty or responsibility.

A major finding from Wellford and Cronin's (1999) homicide clearance study was those departments with specialized crime scene personnel or those who could call on a state or county crime scene unit to process their scenes, had a much higher homicide clearance rates, than those departments that used investigative personnel. This placed specially trained personnel to document and process the scene, while freeing up investigative personnel to concentrate on other aspects of the investigation.

Regardless of who is actually conducting the crime scene examination, traditionally it's the lead detective who is ultimately responsible for the scene and the proper collection of evidence. Meaning the crime scene technicians work for the lead or case detective and should be responsive to their needs and any special requests. At the same time, detectives should listen to the crime scene technicians because they are supposed to be the experts at their job.

As we start looking at aspects of the crime scene examination, there are some very important general concepts to consider in all death investigations. According to Adcock and Chancellor (2016), one important concept is: *the crime scene examination is an opera, not a slam dance.* This concept simply means a crime scene is not just about taking pictures and throwing fingerprint power around; like an Opera the crime scene examination should be processed step by step based on a set and organized plan. Consider the opera, it is written with a set order of music, singing, and other stage movements. It is well organized and scripted and if the same opera were to be performed the following evening, it would have the same music, singing, and stage movements at the same time.

The crime scene examination should generally take place along the same basic order of events and with only minor exceptions because of the particular individual dynamics of each specific scene. For instance, before any examination the scene takes place, it should typically be videotaped, photographed, and sketched before anything is touched or moved. Only after the scene is documented does the actual search for evidence really begin.

Adcock and Chancellor (2016) state another general concept of scene examination:

A crime scene examination is a marathon not a sprint.

Meaning very simply there is, within reason, no real time limit to processing the scene. Therefore, there is no need to pressure or hurry the crime scene techs to complete the scene and there is generally no reason not to do specialized examinations or analysis if they are recommended or believed necessary by the detective or crime scene technician. Sometimes this is a particularly difficult concept to teach and enforce because we, as Americans, tend to be rather impatient and therefore seek instantaneous answers and results. Even worse, they believe a crime scene examination is like what we

The Crime Scene

71

see on television and therefore important evidence should be readily observable and found immediately.

The reality of course is, there are multiple occasions when the crime scene examination has taken several days to several weeks, and in other cases have even taken much longer. It all depends on the scene and the amount of evidence that is contained in the scene. This general concept essentially reminds us we are under no time constraints, or we should not feel we are under any time constraints therefore have to hurry through the scene.

Burned Bridges

One very important concept of crime scene examination deals with the movement of things inside a crime scene. The concept of *burned bridges* expresses an understanding that once an object is picked up or moved, it can never be placed back exactly where it was first found. Examples of this concept being violated were thoroughly described in Case Studies 4.1 and 4.2.

In both of those previous cases studies the initial responding officers by moving items of evidence "*burned the bridge*" so to speak of scene integrity. Those items might be placed close to where it was originally found; but could never be replaced exactly where it was found. The one and only time an item of evidence should be touched, picked up, or moved is when it is collected as evidence.

If those cases when the cause of death is determined to be from natural causes, it is likely that very little investigative effort is going to be necessary. The best example is those people in Hospice care. Police should be called to those deaths but if a quick examination of the deceased notes no signs of trauma, and their enrollment in hospice care is established, then there is probably no requirement to initiate a death investigation. The key here is to confirm their hospice registration. Other examples of natural death may require a little investigation, but typically natural deaths can be confirmed through the age of the victim or through examination of previously medical records to confirm previously identified medical problems.

If the death is the result of some type of accident, then the subsequent investigation is necessary to focus on eliminating any criminal negligence resulting in the death. If not, then it is likely there will be very limited investigation as well.

In cases involving domestic, interpersonal conflicts, which take place within the residence of the suspect and victim, there is a frequent professional disagreement between crime scene technicians and detectives relating to the actual value of the forensic evidence. Because both the victim and the offender may have access to the same area, finding fingerprints, DNA, hairs and fibers, and other such trace evidence from both offender and victim would be expected, and thus may not have the same evidentiary value.

However, regardless of the possible limited value, the scene should be processed in the same general manner as if it was an unknown offender. Adcock and Chancellor (2016) base this idea on several concepts as outlined below.

> First, unless and until the scene is processed normally, we really have no idea what type of forensic evidence is actually present at the scene.

For instance, if the incident took place inside a residence, we might assume to know what is there or what may be found. But without the benefit of processing the scene we truly don't know. Therefore, we have no idea what actual value the evidence might have in the investigation. For instance, we may not know at the initial stages of the investigation any history between the victim and any other person.

> Second, by processing the scene normally it might eliminate an offender from later claiming another unknown offender was actually involved in the death, but the police made no effort to look for anyone else.

In the initial stages of any investigation, we probably are not going to be aware of more than the minimum facts and circumstances of the crime or event. Even when we have the basics and we think we know, the crime scene examination is often completed before we have a chance to really know what happened. But there is a good chance if we don't process the scene as we normally would, we might miss something.

> Third, and actually one of the more important points, every scene should be processed in the same manner as every other scene, because the facts as initially reported and investigated on day one, may change as new information or evidence is obtained.

Basically, what is true and known on the first day is not necessarily what we know to be true the following day or several weeks later. But by then it may be too late to go back and try to redo the scene. We can express these three concepts in a simple statement:

> It is always better to have evidence and not need it, than to need it and not have it.

Although every scene is going to be somewhat different based on the individual circumstances of the scene and the crime itself – there are a few basic steps that are going to be accomplished regardless of the circumstances. Some of these basic steps are described below.

The Crime Scene

Scene Documentation – Photography

Crime scene photography is generally what most people think about when they think about scene documentation. If an agency only had the money to buy one piece of equipment, it should be a good camera to formally document the various scenes and evidence. Especially a digital camera, because of the number of photos that can be taken at minimal cost.

What is a sufficient number of photos; 50, 100, or even 200? There is of course no set number of photographs that you need for a particular scene; rather it's the concept that all aspects of the scene and evidence should be documented.

In addition to the various establishment and close up photos there are also other "*special*" photographs which should be considered as part of the general crime scene documentation. These are photos which center on the victim and properly document their final position. This includes photos of the full body from all possible angles, then separate photos of the body taken in 1/3rds consisting of the lower portions of the legs, the abdomen, and the chest and head. Identification photos should then be taken of the victim's head and face.

These photos of the victim's body are important because they capture not just the body's position, but also the clothing and whatever stains that may be present on the clothing before the body is moved or removed from the scene. It is not unusual once the body is picked up and placed into the body bag and then transported back to the ME's office for autopsy that the clothing may become saturated with blood or receive transfer bloodstains onto the clothing and present quiet a different interpretation of the stains once the clothing is removed and examined.

Additional establishment and close up photographs of all visible injuries and photos of the hands including the dorsal aspect or back of the hand, the palms, and fingers. Photos of the hands are especially important because if the victim attempted or was able to defend themselves it is likely their attempts involved their hands in some manner, therefore these photos will help to validate the presence or absence of any injuries or identify other possible trace evidence.

When the body is eventually moved by the coroner or medical examiner, we also want to photograph the unexposed side of the body, by turning it over or leaning it over and once the body is removed to photograph underneath the area underneath the body and thus hidden from sight.

Depending on the scene and the types of forensic techniques used or evidence collected, it is often a good idea to take a few photographs of the condition of the scene as it was left, to prevent possible complaints by others of damage or destruction of personal property by the police during their examination.

The following case study is a much more extreme example of changes in a suspect's explanation of events. Once it became clear the initial version of events was not being accepted by the police, the woman simply changed

74 Equivocal Death

tact; and initiated an entirely different narrative as to what happened. Not all suspects are able to pivot in midstream and change their story completely, but some do have that talent and can be very believable.

Sketching

Sketching is the third method for documenting a crime scene. This a drawing of the scene typically drawn from a bird's eye view as if we were looking straight down from on top of the scene. The sketch is used to show the spatial relationships between the various items of evidence, and it is an invaluable tool if the scene has to be reconstructed at a later time.

Written Notes

Written notes are the last method of scene documentation and refer to the various observations made at the scene and recorded in the crime scene notes. The importance of the notes is simple, the written descriptions and observations cannot be recorded or observed through video tape or even photographs. Examples would include the ambient temperature, humidity, and other weather considerations around the scene. Additionally, the other documentation mediums cannot provide any information as to any unusual noises, unusual odors, lighting conditions, or the lack thereof present at the scene. This is only going to be documented in written form based on the direct observations by the crime scene technician or detective at the scene.

The documentation of the scene is not just a single initial phase of the examination and then is completed; rather scene documentation continues throughout the examination. As additional evidence is located, then it is further documented through the establishment, close up and close up with measuring device before it is collected, perhaps added to the sketch, and of course adequately described in the crime scene notes.

There are other specialized examinations that might assist in understanding the event such as bloodstain pattern analysis or shooting incident reconstruction. Such examinations would depend on the scene and other evidence but can prove to be very helpful.

Crime Scene from the Detective's Perspective

While the crime scene technician is ensuring the scene is properly documented and examined, the detective is also looking for several other important factors that will add to their investigative effort. These special concerns include establishing the time of death, obtaining additional background

The Crime Scene

information on the victim to assist in their victimology assessment, the general assessment of the crime concerning a possible motive, as well as looking for other offender behavioral clues left behind.

When viewed from an investigative perspective, *the crime scene is the one time the offender actually tells us all about themselves.* Unfortunately, many detectives do not take the time to listen to what the offender is saying by their actions or through their behavior.

An offender does not always leave behind physical or forensic evidence, but they almost always leave some clues about themselves at the crime scene. Sometimes this evidence is left behind quite unintentionally, and the significance must be deduced from the totality of facts and circumstances found at the scene. Other times evidence is left behind quite purposely, as if to make their own unique statement regarding the victim or the reason behind the crimes. Other evidence left behind may be intended to cause a misinterpretation by police of the true evidence and events. What is left behind of course is always dependant upon the individual offender and their specific motive for the crime, the particular victim, and the location of the scene.

In addition to the behavioral evidence, we are also concerned with some more basic facts and circumstances which are covered below.

Time of Death

Determining the time of death as stated before is a very critical finding in any death investigation and should always be one of the main focuses of the detective during the crime scene examination and/or preliminary investigation. The time of death is going to be used to compare to any other event or information such as statements and alibis that are developed throughout the case. All other facts, circumstances, or evidence developed through the course of the investigation are going to be looked at as either *antemortem* (before death events) or *postmortem* (after death events).

Generally, the longer the time period between death and discovery of the body, the more difficult it is to determine the time of death. If the event is not observed by another person or somehow recorded by other means, any time of death determination is likely to be an educated guess covering a span of time. This educated guess can be determined from observation of the various physiological changes after death, such as algor, livor, and rigor mortis. These physiological changes are relevant and can be useful in determining the approximate time of death if the body is discovered within a few hours to 24 hours after death. But, generally if more than a day has passed then the time of death determination becomes somewhat more problematic and other available facts may have to be used.

Fortunately, in this modern age we have many different ways to track a person's whereabouts or activity. Even in a residence we have potential dated material, we may be able to determine if the mail was delivered or picked up, if there are telephone messages, if there are cell phone text messages, if any emails were sent or received and/or opened. With a little extra effort, we can also determine the last time a phone call was made to the victim and received, the last time the internet was accessed, and the last time the victim's ATM or credit cards were used.

Many times, an approximate time of death must be estimated through use of a combination of facts and events as noted in the following case studies:

CASE STUDY 4.3

A mother and father were found murdered in their house on a Sunday afternoon by their two sons. The last contact with them was on Friday around 6:15 when the oldest son called to talk with them. During the call the father mentioned that mother was in the kitchen cooking steak and potatoes, their typical Friday evening meal. During the crime scene examination of the kitchen area the police noted the steak was still in the skillet nearly cooked, and there were potatoes still in the microwave based on the phone call and the steak still in the skillet on the stove the police were able to circumstantially back up the time of the incident to sometime around 6:15 to 6:30. Although the time of death was not exact, it was a logical assumption that the victims were confronted by the offender and their death likely occurred sometime after the phone call. Although not perfect, it provided a fairly good, estimated time frame the police could use.

Release of the Body

At some time the scene examination will reach a point where it is safe to remove the body without the possibility of further contaminating the scene. Removal of the body is the responsibility of the country coroner or the ME and their assistants but any time the body is moved or examined; it is a good idea for the detective to be present to observe. Our main interest of course is to document any additional injuries or determine if the body has any identification documents in their clothing and observe the area underneath the body which was unobservable until the body was moved.

The Crime Scene

Search Beyond the Scene

After the crime scene technicians have documented the scene, completed their forensic examination, have collected all of the visible physical and forensic evidence, and the body has been removed, it is recommended an additional more conventional search of the scene is conducted. This search is focused more on documenting and collecting the non-forensic evidence at the scene and would include a general search through the scene such as desk drawers, closets, dressers, under mattresses, or sofa cushions. Basically, we want to look through the scene for any hidden evidence. It is not uncommon while conducting the search beyond the scene to find very important physical or forensic evidence in the most unusual places. There are many instances after looking in the refrigerator, police have found the suspect's bloody fingerprints on an item in the refrigerator; or the murder weapon is found in between the sofa cushions, or love letters between the mattress and box springs in the bedroom.

There's a wide range of possibilities of what constitutes non-forensic evidence and is really based on the individual facts of the crime. Several examples might include personal day planners, day calendars, address books, notebooks, diaries, letters, phone records, checkbooks or registers, business records, tax records, medical records, personal photographs and papers, or other personal records. There are endless possibilities as to the actual type of documents or other evidence found at a death scene.

Currently, we are finding more and more of this type of information is not always found on paper documents, but rather maintained in some electronic medium such as cellular telephone, blackberries, pagers, computers, portable hard drives and back up devices, recordable CDs, thumb drives, and other personal electronic devices. Making the seizure and later examination of these type items very desirable and often very rewarding with the type and amount of evidence retrieved.

Although we might recover them during the scene examination under the authority of a crime scene search warrant, a second separate warrant, authorizing the examination of the contents of this electronic medium is going to be required. This is also going to be the responsibility of the police detective and will have to be completed before the medium is ever examined.

Completion of Crime Scene Examination

At the completion of the crime scene examination and after the scene is released, it is necessary for the detective to file a search warrant return in the same manner as other search warrants; advising the court of the items seized during the execution of the warrant.

It is also important to coordinate with the crime scene technician to have a clear understanding of all of the items of evidence that have been collected for the search warrant return, as well as a clear understanding of the potential forensic examination at the crime lab. Evidence collected during the examination should be submitted expeditiously to the lab for examination, typically there is a long waiting list of cases pending examination, it is beneficial to get the evidence into the "cue" as rapidly as possible instead of waiting a period of time and then submitting which means, there is an even longer time period to wait for the forensic results.

Chapter Summation

One of our main concerns as detectives is to insure there is no criminality associated with any reported death. It is very difficult to return or try to "redo" a crime scene examination if it is not done correctly or if one is not conducted at all. We generally have one chance to process the scene with as little contamination as possible. We need to do it correctly. We need to work as a team. As we noted in this chapter, the key is always the basics, the scene documentation, scene contamination, and following a standard protocol.

One of the main concepts of crime scene investigation regardless of the crime or event being investigation is: *it is always better to have evidence and not need it, than to need it and not have it.*

References

Adcock, J. M. & Chancellor, A. S. (2016). *Death Investigation* (2nd ed.). Amazon Press.

Chancellor, A.S., and Graham, G.D. (2017). *Crime Scene Staging, Investigating Suspect Misdirection of the Crime Scene.* Springfield, IL: Charles C. Thomas.

Douglas, J. E., & Munn, C. (1992). Violent Crime Scene Analysis: Modus Operandi, Signature, and Staging. *FBI Law Enforcement Bulletin,* 61(2), 9.

Fisher, B.A.J. (2022). *Techniques of Crime Scene Investigation* (9th ed.). Boca Raton, FL: CRC Press.

Gardner, R.M. (2005). *Practical Crime Scene Processing and Investigation.* Boca Raton, FL: CRC Press.

Geberth, V.J. (2015). *Practical Aspects of Homicide. Tactics, Procedures, and Forensic Techniques* (5th ed.). Boca Raton, FL: CRC Press.

Wellford, C., & Cronin, J. (1999). *Analysis of Variables Affecting the Clearance of Homicides: A Multi Site Survey.* Justice Research and Statistics Association, Washington DC, (NCJRS# 181356).

Forensic Autopsy

5

The Need for Autopsy

In many states there is a requirement to conduct an autopsy for any unattended death, but this is not always the case. There are many locations in the United States where the county coroner may decide on their own, that the cause and manner of death is clear and thus no need for an autopsy to be performed. This decision may be based on an effort to save the local jurisdiction money on the autopsy or to win favor from the family who does not wish an autopsy to be performed. Regardless of the reason or rationale, without an autopsy to establish the facts, the cause of death is basically a "*best guess*" made by someone in an elected position without any medical experience or training. Refusing to conduct an autopsy is a frequent complaint by family members, especially when they are disputing the death as the result of suicide.

The main problem with not conducting an autopsy is the cause and manner of death can be challenged or not accepted by the deceased family or friends. Which leads to mistrust and a continuous conflict with the police and the coroner over the investigation. Even after an autopsy, there are still instances when the findings are challenged by the family as *denial* is a very strong emotion. However, the benefit of the autopsy to the police actually comes in those rare instances when later information arises that the death was the result of homicide.

An autopsy is basically an external and internal examination of a body to determine two key questions: (1) the cause of death and (2) the manner of death. The forensic examination of the body is a key step in any death investigation including suspected suicides and other equivocal death events. Timmermans (2005) makes an important point *that "an autopsy alone rarely provides sufficient evidence of a suicide."* This is really an understatement of the need for detectives to actively engage with the pathologist and provide them with detailed information as to the scene, results of the preliminary investigation, and antemortem behaviors of the victim. This type of information is only going to be available for the pathologist if the detectives first collect it then provide it to the Medical Examiner (ME) prior to the autopsy.

DOI: 10.4324/9781003373865-5

79

80 Equivocal Death

Working with the Medical Examiner (ME)

Timmermans (2005) identifies seven different types of information that the ME should have available at the time of an autopsy to properly determine the manner of death, especially in suspected suicide cases.

1. **Witness Reports.** This especially includes when the event has been witnessed by someone, such as police who interacted with the victim prior to the self-inflicted injury, or someone who has witnessed the victim jumping from a bridge or building.
2. **Suicide Notes.** These are important indicators but are only found in limited events.
3. **Suicide Guidelines.** These are the events where the victim has apparently followed the guidance of others outlined in various publications such as Derek Humphry's (1997) *Final Exit.* Such guidance might be found by the mode of death that resembles suggestions outlined in the book, or the book is present at the scene.
4. **Previous Suicide Attempts.** This is always a strong indicator of suicidal intent.
5. **Testimonials.** This is basically the information, or statements obtained from family and friends as to the background of the victim, including any of the previously identified risk factors, or other ante-mortem behaviors.
6. **Life Crisis.** This would include a variety of potential situations including recent relationship problems, death of a loved one, serious health problems, arrests, or pending legal prosecutions or confinement.
7. **Mode of Dying.** Suicidal intent can also be found in the mode or cause of death, for instance the use of a firearm is more lethal than attempts to overdose with pills.

The ME needs as much information and background on the deceased as possible in order to fully understand the event. Much of the information above, such as testimonials and life crises, is obtained from the *victimology assessment* normally initiated during the preliminary investigation, as family and friends are interviewed concerning recent events in the victim's life. As noted above and in the previous chapters, the manner of death determination in suicides and other deaths needs to be a cooperative effort between the police and the ME.

Figure 5.1 and 5.2 are messages written in the deceased blood on the wall next to him. It was considered as his last communication or suicide note and is an example of evidence or information that was found at the scene that should be provided to the ME.

Forensic Autopsy 81

Figures 5.1 and 5.2 These are examples of "messages" found at the scene of a suicide, where the deceased wrote in his blood after cutting himself. Although not necessarily a traditional suicide note, they are consistent with the last thoughts of the deceased.

The Autopsy

There are two general types of autopsies, forensic and clinical. Forensic autopsies are generally performed by a forensic pathologist often referred to as the *Medical Examiner or ME*. Forensic pathology is a subspecialist in pathology, that includes specialized training in the examination of persons who die suddenly, unexpectedly, due to violence, or a criminal act. The main goal of the forensic pathologist is to determine both the *cause*, and *manner of death*. A medicolegal or forensic autopsy is ordered by the coroner or the ME, and can be conducted without prior approval of the next of kin.

Clinical autopsies are conducted by pathologists that may or may not be forensically trained. The purpose of the examination is to evaluate or identify the presence of any disease or injury that may be present for public health, research, or educational purposes. One major difference between the forensic and clinical autopsy is the next of kin must give their permission to conduct the examination of the deceased and may therefore limit the examination to only certain areas of the body. Although the exact cause of death, due to disease maybe already known, one purpose of the clinical autopsy is to determine the extent of the disease and/or the positive or negative effects of any therapy on the disease. It is also beneficial to identify the presence of an undiagnosed disease that might have contributed to death. Therefore, most of the clinical autopsies are performed on those persons who have died in the hospital while being treated for some reason. These deaths are also known as "*attended deaths*" meaning they were under someone's care at the time of death or in the cases of hospice patients, death was expected.

It is important to note that if a patient was brought' to the hospital because they were the victim of some violent act, and then they die days, weeks, or even months after the event, the death would not be considered as an attended death, even when they were in the hospital at the time, because they were injured in a criminal act. Generally, the manner of death would be considered as homicide.

An autopsy is almost always needed when presented with any unattended death, no matter how "obvious" or "routine" the scene appears. An autopsy is a critical step in all death investigations regardless of the circumstances. As noted in previous case studies, there are examples of unattended deaths being considered natural, thus no autopsy was conducted. However, years later, additional information was uncovered that led to the victim being disinterred, autopsied, and found to have been murdered by strangulation. Information and evidence obtained from the autopsy is found in Box 5.1.

To accomplish the above tasks, the forensic pathologist needs to be able to evaluate the entire situation including observations at the scene,

BOX 5.1 LISTS SOME OF THE IMPORTANT INFORMATION AND EVIDENCE OBTAINED THROUGH THE AUTOPSY.

- Determine the deceased's identity.
- Determine the cause of death.
- Determining the manner of death.
- Identify and document all injuries.
- Correlate an injury to potential objects producing the injury.
- Determine the time of injury, onset of illness, and time of death.
- Identify any contributing factors to the death (i.e., toxicology).
- Determine the postmortem interval.
- Confirm medical history.
- Separate complicating medical factors.
- Obtain samples for toxicology.
- For infants, determine live birth and viability.

Forensic Autopsy

statements from witnesses, historical information about all participants, and the evidence thus far collected. To ensure a successful outcome, all agencies involved must work together cooperatively.

Cause of Death vs. Manner of Death

As previously discussed, terms *cause* of *death and manner of death* are often conflated, and many times misunderstood. The cause of death is basically the mechanism or reason that caused the person to die, whether from an act of violence, an accident, or from disease. The manner of death is a medicolegal term that explains the conditions under which the death occurred, i.e., through a criminal or non-criminal event.

There are literally hundreds of ways to commit suicide and it is often a matter of what is available for the person to use. For instance, prisoners in jail or prison may not have access to many things that others in the regular population have, but they can still use what is available to them such as clothing or bedding to make a ligature in order to hang themselves in their cells. They can also make sharp force instruments from various objects to self-inflict injury upon themselves.

Fisher et al (2015) conducted a study of some 2,347 persons committing suicide in Ohio in a 15-year period and identified the causes of death as:

Shooting/firearms 29.7%
Hanging 14.7%
Carbon Monoxide poisoning 8.3%
Poisoning drugs 31.9%
Jumping 5.8%
Stabbing 2.5%
Drowning 1.7%
Asphyxia plastic bag 3.7%
Struck by train/vehicle 1.0%
Burning/fire/explosion 0.2%
Other 0.6%

This type of statistical information is valuable to know but, another study, conducted by the state of Virginia's Chief Medical Examiners' Office (2012) makes an important point concerning suicide statistics:

> Traditional statistical reports of fatal suicide methods do not reflect methods used by subpopulations. For example, a report on suicide in Virginia would note that 57% of suicides were by firearms. This statistic describes suicides

84   Equivocal Death

overall, but obscures method choices made by many subpopulations. Firearms are used in 57% of all suicides largely because most Virginia suicide victims are White males (66%) and most of these White males (64%) commit suicide by firearm. The proportion of persons who are not White males and use a firearm is 42%.

Clearly there is a wide range of modes of death possibilities, but several modes of death that cause questions to be raised from family and friends. This includes deaths resulting from firearms, sharp force, and hanging events. The questions raised are often based on various myths and general misunderstandings surrounding suicide events.

These myths and misunderstandings are among the main reasons it is important for the ME and detectives, to clearly establish that the death was both self-inflicted and intentional (Timmermans 2005 . This finding should be established through the *totality of information and evidence* collected during a proper preliminary investigation and autopsy. The rationale for this effort is best explained by Timmermans (2005) () who quotes a Dr. Cahill a senior ME, explaining her decision-making guidelines as using the "*51% rule of suicides.*" This rule is defined as looking at all the evidence gathered in a case and then being able to defend the manner of death to the deceased's relatives. Basically, she is looking to obtain a 51% certainty based upon all evidence that the death is more likely than not, the result of suicide. Timmermans (2005)() makes perhaps the best explanation as to a suicide manner of death determination, "... *the suicide classification is neither a matter of elimination nor a default option. Rather, it is a manner of death that must be positively demonstrated.*"

The 51% rule is an extremely important concept when conducting suspected suicide investigations and any final determination of suicide should be positively demonstrated to the family and others by the preponderance of evidence. This concept should be applied by all investigative personnel to ensure they are making the right determination. Unfortunately, as previously noted in earlier chapters, this is not always the case.

Time of Death and Postmortem Interval

One of the major areas of concern in all death investigations is establishing the *time of death*. Determining the time of death is a *critical* step because all other times and events, both antemortem and postmortem, of all witnesses or suspects, are going to be compared to this time. Determining the time of death, will also give the *postmortem interval (PMI)*, which is the elapsed time from time of death to body discovery. This is especially important when attempting to confirm any antemortem activities of the deceased and to confirm witness statements or alibies' of persons of interest. However, time of death determination, without an eyewitness to the incident, is not always easy and there are many factors that must be considered.

Determining the time of death is almost always an educated guess based on the physiological changes the body goes through starting at death. These physiological changes begin at the onset of death an continue through body decomposition. Some of the early changes include *algor mortis*, *livor mortis*, and *rigor mortis*. It is important to note that none of these early changes, in and of themselves, are accurate or should be considered absolutes, but collectively they can be of great help. For instance, after death the body begins to lose internal heat and cool down to the ambient temperature, this is known as *algor mortis*. But the body's cooling can be affected by many different things such as the activity of the person just prior to the death, if they were sick, what they were wearing at the time of death, and the ambient environmental temperature where they died. There was a general rule of thumb, under normal conditions, that once death occurs the body's temperature drops about 1.5°F each hour up to four hours; then drops about 1°F per hour. The body's temperature however will never drop below the ambient temperature of the environment. This of course was based on the accepted normal body temperature of 98.6; however, as previously noted there are many factors that could affect the body's temperature prior to death which makes body cooling an undependable way to determine the time of death.

When body cooling may prove to be important is in those cases where the victim has reportedly just died, yet minutes later the body is found to be substantially cooled. This would be inconsistent with the reported death.

These early physiological changes can be influenced by a myriad of factors such as: the last activity of the victim, their overall health condition, how they were dressed, the weather conditions or the environmental temperature. Additionally, information gathered from witnesses as to the last time the victim was seen alive must also be considered. Collectively, this information and the physiological changes in the body can provide a reasonably accurate time of death. The PMI estimations can range from hours to days or even years depending on the evidence present at the scene or the condition of the body when found.

There are few instances when the time of death can be determined inside of two hours. There are instances when the time of death can be reasonably determined such as when a watch or other device was broken during an event, such as a car crash. Case Study 5.1 is another example of how the time of death could be reasonably determined.

CASE STUDY 5.1

A husband returned home in the early morning to find evidence that his house had been forcefully broken into and his wife was murdered in their bed. According to the husband, he had been at an auction that evening and numerous witnesses verified his presence, throughout the night, confirming his whereabouts some 90 miles away. One witness was a local friend that the husband visited at about 6 p.m. that evening, before he went to the auction. The husband further stated that his wife was not feeling well so he ordered supper of roast beef and potatoes from a local restaurant. He drove to retrieve their supper and then returned to the house. The husband stated they had both ate supper between 4:45 and 5 p.m. and afterwards his wife lay down in their bed and he got ready and left the house. However, during the autopsy the forensic pathologist noted that her stomach was full of a recently eaten meal, consisting of undigested potatoes, meat, and other food material.

The stomach contents were consistent with the meal provided by the husband prior to his departure. Primarily based on the stomach contents, the pathologist was able to estimate the time of death roughly 30 minutes after she had eaten. Based on the police investigation this established her time of death was before the husband departed their house. Based on the time of death and many other factors, the husband was arrested and later convicted of her murder.

Identify and Document All Injuries

Usually, it is only at an autopsy when the full unclothed body can be examined. Although most trauma can be observed in an exterior examination, there are some injuries, such as trauma to the soft tissues of the neck, that can only be found during an internal examination of the body. Other important findings may include previous injuries, such as broken bones or scars from other injuries that have healed. Other signs of past trauma are important especially if they are the result of circumstances such as domestic violence.

Most traumatic injuries can be easily identified, such as gunshots, sharp force, blunt force, hanging, or asphyxia. Each injury should be individually photographed, measured, and described within the autopsy report. When dealing with equivocal deaths it is important to identify those injuries that are consistent or inconsistent with being self-inflicted.

Gunshot Injuries

Deaths from gunshot wounds are among the most common modes of death for both homicide and suicide. According to the CDC (2022), firearms were involved in 79% of all homicides and 53% of all suicides within the United States.

For suspected suicide events, using firearms can be seen as a clear or serious intent to end their lives because of the lethality of the choice. More males use firearms to end their lives than females, and at one time a female using a firearm to commit suicide was immediately viewed as suspicious. Because the prevailing thought process for many years was women did not use violent means to end their lives. This is no longer the case and although men still far outnumber females using firearms, there are more females using firearms to end their lives. All firearms, whether rifles, shotguns, or handguns, may be used to self-inflict injuries. In Europe and other countries, shotguns and rifles are used more often in suicide attempts, probably because they are more prevalent than handguns. While in the United States, it is the handgun that is used more often, probably due to the availability of handguns.

There are some common findings at autopsy and the scene that can help differentiate between homicidal and suicidal events involving firearms. These differences include the location of injury, the distance between the firearm and the wound, and in some cases a distinct pattern injury that may correlate the weapon to the injury.

Location of Injury

In homicide cases injuries can literally be inflicted on all parts of the body, depending upon the positions and actions of both suspect and the victim at the time the injuries were inflicted. It is not unusual in homicides for multiple wounds to be found on different parts of the body. Conversely in suicide cases wounds are typically single wound events and are within the range (length of the victim's arms) of the victim to have self-inflicted.

Eisele et al (1981), Karger et al (2002), Nikolić et al (2012), and others have noted in gunshot suicide events, the head was the most favored site. The overall preference of the entrance wound in order was the right temple, intraoral, the forehead, left temple, submental (under the chin), an the parietal region of the head. There are some myths centered on entrance wounds that may cause confusion. One myth that causes perhaps the most questions is the belief that the entrance wound is always smaller than the exit wound. This of course is not true, because the size of the entrance wound is generally based on the location on the body, the range or distance of the weapon when it was fired, and the caliber of the weapon used. Another myth is that suicide victims *"never"* shoot themselves in the eyes or other locations in the face. This is also not true. Although entrance wounds to the eyes, nose, cheeks, or ears are infrequent compared to other locations, they do happen and are not necessarily *suspicious* **or** *inconsistent* when observed.

Strajina et al (2012) noted that self-inflicted gunshot wounds to the chest are a relatively uncommon means of suicide, but they do occur. In these instances, the preferred injury site seems to be left side of the chest, followed by sternum and right side of the chest. The most frequently injured organ was the heart, and the immediate causes of death were exsanguination, heart disruption, and *cardiac tamponade*. In gunshot wounds, a careful examination of the victim may also reveal other evidence consistent with self-inflicted injuries including blood spatter and soot deposition on the victim's hands or clothing. Such findings may prove to be consistent with holding and firing a weapon, or aid in distance determination of the weapon to the injury site.

Typically, in suicidal events there is only one wound, but there are instances where multiple injuries are self-inflicted. Examples include victims who may use automatic weapons and if the weapon was placed into the automatic setting prior to firing, it's possible for a single pull of the trigger to result in multiple rounds being fired, and thus multiple injuries noted (Balci et al 2007). Other possibilities include that the initial shot did not incapacitate or kill the victim, and another round was fired as noted in Case Study 5.2.

CASE STUDY 5.2

A law enforcement officer armed with his .38 caliber service revolver was found in his patrol vehicle with six close contact gunshot wounds to his chest area. He was not wearing a protective vest and the bullets all went through his uniform. The event was initially considered homicide because of the multiple gunshot wounds. However, at autopsy it was noted that although he was shot multiple times, there were no fatal or incapacitating injuries to any of his internal organs except one round that penetrated the heart. The ME opined that fatal wound was likely the last one which struck the heart. He further opined the victim was likely to have survived the other wounds if properly treated. Based on their preliminary investigation, the victim's background, and other evidence the police and ME were able to concluded that the death was the result of suicide. Also, both the victim's hands had traces of soot on them consistent with firing a weapon.

Forensic Autopsy   89

Multiple firearm wounds should normally arouse suspicion of homicide; however, as noted in Case Study 5.2, the wound tracks, relative lethality, and the victim's incapacitation following the wounds, together with other factors found at the scene and victim's background, should be fully assessed by the ME before determining the manner of death.

Distance between Firearm and Injury

The distance determination between the weapon and the injury site is one of the ways to differentiate between homicide and suicide gunshot injuries. It stands to reason that a self-inflicted wound is going to be limited to the weapon and the range of the victim to self-inflict the injury, thus the distance is going to be much shorter than most homicide injuries. Therefore, most suicidal injuries are going to be near contact, when the weapon was fired inches away from the body, contact, where the weapon is placed against the body, or hard contact, when the weapon is pressed into the body when fired.

Karger et al (2002) note in a study of some 624 deaths from gunshot wounds, that 89% of suicidal gunshot injuries from various weapons, were contact or near contact, but only 7.5% of the homicides had contact type wounds. Therefore, distant injuries with a reported suicide should be questioned. Generally, the victim is limited by the length of their arms, the size and type of weapon, and the target area of the body, to be able to point and fire the weapon. An example of the importance of victim's range is demonstrated in Case Study 5.3.

CASE STUDY 5.3

A father reportedly found his son dead in his bed from an apparent suicide. Police found the victim lying in bed, on his back, with a .22 caliber rifle positioned next to the man as if it had fired. The rifle seemed to line up with the entrance wound to the right temple area. The father reports his son had experienced some recent depression but was not aware of any suicidal thoughts. The police were satisfied with the report of suicide and no autopsy was requested by the county coroner. The man was later buried. Several years later, new information was developed that indicated that the father may have murdered his son. Based on new information, the police disinterred the victim for an autopsy and then conducted a scene reenactment. The police discovered that when the

> rifle was placed in the position where it was found, the rifle's trigger was outside the reach of the victim, and thus impossible for the man to have fired the weapon himself. Police noted during the initial scene examination no device was present that could have been used to pull the trigger. The father was later questioned and admitted to killing his son and staging the scene to resemble a suicide.

There are often questions posed by the family or others concerning the location of a gunshot injury being the opposite of the victim's dominant hand. Such as the victim is left-handed, but the wound is located at the right temple, indicating the weapon, usually a handgun, was held and fired by the non-dominate hand. Although it is common sense to think that a victim would normally use their dominant hand to inflict the wound or pull the trigger, this is not necessarily true. This is one of the myths that families and sometimes even police might question. Whereas this is most often true, it is not an absolute and it is not unheard of for the victim to use the non-dominant hand to hold the weapon or pull the trigger while the dominant hand is used to steady the barrel to the targeted area. This is found in handguns, but particularly seen when rifles or shotguns are used. When the non-dominant hand usage becomes important, is when the victim had some type of physical inability to use the non-dominant hand.

When looking at the wound location and distance aspects, remember when a weapon is held to self-inflict a wound it is not held in the same position or manner one uses to normally fire the weapon. Much depends on the target area and the size of the weapon. For handguns sometimes the fingers are wrapped around the butt of the weapon, and it is the thumb that is used to pull the trigger. In rifles and shot guns, typically the butt of the weapon is placed on the floor and the victim then leans forward or stands up to place the weapon against the target area. One hand might hold the barrel while the other hand using the thumb, fires the weapon. In some cases, because of the victim's physical stature, the size of the weapon, and their position, the victim may hold the weapon, such as a rifle, in both hands, then could use their own big toe, to engage the trigger. This method was observed in many suicides committed by Japanese soldiers during World War II.

There are also some cases where the victim might be able to hold the weapon horizontal for a few seconds, placing the barrel against the target area and held in place by one hand, while the otherhand, using the thumb, fires the weapon. Although possible, this is difficult, and as noted in Case Study 5.3, and such cases should be carefully examined and even reenacted to validate the possibility of the wound being self-inflicted.

Forensic Autopsy 91

There are other cases where the victim has taken the time and effort to place a weapon into a position to immobilize it and then use some device or object to push on the trigger and fire the weapon. In such cases, the wound might be more consistent with an intermediate or distant wound rather than a contact wound Such effort does infrequently happen, but in these rare cases the victim's effort will be clearly observable at the scene.

Correlating the Weapon with the Injury

One of the unique factors in gunshot injuries is the possibility to identify or link a particular weapon to the injury site or entrance wound. One example of course is using the aspects of forensically linking the gun to the projectile found in the body through forensic analysis of the lands and grooves that are placed on the projectile as it travels through the barrel of the weapon. This is a recognized and standard forensic examination in homicide investigations, ; because many times the projectile is not recovered in the body of the victim so other means may be necessary. In many hard contact and contact injuries, pattern injuries may be present that outlines the weapons that were used to inflict the wound. These pattern injuries are found surrounding the entrance wound and are consistent with hard contact and close contact type injuries. These injuries are caused as the weapon is pressed against the skin of the victim and fired, the gas from the propellant also enters the body and pushes the skin back against the weapon and creates an injury that mimics the end of the barrel.

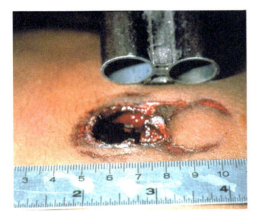 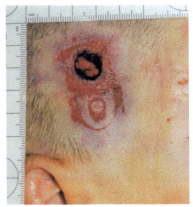

Figures 5.3 and 5.4, are gunshot pattern injuries. 5.3 is the outline of a double barrel shotgun and 5.4 is from a pistol, and depicts a hard contact wound, from a semi-automatic pistol. Note the outline of the end of the weapon at the entrance wound. A weapon found at the scene can be compared to the injury site.

92   Equivocal Death

Other examples of pattern injuries are found in 6 and 7.

In suspected suicide cases, firearm entrance wounds that are not contact, near contact, or hard contact, should be carefully examined. Such wounds are identified by the presence of soot, and stippling, which are small burns surrounding the entrance wounds made by gunshot powder that exits the barrel behind the projectile and impacts on the skin (Figure 5.5, Figure 5.6 and Figure 5.7)

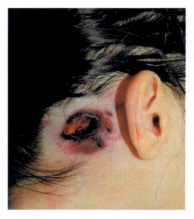

Figure 5.5 This figure depicts a contact gunshot wounds. Note the presence of soot surrounding the entrance wounds. There is no stippling present but head hair may have prevented any stippling or unburnt power from striking the skin surface.

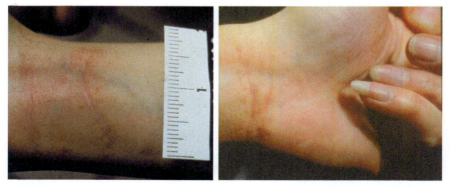

Figures 5.6 and 5.7 These figures depicts old scars on the wrists of a suicide victim found at autopsy from a previous suicide attempt.

Sharp Force Injuries

Sharp force injuries are common in homicide events and to a smaller extent are also found in suicide events. In a homicide, the wounds are often found scattered or haphazardly inflicted and may be found in the back and front of the victim during the same event. In both homicide and suicides involving sharp force trauma, there are often multiple non-fatal injuries present on the victim. The presence or absence of these non-fatal injuries is extremely useful in the differentiation between homicide and suicide. In homicides events, some of the non-fatal injuries are known as *defensive wounds* and are inflicted as the victim attempts to escape, defend themselves, or ward off their attacker. They tend to be found on the hands, forearms, and even legs and may be incised or stab wounds. Although not fatal they may cause severe injuries. It is important to note that such injuries are not found in suicide events as the injuries are self-inflected.

There are other type of non-fatal sharp force trauma consistent with suicidal events, these are known as *"tentative or hesitation wounds."* Such injuries are characterized as superficial incised or sometimes shallow stab wounds. Some wounds are so shallow they often do not even damage the underlying tissue, and hesitation stab wounds are often only observed as pin pricks on the skin or ¼ to ½ inch deep wounds. Hesitation wounds are often found near the fatal injury site. The explanation for these wounds is the victim is building up their courage to end their life or determining the pain level, before the final fatal wound is inflicted.

Evidence of prior suicide attempts, such as healed wounds and scars, may establish a history of prior suicide attempts. Some of these injuries are scars from prior hesitation wounds or true suicidal attempts and are important evidence when found during the autopsy. See Figure 5.8 as examples of previous hesitation and prior suicidal attempts.

An example of hesitation wounds that were inflicted contemporaneously with the suicide is depicted in Figure 5.9. Hesitation wounds are typically found adjacent to deeper wounds that actually caused the serious injury.

Prior healed injuries as depicted in Figures 5.7 and 5.8 and any similar injuries observed contemporaneously with the death of the victim are extremely important to document because the injury is consistent with prior suicidal behaviors. Karlsson (1998) noted in his study that hesitation injuries were present in 80% of suicide cases involving sharp force means. In sharp force deaths the presence, or the absence of defensive or hesitation injuries are important to document. Hesitation and defensive wounds are the result of distinctly different actions.

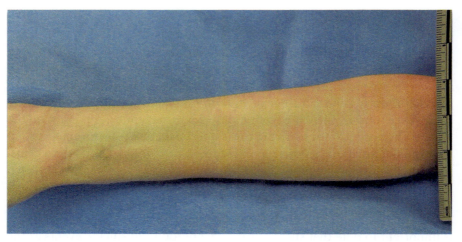

Figure 5.8 This figure depicts scars from a victim described as a "cutter." It is unknown if these injuries were previous suicide attempts or not, but their presence should be clarified by family or friends.

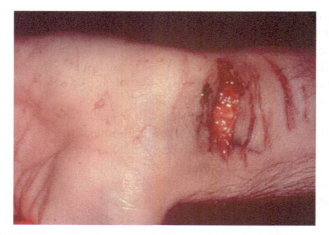

Figure 5.9 This figure depicts several shallow incised wounds across the wrist area that did not penetrate the underlying tissue and one deeper cut that did cause some bleeding. These injuries are consistent with hesitation wounds and suicidal intent.

Hesitation wounds are scratches or shallow cuts that are inflicted on the body generally near the more serious injuries. These smaller cuts are depicted in Figure 5.10 and are made as the victim judges the pain, gains courage, or resolution to cut deeper.

Forensic Autopsy 95

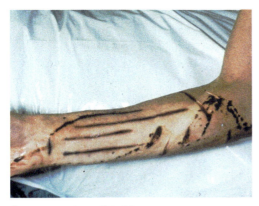 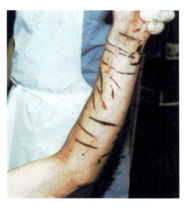

Figures 5.10 and 5.11 These figures depict incised wounds of a successful suicide at autopsy. Note the multiple linear type injuries on one arm and the multiple cuts on the other arm.

One simple rule to remember: *defensive wounds are inconsistent with suicides and hesitation wounds are inconsistent with homicides.*

Incised Wounds

One example of a sharp force injury that can be found in both homicides and suicides is the incised wound, defined as being longer than they are deep. Such injuries are often referred to as "cuts" and sometimes misidentified as "*lacerations.*" However, a laceration is an injury caused by blunt force and not sharp force. Incised wounds are perhaps the "traditional" or most common sharp force injuries to be found in suicides. The general intent is to open blood vessels and then bleed to death. Brunel et al (2010) noted that most sharp force suicide wounds tended to be isolated incised wounds located solely at the anterior parts of the trunk, neck, forearms, or wrist area. These areas are probably chosen because of the ease of access and presence of major blood vessels in those areas.

Note that in the previous Figures 5.8 and 5.9 depict examples of incised wounds. However, quite often many of these injuries prove to be non-fatal because they did not cause sufficient damage such as severing a major artery, that would have prevented the body from naturally stopping the flow of blood through coagulation. Figures 5.11 and 5.12, depict multiple injuries that are more linear and deeper and thus causing considerably more trauma and thus more bleeding from injuries to multiple blood vessels. These injuries were so

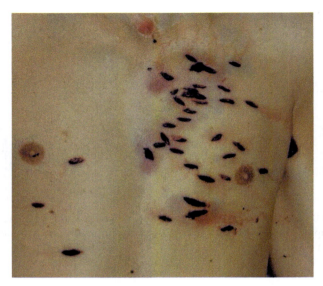

Figure 5.12 Depicts multiple shallow cuts or hesitation wounds made as the victim gains courage or resolution to cut deeper.

severe it made it impossible for the body to stop the bleeding. These injuries caused the victim's death.

There are other aspects of sharp force injures that differs from other modes of death and this is the number of actual injuries that the victim might inflict upon themselves to cause death. Multiple stab or incised wounds are common features in homicide incidents, but they are also present in suicide events as well. It is not uncommon for the suicide victim to have self-inflicted numerous stab or incised wounds upon their body before causing their death.

Stab Wounds

A stab wound is defined as a sharp force injury that is deeper than it is long and is a common injury associated with homicides. Although much rarer than other means, they can also be found in suicides. Sabale and Kumar (2018) and other similar studies note that suicidal stabbing is only found in between 1.6% and 3% of all suicides. Therefore, all stabbing events should be carefully examined initially as potential homicides. There are some common findings that can help to differentiate between homicidal and suicidal stabbing events. These differences include the location of injury, the shape, and orientation of the wounds.

Location of Injury

The location of injury is important because if suicide is suspected, the injuries must be within the "range" or ability for the victim to have self-inflicted. For instance, it is difficult if not impossible for someone to stab themselves in the back. Brunel et al (2010) noted that in homicide cases wounds are often scattered around the body and might include both stab and incised wounds. Injury locations in one homicidal event might include head, limbs, hands, neck, or back.

In suicidal stab wounds the victim typically chooses bodily regions that are easily accessible and tend to be centered on vital organs, i.e., the heart, which would lead to a faster fatal outcome. Karlsson (1998) notes that stab wounds to the face, the back, genitals, or other sensitive parts of the body are uncommon with suicide events. The common regions in self-inflicted stabbings are the neck, the heart area, and the abdomen. In right-handed people, the injury locations tend to be on the upper left side of the body targeting the heart. Karlsson (1998) observed that in many suicidal stab events the victim tended to expose the target area by removing their outer clothing before stabbing themselves.In suicidal stab events, there may be multiple injuries present, as victims are seldom able to inflict a single fatal injury. Some of these injuries could be considered as hesitation wounds as they tend to be very shallow in depth. Case studies have documented injuries numbering from just a few to over 90 stab wounds, all self-inflicted by the victim.

Generally, in suicidal stab events, there is one deep fatal wound but there may be multiple non-fatal wounds are present. Multiple deep fatal wounds might be possible but should be questioned.

Shape of Wounds

In homicidal attacks the victim will often present with distorted wounds as the victim struggles or responds to the instrument being inserted or withdrawn from their body. Also depending on the angle, a weapon that enters the body may cause distortions by severing muscle tissue that is holding the body together. Cutting through the muscles or the *lines of Langer* may cause gaping wounds that do not seem to match other wounds inflicted by the same instrument. The muscles that are holding the body together are much like a rubber band. If the angle of the blade enters horizontally, then the rubber band might not show great damage and still be able to function. However, if it is struck vertically, it might cause the rubber band to separate. This is why some stab wounds seem more severe and gaping while others may only appear as small linear defects. The same knife may create different sized and shaped wounds depending upon where it entered the body and the orientation of the knife or object as it enters the body.

Wound Orientation

Another important consideration is *wound orientation*. Karlsson (1988), Brunel et al (2010), and others have noted that the wound orientation in stabbing injuries is very important and may help to differentiate between a homicide and a suicide. Wound orientation refers to the stab wounds and if they appear to be on a vertical or a horizontal plane in relation to the victim. Generally, in a homicidal stabbing incident the wounds appear to be more vertical as the weapon is usually thrust in a downward motion into the victim. Whereas a suicidal injury the wound appears to be more horizontal based on the way the injury is inflicted from a sideways position (Figure 5.13).

Brunel et al (2010) explain the higher frequency of horizontal wounds in suicides may be the result of victims holding the instrument on a plane that was parallel to their ribs. Figures 5.13a and 5.13b illustrate how horizontal injuries can be self-inflicted.

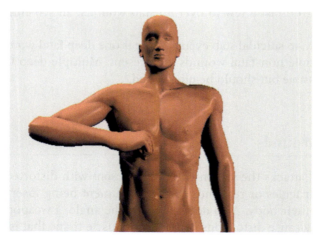

Figure 5.13a This figure depicts multiple stab wounds of a "stabbing" suicide. It is important to note that all of the wounds are within the range or could have been self-inflicted by the victim. Some of these injuries were shallow penetrating only about ¼" to ½" in depth and were identified as hesitation wounds. Note the orientation of the wounds. Although there are some vertically orientated injuries, the majority are horizontal and are more consistent with suicide.

Forensic Autopsy   99

Figure 5.13 b These figures illustrate how a knife may be held by a person to inflict stab wound injuries onto themselves. This is how horizontal orientated injuries are inflicted. Compare these figures to the wounds in Figure 5.12.

A mixture of horizontal and vertical orientated injuries is not uncommon because the orientation of the wound is really based on the position of the instrument as it is inserted into the body. A change in hand position or the way the instrument is held could change the orientation of the entrance wound, even in self-inflicted events. Figures 5.13a and 5.13b also illustrate the range that someone would have to self-inflict injuries to themselves.

Wound orientation is important to note, but such observations are only a part of the totality of information and evidence. It is also important to remember that not all self-inflicted sharp force stab wounds are necessarily immediately fatal or will cause death instantaneously. The following two case studies are examples of sharp force injuries that were not immediately fatal.

CASE STUDY 5.4

Shiono and Takaesu (1986) describe a 44-year-old man who stabbed himself in the heart with a kitchen knife. Although injured, he changed his bloody clothing and then proceeded to eat lunch with his aunt who apparently did not notice his injury. After two hours he collapsed and died. His cause of death was due to *cardiac tamponade.* In this case although the heart was stabbed, it was not initially fatal, instead blood from the injury filled up the pericardium, the sac that covers the heart. Once filled with blood, it causes pressure against the heart, to the point it could not function as a pump and deliver blood to the rest of the body.

> **CASE STUDY 5.5**
>
> Fekete and Fox (1980) describe a case wherein a 53-year-old male stabbed himself in the abdomen and chest, and then asked another person to drive him to another location seven miles away. No one was aware of his injuries until he arrived at his requested location. Once there, he exited the vehicle and then stabbed himself again, this time through the calvarium or skull, which finally caused his death.

One of the frequent comments or beliefs expressed by the public and even by some police are serious doubts that multiple injuries, such as stab or incised wounds, could be inflicted onto oneself, because of the pain that's involved. That of course is another one of the myths that surround the whole concept of self-inflicted wounds. There is another general rule that needs to be understood when looking at the mode or cause of death in suspected suicides:

There is no such thing as too much pain when committing suicide.

There are multiple examples of unusual and certainly painful modes of death that has been used to end someone's life. Such examples include self-immolation, swallowing caustic liquid, using a saber saw or even a chain saw to cut their throat. Therefore, multiple injuries should not necessarily be considered inconsistent with suicide. This concept is especially important when explaining injuries to the family if they raise such concerns.

Correlate an Injury to Objects Producing the Injury

In self-inflicted injuries it would be expected to find the object or instrument that caused the injuries at the crime scene. If it is not found, then this would be inconsistent with a self-inflicted act. It is very difficult if not impossible to positively link a sharp force injury to a specific wound unless during the event, a portion of the object, i.e., knife broke off and was found during the autopsy and can be matched to the weapon. However, there are sometimes hilt marks or injuries from serrated edged objects that might provide additional evidence to link the object to the injury. Generally, when comparing injuries to sharp force objects the finding is liable to be just consistent or inconsistent with the injuries.

Forensic Autopsy

Hanging

Hanging and asphyxia is a popular method to cause death, but typically only hanging produces any real injuries that can be observed during the autopsy. Although possible, there are very few hanging deaths attributed to homicides, but it is a popular method for suicide because it takes very little preparation and does not require any specialized equipment. It is also thought to be a relatively painless way to die. There are some important factors relating to hanging deaths that are important to remember especially when talking to the next of kin who may question the cause and manner of death based on some common myths or misunderstanding of the cause of death in hangings. Suicidal hangings differ greatly from judicial hangings carried out as a form of execution. The cause of death from judicial hangings is the result of falling through a trap door for a certain distance and the sudden stop that breaks the neck of the victim. Thus, the cause of death from a judicial hanging is a broken neck and not asphyxia.

In a suicidal hanging, it is not necessary for the person to be fully suspended off the ground to hang themselves. It is only necessary to be able apply pressure to the neck and the major arteries leading to the brain. Death is not caused from being unable to breath, but the result of pressure on the major blood vessels that cut off the flow of oxygenated blood to the brain. Generally, when thinking of hanging most people vision a rope or similar object used to create a ligature around the neck. Although this is common, there are really an unlimited number of items that can be used including bedding, towels, or clothing. In many *in custody* hanging deaths in jails the victim may use sheets, blankets, towels, cothing, or other material to use as a ligature to place around their necks.

Hanging Injuries

One of the findings at autopsy are patterned abrasions caused by a ligature placed against the neck. These abrasions are found in both homicidal strangulation as well as suicidal hangings and are caused by the friction of the ligature against the skin leading to blister formation. But there is a difference in the appearance of abrasions or ligature marks in homicides and suicides.

In homicidal ligature strangulation the abrasions appear as horizontal marks across the throat area. Other injuries such as fingernail scratches or cuts are often found adjacent to the ligature marks made by the victim attempting to remove or loosen the ligature or attempt to place their fingers between the ligature and their throat. Such injuries are generally suggestive of homicide.

In hangings, the abrasion is observed as an inverted "V" pattern, at the site of the knot. See Figure 5.14.

Accidental Hanging

There is another circumstance when a victim is found hanging that is not a homicide or a suicide but is actually an accidental death. These incidents are known as *autoerotic deaths* or *autoerotic misadventures*. As noted by Chancellor (2017) autoeroticism or *asphyxiophilia*, comprises sexual feelings, arousal, or gratification achieved through *anoxia*, or depleting the oxygen supply to the brain. To achieve this the practitioners will cut off oxygen to the brain by using ligatures, by hanging, or placing a plastic bag over the head and it is an extremely dangerous practice. Generally, practitioners will often plan these events with safety mechanisms in place to prevent accidental deaths. However, many times the safety mechanisms fail which leads to the accidental death of the practitioners.

To the untrained, these events are often misinterpreted as suicides, because the deceased did in fact die by their own means. However, these deaths are unplanned and unintended, therefore they should be considered as *accidental* deaths and not suicide. The intent behind this activity was sexual gratification and not suicide.

To differentiate between a suicide and an accidental death by *autoerotic misadventure*, it is important to observe the scene and victim. In

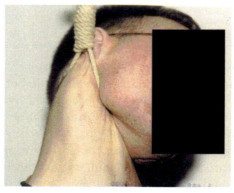

Figure 5.14 This figure depicts how the inverted "V" pattern injury is caused as the ligature holds the body weight the ligature causes friction marks on the neck.

Forensic Autopsy

an autoerotic death, it typically occurs in a secluded spot where they are unlikely to be disturbed. If the deceased is found hanging there is often material placed between the ligature and the skin to prevent the abrasions to the neck that are common in homicidal ligature strangulation or suicidal hanging deaths.

The scene may have evidence that the deceased may have engaged in such activity before. Examples include wear marks on exposed wood or hooks placed into the ceiling or walls used to support the victim. Often present at the scene are examples of multiple sexual paraphilias including the deceased is nude or dressed in female attire including wigs and make up. Elements of sadomasochism and bondage tend to be prevalent, as well as foreign objects are sometimes inserted into the anus, known as anorectal eroticism. Pornography is often present and many times these events are videotaped by the deceased, for the purpose of viewing and masturbating later.

Sheleg and Ehrlich (2006) noted four key factors when comparing a possible accidental autoerotic death to a possible suicidal event.

1. The deaths are a surprise to relatives. Meaning they had no idea that the victim was practicing such activity.
2. There was no known history of psychiatric problems or obvious motivation for suicide.
3. There are signs of preparation (i.e., material placed between ligature and neck. a safety or escape mechanism is in place but failed.)
4. The victim is typically an intelligent white male.

Most practitioners are white males, but other races, and women also participate in this activity. Generally, a complete scene examination can establish or refute whether the act was accidental or suicidal and often determine if there were previous events.

Drug Overdose

Death caused by drug overdose or mixing legal prescription or illicit drugs and alcohol together are also prevalent means to commit suicide. Perhaps this is the most painless way to die as the mixture of drugs and alcohol typically induced sleep and the depressant effect of the drugs cause the body to eventually quit breathing and death follows. For many years drug overdoses or poisons were considered the main method for women to commit suicide as it was typically not very violent. Although this is not necessarily the case in our current culture, it is still used predominantly by females to end their lives.

Like other examples in this chapter if this is an unattended death there should be an autopsy performed, if for no other reason to establish no other evidence of trauma and especially in the case of females, that there is no evidence of sexual assault. One important factor would be the stomach contents, looking for any undigested pills or substances, to compare to any pills, vials, or other medications found at the scene. Above all it is critical to conduct a toxicology analysis of blood and urine of the victim. This is to confirm or refute the presences of such material or to identify what drugs or substances were consumed by the deceased.

Toxicology

Toxicology is obtained from the blood or urine obtained during the autopsy. This is necessary to determine if drugs or alcohol present or had been consumed by the victim. Many times, the cause of death may be determined through toxicology analysis, especially in those instances when drugs or other substances as ethylene glycol, or anti-freeze, that have been consumed or given to the deceased. In many instances the cause of death may be readily apparent such as those rare occasions when the deceased has actually recorded or filmed their death. This is much more prevalent now with the advent and popularity of cell phones. But, even in these cases as a minimum a toxicology should be conducted to confirm or refute the presence of any drugs or alcohol in their system. This may help to further explain their actions.

Chapter Summation

A forensic autopsy is a critical step in every death investigation and without such an examination, the cause of death is really just an educated guess. There are many reasons or justifications for not conducting an autopsy of a suspected suicide, but no one can dispute the fact that an autopsy can almost always rule out any other cause or manner of death. The biggest danger is not conducting an autopsy and later new information surfaces that the death is consistent with a homicide, but no autopsy was conducted. Sadly, on multiple occasions when this occurred, the police discovered the deceased was cremated soon after death.

Determining the cause and manner of death is really a team effort as the pathologist relies on the detective to provide information as to the crime

Forensic Autopsy

scene and background of the victim, particularly the presence or absence of risk factors in their lives or prior suicide attempts.

There are several other important concepts that will aid in the investigative effort and should be considered when conducting any suspected suicide. First is the concept of the *51% rule*, wherein the totality of evidence and information collected has led to the conclusion of suicide rather than just a quick scene examination. Second is the concept that *suicide classification is neither a matter of elimination nor a default option. Rather, it is a manner of death that must be positively demonstrated.*

If these last two concepts are applied there will likely be fewer family questions, complaints, or disagreements with the investigative findings. It will also ensure that someone has not gotten away with murder by staging the scene to look like something else happened.

Bibliography

www.merriam-webster.com/dictionary/autopsy

Balci, Y., Canogulari, G., & Ulupinar, E. (2007). Characterization of the Gunshot Suicides. *Journal of Forensic and Legal Medicine*, 14(4), 203–208. https://doi.org/10.1016/j.jcfm.2006.06.025

Brunel, C., et al. (2010). Homicidal and Suicidal Sharp Force Fatalities: Autopsy Parameters in Relation to the Manner of Death. *Forensic Science International*, 198(1–3), 150–154.

Centers for Disease Control and Prevention (CDC). (2022). *Morbidity and Mortality Weekly Report (MMWR)*, 71(19), 656–663.

Chancellor, A. S. (2017). *Investigating Sexual Assault Cases* (2nd ed.). Boca Raton, FL: CRC Press.

Eisele, J. W., Reay, D. T., & Cook, A. (1981). Sites of Suicidal Gunshot Wounds. *Journal of Forensic Sciences*, 26(3), 480–485. PMID: 7252463.

Fekete, J. F., & Fox, A. D. (1980). Successful Suicide by Self-Inflicted Multiple Stab Wounds of the Skull, Abdomen, and Chest. *Journal of Forensic Sciences*, 25(3), 634–637. PMID: 7400770.

Fisher, L. B., Overholser, J. C., & Dieter, L. (2015). Methods of Committing Suicide among 2,347 People in Ohio. *Death Studies*, 39(1–5), 39–43. https://doi.org/10.1030/07481187.2013.851130. Epub 2014 Jun 23. PMID: 24932592; PMCID: PMC4268074.

Humphry, D. (1997). *Final Exit, The Practicalities of Self-Deliverance and Assisted Suicide for the Dying*. New York City, NY: Dell Publishing CO.

Karger, B., Billeb, E., Koops, E., & Brinkmann, B. (2002). Autopsy Features Relevant for Discrimination between Suicidal and Homicidal Gunshot Injuries. *International Journal of Legal Medicine*, 116(5), 273–278. https://doi.org/10.1007/s00414-002-0325-8. Epub 2002 Aug 16. PMID: 12376836.

Karlsson, T. (1998). Homicidal and Suicidal Sharp Force Fatalities in Stockholm, Sweden. Orientation of Entrance Wounds in Stabs Gives Information in the Classification. *Forensic Science International*, 93(1), 21–31.

Karlsson, T., Ormstad, K., & Rajas, J. (2007). Patterns in Sharp Force Fatalities—A Comprehensive Forensic Medical Study: Part 2. Suicidal Sharp Force Injury in the Stockholm Area 1972–1984. *Journal of Forensic Sciences*, 33(2), 448–461.

Manso, N. L., Riberiro, I. P., & Inacio, A. R. (2021). Sharp Force Fatalities: Differentiating Homicide from Suicide Through a Retrospective Review (2012–2019) of Autopsy Findings in Lisbon (Portugal). *Forensic Science International*, 327, 110959.

Nikolić, S., Zivković, V., Babić, D., & Juković, F. (2012). Suicidal Single Gunshot Injury to the Head: Differences in site of Entrance Wound and Direction of the Bullet Path Between Right- and Left-Handed—An Autopsy Study. *American Journal of Forensic Medicine and Pathology*, 33(1), 43–46. https://doi.org/10.1097/PAF.0b013e31823a8a32. PMID: 22083074.

Sabale, M. R., & Kumar, N. B. (2018). An Unusual Case of Multiple Self-Inflicted Stab Wounds. *International Journal of Scientific Research*, 7(2), 46–47.

Sheleg, S., & Ehrlich, E. (2006). *Autoerotic Asphyxiation: Forensic Medical and Social Aspects*. Tucson, AZ: Wheatmark.

Shiono, H. M. D., & Takaesu, Y. (1986). Suicide by Self-Inflicted Stab Wound of the Chest. *The American Journal of Forensic Medicine and Pathology*, 7(1), 72–73.

Strajina, V., Živković, V., & Nikolić, S. (2012). Forensic Issues in Suicidal Single Gunshot Injuries to the Chest: An Autopsy Study. *American Journal of Forensic Medicine and Pathology*, 33(4), 373–376. https://doi.org/10.1097/PAF.0b013e31824a4797. PMID: 22354080.

Timmermans, S. (2005). Suicide Determination and the Professional Authority of Medical Examiners. *American Sociological Review*, 70, 311–333.

Virginia Violent Death Reporting System (VVDRS), Office of the Chief Medical Examiner, Virginia Department of Health. (2011). *Suicide Methods in Virginia: Patterns by Race, Gender, Age, and Birthplace (2003–2008)*. April, 2011.

Victimology

6

Victimology Concept

When conducting investigations into any crime of violence, detectives traditionally focus on identifying the suspect through forensic evidence, the motive, or witness testimony. Whereas this is an acceptable initial focus of most investigations, it is also critical to examine the victim and their background. This focus on the victim's background is referred to herein as a *victimology assessment*. This is an important concept in all death investigations but perhaps especially important in equivocal death situations because many times the police are trying to determine if the death is consistent with a homicide, suicide, or in some cases accidental. The answer is often found in the victim's background or what was going on in their lives before their deaths.

In homicides a background investigation can be used to determine the last known time and location where the victim was known to be alive and who had last contact with them. It can also provide information relative to their possible participation in illegal activities or associating with the criminal element. Such information may prove helpful in determining a possible motive for their death and in some cases identify potential suspects. The absence of such conduct may point the investigation in another direction.

In sex crimes, Roy Hazelwood, one of the original members of the FBI Behavioral Science Unit, summed up the importance and necessity of *victimology* slightly differently. He stressed using victimology and the background of the victim, to help understand the offender and why a particular victim was targeted. His teaching point was: "*Tell me about your victim, and I'll tell you about the offender.*" Thus, victimology was one of the more important concepts covered during his training courses on investigating sexual assaults.

Prior to the 1980s the background and personality characteristics of victims were largely ignored or considered a relatively minor part of the overall investigative effort. If the victim's background was deemed important by detectives, it was typically because they were suspicious of the validity of

DOI: 10.4324/9781003373865-6

108 Equivocal Death

the victim's complaint, or the victim was some type of celebrity. Traditionally, the police effort to obtain background information often amounted to a cursory criminal history check or a collection of tidbits of information provided by witnesses. With this lack of real effort, it is not surprising that the actual value of a *victimology assessment* is not understood or appreciated by most detectives.

A *victimology assessment* is a detailed study of the deceased, which includes their individual background and personality characteristics. In homicide investigations, this information is used to understand how they became a victim or why they were selected by the offender in the first place. In suicide investigations, it provides insight and identifies any risk factors, personality characteristics, or antemortem suicidal behaviors which may provide their *intent* to end their lives.

As noted by Joiner (2010) the concept of someone deciding impulsively or a *"whim"* to commit suicide is incorrect. Therefore, it is imperative in the preliminary stages to conduct a thorough background investigation to establish a motive or a reason for someone to end their life. In most reported suicides, even a cursory background check will quickly identify problem areas or difficulties in the deceased's life, that could lead to their self-destruction. Based on these issues and the crime scene, the manner of death as suicide, becomes relatively clear and is not necessarily a surprise to family or friends.

The value and importance of the victimology assessment comes during the preliminary investigation, when police discover an absence of risk factors, motives, or antemortem behaviors that are consistent with suicide. This is when the victimology assessment becomes more than just a check the box exercise, but now a critical step in the investigative process, because if suicide is inconsistent then the death is likely a homicide.

The concept of victimology is also relative to the circumstances of the crime under investigation; therefore, it may not always focus solely on the victim themselves. For instance, in other cases such as child abduction, child injury, or accidental death, the study of the actual victim's background may prove to be pointless. Because how many life experiences does a child really have? But a *victimology assessment* centered on the child's caregiver, the parents, or the family dynamic might prove to be more important and helpful to the investigation. As an example, some parents or families may give an outward appearance of being financially secure, kind, and loving spouses or parents, basically the ideal "all *American* family." However, a victimology assessment on the individual parents, their marriage or relationship, and the family dynamic, may uncover a totally different picture than what is presented to the outside world at a casual glance. Financial problems, infidelity, incest, or just the normal stresses of life and raising children may

Victimology   109

be contributing factors to the original crime that are being cloaked through a staged crime scene.

Victimology Assessment

A victimology assessment is not complicated and is essentially a detailed, in-depth study of the victim, based on their individual background. The *victimology assessment* provides an insight into the victim and who they were as a person and more importantly helps to identify certain personality characteristics. This is an important exercise in all violent crimes because people do not live in a vacuum, meaning there is always a before, during, and after to every event. Often detectives concentrate only on the "during and after" of the crime and miss other potential evidence from events that may have taken place leading up to the event. In cases of suspected suicide, the victimology assessment might determine if the victim had a history of mental issues, suicidal behaviors, or had recently experienced additional or elevated risk factors. Identifying these risk factors and suicidal behaviors can often firmly establish the death as a suicide or in the absence of such risk factors or behaviors, rule it out as a manner of death.

The victimology assessment is based on both *factual* and *subjective* criteria, and as a general guideline there is no unimportant piece of information relative to the victim. In all instances one general concept is critical; and that is to establish if the conduct or behavior of the victim observed at the scene or alleged through witness statements is consistent or inconsistent with their previous behavior or conduct. This is not to say that under certain circumstances people cannot make an irrational decision or suddenly engage in high-risk behaviors. But our individual behavior is relatively constant throughout our lives. So, if any victim's behavior seems suddenly or unexpectedly out of the ordinary from their normal behaviors, it probably bears further investigation.

Factual Information

Examples of the factual type of information are found in Box 6.1.

Box 6.1 lists factual information about the victim, which are essentially undisputed.

As noted in Box 6.1, most of the *factual information* is basic and can be obtained fairly quickly because they are just the basic facts about the deceased or victim. Such factual information is seldom in dispute and will provide the foundation to the victimology assessment.

BOX 6.1 EXAMPLES OF FACTUAL INFORMATION.

- Age and sex.
- Race.
- Physical features or traits (hair or eye color, height, weight).
- Basic family structure (mother, father, and siblings).
- Current relationship status (single, married, separated, divorced, widowed, "domestic partner").
- Education level.
- Basic employment history (occupational history).
- Criminal history.
- Medical history, including disabilities and other physical attributes.
- Mental or physical disabilities or impairment.
- Military service.

Subjective Criteria

Subjective criteria are somewhat different and a little more complex, because they cover a wider range of issues. This aspect of their background relates to different conditions regarding the victim and their lives which may or may not have contributed to their victimization or elevated their risk factors for self-harm. Thus, the information gathered is *"subjective"* meaning an evaluation is made to determine if such background factors were contributory to their victimization or not.

The subjective criteria also include aspects of their individual *personality characteristics* and what was going on in their lives before the event. Examples of subjective criteria are found in Box 6.2.

Depending on the particulars of the event, information might also include the victim's *residence or current living conditions.* Information concerning the victim's living conditions or situation is not always considered during a death investigation. However, this aspect may prove to be important because it may provide additional personal information about the victim and how they were living at the time. Examples of this general information is found in Box 6.3.

Box 6.3 are questions about the victim's residence or living conditions.

Such basic information about their residence may provide subtle but important elements of additional stress. Especially if they are living in a high crime area or are in a location that they might not be able to afford. Also, it is important to note if there were any noticeable changes in their living

Victimology

111

BOX 6.2 INDIVIDUAL SUBJECTIVE CRITERIA.

- The victim's use of alcohol or drugs (recent increase).
- Their socioeconomic level (any recent changes).
- Financial situation (any recent changes?)
- Type of employment (any recent changes, i.e., layoff, termination, new job, transfer).
- Their sexual preference/orientation (heterosexual, homosexual, bisexual, trans, or other).
- Availability of family or other support structure.
- Presence of children in home (how many: are they bio, step, or adopted?).
- Current relationship status (any recent changes?) (separated, pending divorce, recent break up).
- Hobbies and social activities (any recent changes?).
- Relative successes or failures in life (recent changes).
- Last known activity (days, weeks, months).
- Participation in religious events/activities (any recent changes increase or decrease).
- Participation in recent social events.

BOX 6.3 LIVING CONDITIONS.

- Do they live in a house or apartment?
- Do they own or rent their residence?
- Do they live with non-related roommates/housemates?
- Is their residence adequate for the number of residents?
- Are they able to afford the residence?
- Living conditions of the residence (i.e., clean and orderly or dirty and disorganized): any major problems (i.e., plumbing or HVAC).
- Are there any recent changes in the condition of the residence?
- How long have they lived at present residence?
- If recently moved, the reason for the move.
- How long have they lived in the same town?
- Local area of the residence (high crime, residential, apartment complex).
- Contact or relationship with neighbors.
- Living separately from spouse or significant other.

conditions, such as the residence is normally clean and orderly, but recently has become dirty or disorganized. Conversely, someone with poor house-keeping skills has unexpectedly begun to clean up their residence. In either case the change noted in the residence is important antemortem behavior.

It some cases the victim may be living separately from their spouse or significant other because of some domestic or relationship issue. Moving away from a partner because of a failing relationship is an additional stressor that must be considered. Moving out because of domestic physical or sexual abuse situation may be stressful, and it bears closer attention because many times the act of leaving the home or relationship is the precursor to additional physical violence, including death by the offending party.

Other important subjective criteria focus on aspects of the individual's *personality and emotional maturity*. Examples would include but are not limited to those found in Box 6.4.

BOX 6.4   PERSONALITY CHARACTERISTICS AND EMOTIONAL MATURITY.

- Current and past medical conditions.
- Current or prior mental health issues (i.e., depression, bipolar, other).
- Church attendance or religious beliefs (sudden attendance or avoidance)?
- Personality: outgoing or shy.
- Relationship with family (mother, father, and siblings).
- Recognized best friend.
- Recent increase or decrease of stressors.
- How do they normally handle stress?
- Did they take responsibility for their actions?
- Recent noticeable changes in attitude or lifestyle?
- Overall maturity and life experiences.
- Normal personal hygiene? Any recent changes?
- Normal temperament, are they calm or prone to emotional outbursts?
- Are they impulsive or reflective?
- Type of vehicle they owned/drove.
- How did they normally dress? Any recent changes?
- What is the victim's best and worse personality characteristic?
- Did the victim have any normal routine (was there any recent change to their routine?)?

Victimology   113

Box 6.4 are examples of subjective criteria based on personality characteristics and their emotional maturity.

This type of information is considered *subjective* because the amount of weight or consideration given to them is based on each individual victim and the event dynamics of what happened. For example, consider the victim's attendance at church or other religious activity. This may prove to be relatively important in the lifestyle or personality characteristics of one victim but play no role in another. These examples of information and subjective criteria listed above are obviously not all inclusive but just a relative sample of the type of information about the victim that may prove useful to complete the assessment.

Box 6.5 provides some additional subjective criteria but is more focused on recent issues that may increase the risk factors or result in potential suicidal behaviors. Again, a lot of these questions may or may not apply to each victim. For instance, being the victim of a sexual offense or domestic violence may be applicable to some victims, but not to others. Many of these behaviors can be identified as the victim planning or considering suicide as an option to solve a problem.

Box 6.5 questions that focus on increased risk factors, suicidal behaviors, or potential plans to end their life.

Note that many of the questions in Boxes 6.4 and 6.5 may also identify life stressors that may not be known or readily understood by family and friends. In a victimology assessment it is seldom one aspect or factor in the victim's background that leads to increasing their risk level for suicide or becoming a victim of a crime. Instead, it is the totality of information collected that is used to formulate the assessment. The type of information needed for the assessment may change or be adapted based on a particular crime or for different victims. For instance, we would want some of the same basic *factual information* on every victim, but we may adapt and exclude or include other factors based on the specific individual victim, the individual crime, or the specific event. Examples of specific information sought based on the "type of victim" and the crime. Boxes 6.4 and 6.5 can be used or adapted for both male or female adults. But there are other subjective criteria that might be more relevant for teens and adolescents.

Teenagers

Teens are somewhat different because they are at the stage in life where they are more mature than children, but do not yet have the life experiences of an adult. Therefore, their victimology is somewhat more complicated or nuanced than adults and may require additional questions. Part of the problem with

BOX 6.5   RISK FACTORS AND ANTEMORTEM BEHAVIORS.

- Prior victimization (i.e., incest, sexual assaults, or domestic violence).
- Recent personal or romantic relationship issues (divorce or separation or breakup).
- Money or financial problems (i.e., change of income bankruptcy).
- Legal issues particularly pending prosecutions or recent convictions of a criminal act.
- Recent loss/death of a spouse.
- Living an alternate lifestyle.
- Looking up facts on suicide online.
- Serious eating disorders.
- Changes in personal hygiene or dress?
- Losing interest in subjects or people once cherished.
- Significant changes in sleeping patterns (i.e., too much or not enough).
- Become withdrawn from routine activities.
- Expressing loss of purpose or hopelessness?
- Changes in self-esteem or self-worth.
- Unusual or increasing agitation or anger.
- Changes in last wills.
- Increases of life insurance policies.
- Previous suicide attempts.
- Any recent end of life plans (i.e., funeral, burial requests)?
- Did they express any short term or long-term plans?

teems, they often want to be older than they are, and seek the same excitement, adventure, or privileges they see older teens or young adults enjoy. But often they are not emotionally mature enough to handle what might come along with that excitement or privileges. This can lead to embarrassment, potential danger, with little experience of how to extract themselves from such situations. Some of the important questions are noted in Box 6.6.

Subjective Criteria for Teens

With teens there are several areas which require special attention. The first is how friends or peers of the victim may be able to apply pressure to engage

Victimology

BOX 6.6   LISTS SOME SPECIAL QUESTIONS AND SUBJECTIVE CRITERIA FOR TEENAGERS.

- What is their maturity level and is it age appropriate?
- Do they have a dependent or independent personality?
- Are they outgoing or shy?
- Do they have age-appropriate friends or generally older friends?
- Do they actively engage in online social networking?
- Do they have profiles on any dating sites?
- Are they active on any chatting aps?
- Do they have cell phones with texting abilities?
- Do they have unsupervised telephone or computer privileges?
- Do they participate in school activities and what is their grades/success in school?
- Are there disciplinary or school attendance problems?
- What is their current dating status?
- Do they have boyfriends or girlfriends or any "romance" problems?
- Any problems at school (i.e., learning disabilities or bullying)?
- "Teen age" problems at home or with other siblings?
- What were some recent events in their lives?
- Do they have clear plans for the future?
- Do they engage in high-risk behaviors such as drug and alcohol abuse?
- Have they identified as Gay or Trans?
- Are they undergoing or considering gender reassignment?

in some activity they would not normally do themselves. Because teens are younger and less mature, they are generally more easily influenced by peers and especially through *social media*, and therefore may be more likely to participate in certain activities because they want to "belong." This peer pressure could include anything from smoking tobacco to drug usage, and even to participating in minor crimes such as shoplifting. Peer pressure and efforts to be socially accepted is obviously a greater problem in teenagers and adolescents than in adults and how they are seen by peers may significantly impact their lives.

Teens may also attempt to engage in more adult activities such as exchange of intimate photos with strangers, online dating, or meeting up with someone they met online. It is not unusual that the teen after participating in such activities find themselves being blackmailed or coerced into some activity they have not counted on, but because of the embarrassing nature of their acts may not be able to seek help with their parents, Therefore, a self-destructive act may become an option they look at to end the problem.

One of the major correlating factors for becoming a victim of a crime or suicide is found in the amount of social media participation of teens. Sedgwick et al (2019) looked at nine independent studies correlating social media/internet use and suicide attempts in persons younger than 19 years old. They found a direct association between heavy social media/internet use and increased suicide attempts in seven of those studies. In another study, Twenge (2020) notes the increase in depression of adolescents is concurrent with their increased usage and exposure to social media. Along with depression, there were increases in anxiety, loneliness, self-harm, and unhappiness, which often led to suicidal ideation, suicide attempts, and suicide. These increases tend to be more pronounced among girls and young women.

In the past, the concern was such activity that was occurring while teens or adolescents were on home computers. However, that is not the problem currently. The problem now is the cell phone, which is basically a small computer and nearly every teenager has one or has access to one. It is a cell phone with a multitude of choices to chat, message, and send photos or videos to others that now presents the greatest danger for bullying, peer pressure, or even potential contact with offenders.

The combination of access to cell phones and social media obviously puts a portion of the teen population at an increased risk for developing suicidal thoughts and behaviors. Some of these issues revolve around both the pros and cons of current technology. The pro includes the ability to instantaneously respond and give our thoughts or comment to something seen on social media sites. However, the con comes from this same ability to instantaneously respond. Unfortunately, these impulsive responses may reflect a feeling or thought in the moment but may not be true a day later. The problem is these impulsive thoughts are difficult if not impossible to retrieve. Many times, when later confronted with these postings, there is often severe critiques from peers, followed by embarrassment, shame, and regret. In the teen world this is sometimes extremely difficult to overcome.

Burnett (2017) notes another con to the internet that many parents are not aware include the number of pro suicide websites that actually encourage or give tips on how to end your life.

Another potential problem causing problems teens and adolescents participating in social media are teenagers exchanging personal information

Victimology

including sexual photographs of themselves and sending them to those they're personally acquainted with or others they have only met over the internet in what has become known as *sexting*. This of course is very high-risk behavior of which many parents may be totally unaware. The problems come when those personal often intimate or revealing photos are first shared with a "friend" but then are forwarded to others. In many cases photos are passed around from friend to friend, throughout the entire school, resulting in embarrassment and humiliation for the victim. There are instances when such embarrassment has led to or at least contributed to thoughts of suicide to escape their humiliation.

One last aspect of the dangers of social media that must be considered is the sexual offender who is constantly searching for potential victims. As noted previously, this search for victims no longer requires an offender to create a profile and contact someone through one of the normal social media sites such as Facebook. Now contact is established through cell phones in Aps such as TikTok, Instagram, What's Ap, and many others. So, it's no longer necessary for a person with devious intentions to try to establish contact with adolescents or teens through a regular home computer that might be monitored by parents. The use of personal cell phones by kids makes it very easy for them to become targeted victims without the parents' knowledge.

Adolescents

Adolescents present similar issues as teenagers, but with even less maturity and life experiences. With limited life experiences, issues confronting some adolescents take on an even greater impact in their lives than would teenagers or adults. The family dynamic or living conditions, particularly divorce or family separation, may affect adolescents more than younger children or teenagers, because they are at the age to recognize certain problems or issues but lack the maturity to understand or properly deal with them.

The same issues revolving around social media usage often play an important role in an adolescent's life. Therefore, it is critical to determine if the adolescent had access to a computer or cell phone and then exploit them to determine what was going on in their lives prior to their deaths.

Some of the factors and areas of inquiry in deaths of adolescents and children are found in Box 6.7.

One of the more prevalent aspects of teen and adolescent suicides revolves around *bullying*. Such activity was traditionally found in face-to-face confrontations generally within school or other social environments, but

BOX 6.7 SUBJECTIVE CRITERIA FOR ADOLESCENTS OR YOUNGER CHILDREN.

- Are they a dependent or independent personality type?
- Are they outgoing and warm to strangers, or shy and fearful?
- Do they easily make friends and playmates or have difficulty establishing peer relationships with someone of their own age?
- Living conditions: single parent (which one) or both parents in home?
- Was child's parent living with "non married partner" or multiple non-married partners?
- Presence of other children in the home?
- Relationship with siblings.
- Family economic situation.
- Use of drugs or alcohol in house by parents?
- Evidence of physical or sexual abuse?
- Evidence of bullying?
- Social Media exposure.
- Online harassment.
- Owning or private use of cell phone.
- Private or unsupervised access to the internet.

such activity can also take place within social media online. This is referred to as *cyber bullying* or online harassment. Cyber bullying takes on many forms ranging from disrespectful or humiliating postings to actual threats. The difference is cyber bullies tend to be more aggressive and their posts can reach a larger audience than a face-to-face confrontation. Burnett (2017) notes that more males experience physical bullying, but more females are targeted in cyber bullying events.

Bullying, even among pre-adolescents, exists more than many adults realize. Surveys conducted by Nansel et al (2001) and Losey and Graham (2004) of students at various elementary grade levels, found that between 19% and 50% students surveyed had experienced some type of bullying within the previous month. Bullying takes all forms from threats, to intimidation, to actual physical assaults. It is important to always view *bullying* not as an adult, but as the younger victim and what they may have been subjected to. This becomes important as noted by Losey & Graham (2004) that for many children who are bullied relentlessly, they see no hope for resolving the situation.

Victimology 119

Their hopelessness, enhanced by irrational thinking, and combined with a lack of maturity and life experiences, *suicide* is seen as their way of escaping what is happening to them.

Unfortunately, children and teens often lack the maturity to understand they are seeking a permanent solution to a temporary problem and are not thinking about other ways to deal with the situation, including involving their parents. Instead, they often view their problems as being not only overwhelming for themselves, but because of their situation they are also *burdening* others. Therefore, choosing suicide is an escape for them, and a way to stop being a *burden* for their families.

Many times, parents are either not aware of the bullying, or were not aware of the extent of the bullying activity. But peers and fellow students are generally aware and may have observed some of the activity. Often aspects of bullying and other antemortem activities are only discovered during the investigation.

Regardless of the circumstances, whenever confronted with the deaths of teens, adolescents, or younger children, aspects of their online and social media exposure should be examined to see if they are related to the death.

There is one thing to consider whenever conducting a victimology relating to a young person's death. Because of their life experiences and maturity, personal problems or issues confronting teens and adolescents tend to be magnified much more than they might be for an adult. Thus, their instant problems confronting them may seem insurmountable, so they unwisely choose self-destruction as a solution for what an adult may consider as a temporary problem.

Risk Factors

Much of this text revolves around the concept of risk factors, basically those events in the victim's life that may lead to their thoughts of suicide. Some risk factors may be well known to family and friends, while others may be subtle and unknown to even family members. It is during the collection of background information of the victim that these risk factors can be identified. Risk factors are not always black and white and are dependent on the personality characteristics of the victim and the circumstances of the crime or death.

Risk factors for suicide cover a wide range of issues. Juhnke et al (2007) created a mnemonic to help identify some of the more common risk factors for potential suicides. The mnemonic is *"IS PATH WARM?"* and was designed for counselors to recognize signs of potential suicidal thoughts or behavior in their patients, with the intent to help prevent suicides. However, this simple mnemonic can also be used by police when conducting a victimology assessment to identify the presence or absence of these same risk factors. The specific risk factors identified in *IS PATH WARM* are listed below but are adapted to help in conducting the victimology assessment:

Suicide Ideation: Did the victim ever express any suicidal ideations or their death verbally or in writing?

Substance Abuse: Was the victim abusing alcohol or drugs? Did they recently *begin* using or did they increase their use of alcohol or drugs?

Purposelessness: Did the victim ever express a lack or loss of purpose in their life, or no reason for continued living?

Anger: Did the victim express feelings of anger directed at themselves or others that may have wronged them?

Trapped: Did the victim ever express a belief that there was no way out of their current situation?

Hopelessness: Did the victim ever express feelings of hopelessness about their current life situation or the future?

Withdrawing: Was the victim withdrawing from significant others, family, or friends?

Anxiety: Was the victim feeling anxious with an inability to relax? Was there a change in their sleeping patterns?

Recklessness: Did the victim begin to act recklessly or engage in risky activities?

Mood Change: Was there any noticeable or dramatic mood shifts or states?

Gathering Victimology Information

Information concerning the victim can be gathered through a wide variety of sources including family, friends, coworkers, neighbors, school, medical, or work records including supervisory evaluations of their work performance. These types of questions are best asked in an open-ended manner, requiring hopefully more than a simple yes and no answer. This allows the interviewee to expand their answer and focus on what they believe is important about the victim. Examples of basic opened ended questions include:

Tell me about____ and what was going on in their lives?

Has anything significant taken place in their lives recently?

What changes have you noticed in them personally or in their lifestyle?
Did ___ ever talk about any problems or indicate they were having difficulty with anything?
Tell me about _____'s relationship with their family.
Tell me about ___'s relationship with their husband/wife/boyfriend/girlfriend/partner.

One of the problems in conducting canvass interviews is that there are some people who may feel obligated out of friendship and loyalty to paint the victim in a much better light or to avoid any negative statements. The purpose of these questions of course is not to criticize or degrade the victim, but to understand who they were and if their personality, lifestyle, or other aspects of their lives played any role in what happened. Extra effort may be needed to explain the importance of these background questions to obtain an accurate assessment.

Employment

For adults, their employment history is another important aspect of the victimology assessment. Employment is important because this is typically where we spend approximately 1/3rd of our normal day, thus work plays a very important part in our normal lives. Employment is understood to be either the source of pleasure and satisfaction or a source of stress and frustration. So, the type of work and the victim's satisfaction with their current employment may be very helpful in determining what was going on in their lives at the time of the incident. Especially important for some "victims" is not just their type of employment, but because they may be business owners, other questions also become important, such as how is the business faring; was it successful or going through difficult times? Are there conflicts with any business partners? Would the victim's removal from the business benefit someone at the business?

Other issues to note are if the "victim" was under employed or forced to work below their qualifications. An example is an intelligent and well driven person, with a master's degree, but because of where they are living, or family situation, they are unable to find a job other than for minimum wages. As noted previously, employment, salary, and in many cases the "status," in the workplace can be very important to the victim and loss or changes to their status could contribute to increasing their risk factors. If employment seems to be a key factor in their lives, the victimology assessment should determine the reason for the change in position, title, or loss of employment. There may be a difference in risk factors if the loss of employment was the result of the company downsizing and they were laid off; to the person was terminated for some reason. Obviously, both situations impact the standing of the victim, but termination will probably be a higher risk factor. The reasons for the termination should be a critical step in the victimology assessment.

If there are no issues with employment and the victim was satisfied with their job, status, and salary, then this might prove to be a plus in their lives, thus an argument or inconsistency to suicide.

Investigative Uses of Victimology

The following case study is an example of how a victimology assessment can become important evidence in establishing the circumstances behind a death. In the below case study, the initial report to police was that of an accidental death and although there were minor scene alterations, the real effort to misdirect a police investigation was really limited to the false statement by the two offenders.

CASE STUDY 6.1

A man reported to the county sheriff's department that he, his wife, and his best friend were all hiking up the back side of a mountain, intending to get to the top and look out over a sheer cliff on the other side. They arrived on the mountain top, and the other side was a sheer straight drop some 300 feet above a small stream. Once at the top, the husband reported his wife wanted to take a picture of the area. She then walked toward the edge of the cliff, but apparently got too close and accidentally slipped or the ground underneath her had given way and she fell over the cliff before they could come to her aid. She fell over 300 feet to the creek bed below, dying from her injuries sustained by the fall. Suspicions of the police were raised when the husband left the scene even before his wife's body was recovered from the creek bed by the county Sheriff's search and rescue team. The husband returned to his residence some 50 miles away. Shortly after his arrival, his church's pastor arrived to comfort him. Once inside the house, the pastor noted the husband was sitting on a sofa, drinking iced tea, and had five different life insurance policies spread out on the coffee table. The husband seemed unconcerned with being consoled over the loss of his wife, and instead asked the pastor if he had ever filed a life insurance claim as he was uncertain exactly what to do. In the follow-up investigation, the police walked to the top of the mountain and found some soil disturbances on the edge of the cliff and noted a few bent and broken branches of Manzanita bushes located at the edge of the cliff. But, during interviews with the woman's family, they learned the victim was absolutely terrified of heights; to the point of her being unable to even climb a small ladder or even stand on a step stool to hang pictures on the wall. According to the family, she was so terrified of heights that she could not even look out of a second floor window of a house because it made her dizzy. Thus, the husband's claim of the wife walking on her own toward the edge of a cliff and looking out over the area was totally out of character and diametrically opposite of her known behavior and height phobia. Eventually through an event reconstruction, the police were able to show it was impossible for the victim to have struck the various places on the cliff as she fell and landed where she did at the bottom of the cliff if she had simply slipped. Instead, through a reconstruction effort, they established the husband, and friend had swung her by the hands and feet until they launched her over the side. Both the husband and best friend were later convicted of premeditated murder.

In the above case study, the husband's postmortem behavior of leaving the scene prior to his wife's body recovery and his immediately interests over the various life insurance policies were suspicious and led to a closer look at the event; but, it was the *victim's background* that clearly established the victim's absolute fear of heights; and therefore the victim was unlikely ever to be in any position to look out over such heights as the husband and best friend alleged. The above case study was one of the few cases where one of the most powerful pieces of evidence in court was the *victimology* which completely countered the false statements and elements of staging by the coconspirators.

Another investigative use of a *victimology assessment* are the physical attributes of the victim and their ability to carry out or complete the event that was alleged or depicted at the death scene. The consideration of the physical attributes of the victim to complete the act that is reported is really a combination of factual and subjective criteria. The best examples of this concept of a physical inability to perform certain acts are found in the following case study.

124   Equivocal Death

CASE STUDY 6.2

A suspect reported to the police he had taken a young female teenager on a ride with his jet ski at a local lake. According to the suspect, she asked to go out on her own, so he got off the jet ski on a small island in the lake and she got on and rode around for a while. The suspect claimed she was speeding along the lake and even started to jump the wakes of other boats as they went by. But according to the suspect, she misjudged what she was doing and hit a wake incorrectly and flipped the jet ski. He said he swam out to her, but by the time he got to her she had drowned. The police were initially accepting the suspect's claim, but at autopsy they noted the teenager was born with a deformed right hand, and only had a thumb and little finger, which would have made it *physically impossible* for her to control the throttle of the jet ski or to properly hold onto the handlebars.

In the previous case study, it was really the physical attributes of the victim that caused the police to take an additional look at the incident that was being reported, because the victim was incapable of physically doing what was reported by the suspect. Other examples include if the victim was physically unable to handle or use the weapon in cases of self-inflicted injuries or to physically be unable to do whatever else the scene has been staged to resemble.

Case Study 6.3 is from a homicide case, but it provides the importance of conducting a general background check or victimology assessment of victims and what was going on in their lives prior to their death.

CASE STUDY 6.3

A mid 20-year-old female was found brutally murdered and raped in her apartment. She had been stabbed multiple times and her throat was cut while on her bed. She was then left naked, sexually posed, and propped up against the wall. There were indications of forced entry through the kitchen window, but no suspects were immediately identified. During the victimology canvas interview of her friends, several reported the victim's comments about a certain *"creepy"* male neighbor who lived in the apartment building next door that would stand out on the balcony

Victimology   125

> of his second floor apartment smoking cigarettes at night and look down into her ground floor apartment as she was washing dishes or cooking. Friends reported that his actions "gave her the creeps," but he had never actually approached her, nor had they ever had any face-to-face contact. Based on this information, the police turned their focus onto the neighbor and eventually through their investigation and later DNA analysis; he was connected to the scene and was convicted of the homicide.

The victim in the above case study had never reported her feelings or concern to any authorities and the only way detectives became aware was asking about any concerns expressed by the victim to her friends or family members. Case Study 6.3 highlights the importance of conducting a victimology assessment in all death investigations.

In potential or suspected suicide cases, such canvass questions are important because many times the victim may have openly discussed or made statements that indicated their contemplation of suicide. Statements such as *"no one would miss me if I were gone, I might as well be dead, I wish I was dead,"* may have been misinterpreted or considered unimportant at the time. But clearly any mentions of self-destruction or suicide are important to uncover. Such statements by children, teens, or young adults are seldom made to parents, and are more likely to have been made to their close friends.

Domestic Issues

Because the basis of many homicides and suicides are the result of some type of interpersonal or interfamilial conflicts, questions regarding the family dynamic are critical. Because, if the victim has been murdered and the suspect attempts to stage the scene as a suicide, the offender typically will *"paint themselves"* in the best possible light and may not accurately state their current or past relationship problems with the victim. An example is the surviving spouse who flatly states that there were no problems they were aware of, that suicide has taken them completely by surprise. According to them, everything was fine, they were in a happy relationship. However, such self-serving statements are not always accurate.

Canvass interviews of family and friends will often provide information concerning conflicts between the victim and their husband/wife or significant other, that may not have been officially reported to the police. Such conflicts within a relationship are not always contained within the residence, and many times the family and close friends are often aware of conflicts and issues within the relationship.

Assessing Risk

Once the background information is collected, the potential "risk factors" and the victim's individual personality characteristics can be identified and evaluated. It is important to remember that the risk factors will basically equate to the motive for self-harm. So, the more risk factors that are found, the greater the chance or higher risk for self-harm, as the victim's way to avoid or solve those problems. The absence of such factors may lower the risk for self-harm. In normal crimes of violence, the concept of victimology is to then place the victim into one of three risk categories of *High, Moderate, or Low*. These risk categories simply refer to the likelihood or *risk* of the victim becoming the victim of a crime based on their lifestyle and personality characteristics. The higher the risk category, the more likely they are to become a victim of crime or are likely to have committed suicide.

High-Risk Victims

A *high-risk* victim is someone that is almost expected to eventually be a victim of crime based on their age, sex, and maturity levels in combination with their general lifestyle, residence, and employment. Examples would include but are not limited to runaways, homeless, drug abusers, criminals, and prostitutes. These are obvious potential crime victims because they routinely put themselves into contact with the public or the criminal element. Many times, they are also living within a high crime area, or interact with other criminals. Because of their general lifestyle, it is considered only a matter of time before they are eventually victimized. Additionally, engaging in criminal conduct should automatically place the victim into a high-risk category because those who are engaged in criminal conduct often associate themselves with others involved in criminal conduct.

A *high risk* for suicide is generally centered around the presence of those risk factors and antemortem behaviors that have been covered throughout the text. The real high factors generally include relationship or interpersonal problems, legal problems, health problems, and financial problems. Conceptually the more risk factors and antemortem behaviors that are

Victimology

present in their lives, the greater risk for suicide and would be a consistent finding in a suicide investigation.

Moderate or Medium Risk

Moving down the scale is the *moderate or medium risk*; these are generally those persons who would probably be placed in a low-risk category and thus very unlikely to come into contact with the criminal element or become victims of a crime; but something in which they were engaged at the time, may have placed them into a higher risk category. For instance, a housewife who is out shopping after dark and their car breaks down on the highway. Although she may normally be considered a low-risk person, the fact they now find themselves alone on the highway with a broken-down vehicle now places them into a moderate risk category to reflect situational risk factors. Another example would include a traveler who takes a wrong turn off the interstate and finds themselves lost and driving around in a high crime area in an unfamiliar city. Their normal lifestyle would not place them into such a position, but through situational circumstances, their risk factors were elevated.

The concept of a moderate or medium risk in relation to a suicide might include those that have only recently experience any of the risk factors but have not yet expressed suicidal thoughts or exhibited antemortem behaviors.

Low Risk

A *low-risk* victim is someone, based on their age, sex, lifestyle, and personality characteristics, is unlikely to become a victim of crime. Primarily because they are not engaged in the typical high-risk behaviors, or they are seldom in the public enough to come into more than happenstance contact with a *stranger offender*. An example of a typical low risk victim would be a stay-at-home mother and wife, with a stable marriage, who has no outside employment, does not abuse drugs or alcohol, is not involved in any extra marital affairs, and lives in a nice residential neighborhood.

Recognizing a low-risk victim is important because they are more often specifically targeted by an offender, rather than routine contact with an offender. Meaning, the offender may have some amount of prior knowledge of the victim and has specifically planned to assault that specific victim, as opposed to another victim they contact by chance. This does not mean that the offender knew the victim personally; it maybe a case of the victim being observed at some prior

128

Equivocal Death

time by the offender who returns later to commit the assault when it was to their advantage to do so. This is not an absolute rule, but with all things being equal and no other evidence pointing in another direction, it is a good course of action and assumption until additional evidence can be developed.

In potential suicide cases, a low-risk person would have an absence of any risk factors or antemortem suicidal behaviors. Basically, there is no motive for their self-harm. Turecki and Brent (2016) and Steele et al (2018) identify several factors that may act or influence someone away from suicidal thoughts and behaviors. These *protective factors* are essentially conditions that tend to promote strength and resilience and thereby provide vulnerable individuals with support during difficult times. Thus, making suicide or thoughts of suicide less likely. These factors include:

Reasons for living (e.g., responsibility for young children, future goals).
Being married.
Satisfied with their life and optimistic about the future.
Cultural, religious, or personal beliefs that discourage suicide.
Life skills (including problem solving and coping skills).
Having a supportive social network and access to mental health care.
Being in good mental and physical health.

Therefore, when there is an absence of such risk factors or antemortem behaviors and there may be positive factors in their life, the death would be inconsistent with suicide. These same background and personality characteristics that make them low risk will generally allow them to deal with and accept even devastating potential life problems that come up. Therefore, a low-risk victim committing suicide should be looked at carefully before a final decision on the manner of death is made.

Chapter Summary

Victimology is one of the most underused concepts in death investigations, and when used correctly, a victimology assessment can be a valuable tool in all crimes of violence but especially in equivocal cases. Understanding what was going on in the victim's life and what they were doing prior to their deaths will provide a great deal of information if detectives only take the time to ask and collect it. As noted by Joiner (2010) the concept of someone deciding impulsively or by a "whim" to commit suicide is incorrect. It is the victimology assessment that can be used to identify what is consistent or inconsistent with the scene or the manner of death. Based on the victim's background and

Victimology

other related information, such risk factors or behaviors should be quickly identified and documented. Added together with the autopsy results as note in Chapter 5, this could provide the detective and Medical Examiner the necessary 51% of information to conclude the death is a suicide.

However, if there are no identified risk factors or antemortem suicidal behaviors present, then the scene and event must be looked at much closer because something is wrong. As noted previously by Chancellor and Graham (2017), suicide is among the top four themes used to stage a homicide so suspected suicides involving low-risk victims should always be looked at carefully before the manner of death is finally determined.

Bibliography

Brown, S., & Seals, J. (2019). Intimate Partner Problems and Suicide: Are We Missing the Violence? *Journal of Injury and Violence Research*, 11(1), 53–64. https://doi.org/10.5249/jivr. v11i1.997

Burnett, A. L. (2017). The Internet and Suicide. In Omar, H. A. (Ed.), *Youth Suicide Prevention: Everybody's Business*. New York, NY: Nova Science Publishers Inc.

Chancellor, A.S. & Graham. (2017). *Crime Scene Staging: Suspect misdirection of the crime scene*. Springfield, IL: Charles C. Thomas.

Cross, T., Gust-Berry, K., & Ball, P. (2002). A Psychological Autopsy of the Suicide of an Academically Gifted Student: Researcher's and Parents' Perspective. *Gifted Child Quarterly*, 46(4), 1–18.

Johnson, H., & Hotton, T. (2003). Losing Control: Homicide Risk in Estranged and Intact Intimate Relationships. *Homicide Studies*, 7(1), 58–84. https://doi.org/10.1177/1088767902239243

Joiner, T. E. (2010). *Myths about Suicide*. Cambridge, MA: First Harvard University Press.

Juhnke, G. A., Granello, P., & Lebron-Striker, M. (2007). *Is Path Warm? A Suicide Assessment Mnemonic for Counselors*. Alexandria, VA: Professional Counseling Digest (ACAPD-03).

Losey, B., & Graham, S. (2004). *The Scope of Bullying in Rural School Communities: A Survey of Elementary Students in Clermont County, Ohio. Community Report*. Cincinnati, OH: Child Focus Incorporated.

Nansel, T. R., Overpeck, M., Pilla, R. S., Ruan, W. J., Simon-Morton, B., & Scheidt, P. (2001). Bullying Behaviors Among US youth: Prevalence and Association with Psychosocial Adjustment. *Journal of American Medical Association*, 285(16), 2094–2100.

Sedgwick, R., Epstein, S., Dutta, R., & Ougrin, D. (2019). Social Media, Internet Use and Suicide Attempts in Adolescents. *Current Opinion in Psychiatry*, 32(6), 534–541. https://doi.org/10.1097/YCO.0000000000000547. PMID: 31306245; PMCID: PMC6791504.

Steele, I. H., Thrower, N., Noroian, P., & Saleh, F. M. (2018). Understanding Suicide Across the Lifespan: A United States Perspective of Suicide Risk Factors, Assessment & Management. *Journal of Forensic Sciences*, 63(1), 162–171. https://doi.org/10.1111/1556-4029.13519.

Turecki, G., & Brent, D. A. (2016). Suicide and Suicidal Behaviour. *Lancet*, 387(10024), 1227–1239. https://doi.org/10.1016/S0140-6736(15)00234-2.

Twenge, J. M. (2020). Increases in Depression, Self-Harm, and Suicide among US Adolescents after 2012 and Links to Technology Use: Possible Mechanism. *Psychiatric Research and Clinic Research and Clinical Practice*. https://doi.org/10.1176/appi.prcp.20190015.

The Latent Investigation

7

After the Preliminary

After the crime scene examination, the autopsy, the preliminary investigation, and the initiation of the victimology are completed or are in process, the investigation continues. But now should proceed in a more organized and planned event. One of the most important tasks at this stage of the investigation is to organize the investigative file, and make sure all of the documents produced during the preliminary and crime scene are present. Most questions about the event were likely answered and a determination made whether a criminal offense has or has not taken place. In those cases where evidence has clearly shown that a criminal offense has taken place, the investigation now shifts to a traditional investigation.

In other cases, the manner of death might still remain equivocal, and therefore additional investigation is necessary to make the final determination. Case Study 7.1 is a good example of how questions can remain after the preliminary investigations based on the confusing nature of the scene.

CASE STUDY 7.1

A soldier's body was found on a military reservation floating in a small waterway used for training. Two fishermen in a small boat found the body and alerted the authorities. The deceased was removed from the water and was found to be dressed in civilian clothes but was wearing a military rucksack and other military gear. He was identified initially through his wallet found in the rucksack, and it matched a soldier that had been reported AWOL or missing from his unit for over three weeks. The appearance of the body seemed consistent with being in the water for that length of time. An autopsy was performed, "and the soldiers" identity was confirmed by dental records and the cause of death was determined to be a single gunshot wound to the back of his head that exited through his forehead. The injury and other facts seemed consistent with homicide and an investigation was immediately

---

DOI: 10.4324/9781003373865-7

launched. The police quickly learned that the deceased soldier was known as a "womanizer" and specifically was interested and seemed to target in married women. The police then learned that he had or was suspected of having relations with at least three specific women and their husbands all became potential suspects. For several months the other three soldiers were intensively investigated but none of them could be eliminated or confirmed to be involved in the death. After a few months, the investigation seemed to stall. Eventually the detectives went to the location where the deceased was found and arranged for the water to be drained. When the waterbed was exposed, the police found a 9 mm pistol and one expended shell casing. The pistol was later determined to belong to the deceased and the crime lab was able to link the shell casing to the pistol. A background on the deceased soldier found that he did not want to be in the army, he wanted to be a police officer. So, he had previously let his enlistment lapse and then went to a large city and applied for the police department. Unfortunately, after a psychological assessment he was not hired. He then found a job with a Sherriff's department but was forced to work in the jail which he did not like. After a few months he re-enlisted in the army. But again, he was not very happy in the army and began engaging in affairs with married women, but according to a civilian friend he was not proud of himself for such activity. Eventually the concept of suicide was raised and reviewed as a possible explanation. But the detectives were adamant that this was a homicide and discounted any possibility of suicide. The case eventually got cold and was closed as an unsolved homicide. Twenty years later the case was reopened and after going through the entire file, the three husbands earlier consisted potential suspects, were actually eliminated, based on their alibies and some additional information. One factor in particular raised doubts as to their involvement. Noone was aware that the soldier went on a hike the day he disappeared. All of his friends indicated this was a common occurrence that the soldier would on the spur of the moment just get up and take a long hike. He was known to carry around the pistol, but no one could explain how an offender would know he was out hiking, would know where he would be hiking, would know about his pistol, would use his pistol to kill him and then throw the pistol in the water. A reenactment was staged that showed that it was possible for someone to shoot themselves in the back of the head without a lot of difficulty. A panel of six experienced detectives and a forensic psychologist reviewed the entire file as part of a cold case review. Their unanimous opinion was the deceased died as a result of suicide but staged the scene to appear as if he were murdered. However, members of the panel were later reconnected by the original detectives, who did not accept their findings. The detectives continued to believe that the soldier had been murdered by one of the three original suspects. Interesting, none of the detectives could name which of the three men were the most logical suspect. As with other examples of tunnel vision, the other detectives discounted or ignored any evidence that led away from their own theory of what happened.

Case Study 7.1 is a little unusual in that it was the detectives that refused to consider or accept the death was a suicide, rather than the family. As demonstrated in the previous case study, there are some events, although rare, when the initial effort has not completely established what happened and the event is still *equivocal* or uncertain. For those events, the investigation must continue to completely establish that a criminal event has or has not taken place. In these rare instances, the investigation should continue as if it was a homicide.

The next step after the preliminary investigation is known as the *latent phase*. By definition, *latent* simply refers to *something that exists but is not current visible, apparent, or activated. It is something that lies hidden waiting to emerge or become active.* Finding that evidence that lies hidden among the facts and circumstances of the event is exactly what the detective seeks during this stage of the investigation.

The Latent Investigation

After organizing the file, the detective should go through and read the complete file. This is a critical step, because so many different things occur during the preliminary investigation, it is imperative for the detective to sit down and understand exactly what has transpired. Many detectives ignore this step because they have just completed the preliminary investigation and therefore, they think they know exactly what happened. But the preliminary investigation can be a confusing time, so the detective needs to know exactly what was done and what was said and not rely on memory of verbal conversations of what was done.

Unfortunately, many times it is not until the closing of the case or preparing for prosecution that the detective discovers that some lead or action, they had directed another to complete, or they forgot to complete was not done, or was not done correctly. Now weeks or months later they realize the mistake and not are scrambling to complete that lead. This could have been prevented if they had taken the time to read their case file after the preliminary investigation. Even worse when the prosecutor or supervisory personnel finds an inconsistency between statements and physical or forensic evidence that has not been addressed. Even worse is when this error is found and addressed by the defense during a trial.

Another important rationale for this seemingly common-sense task is quite simple: to get organized and stay focused. Whereas during the preliminary investigation the detective may be subjected to several twists and turns as often conflicting information is funneled into them, the latent investigation is marked by more planning and prioritizing of the remainder of the investigation. Basically, this is the time to map out what has to be done and then prioritize those tasks.

Evidence

Part of the case file review includes a thorough understanding of the crime scene examination, and the evidence collected. In many police departments a specialized crime scene unit may have processed the scene and is responsible for submitting the evidence directly into the crime lab. If someone other than the detective has completed the scene examination, then it is doubly important for the responsible detective to become familiar with the evidence collected at the scene and/or the autopsy. Then make sure the evidence has been submitted to the laboratory and the appropriate examinations are requested. Careful consideration should be given to submitting evidence to the laboratory even in those instances when after the preliminary investigation and victimology assessment, the event appears consistent with suicide.

Special attention should be given to any digital evidence including phones, iPads, or computers that the deceased was using or had access to. As noted previously, in our modern society, particularly the younger generations, we practically live with our cell phones. Therefore, they typically contain a plethora of information about the user and what was going on in their lives prior to their death. Such evidence has proved to be extremely helpful in all violent crimes because it often contains evidence of the owner's activity before, during, and in some cases even after the event. Much of their recent and past antemortem activity can be gleaned through examination of their text messages, phone logs, social media applications, photographs, fit bits, and internet searches. There are multiple examples of internet searches relevant to different methods of committing suicide, calls to suicide hot lines found in phone logs, and text to friends contained suicidal thoughts. Such findings are critical for all death investigations but especially when looking at any potential antemortem suicidal behaviors.

The Latent Investigation   135

There are some that might feel this extra effort is not needed or even a waste of time and resources if they are certain the death is believed to be a suicide. Timmermans (2005) notes that such investigative activity is generally necessary based on the *51% rule of suicide*, and what may seem to be a wasted effort, actually ensures police are able to defend the investigation and manner of death to the deceased's relatives and just as important, to eliminate other manners of death. Although suicide is not presented in court for prosecution, it may have to stand up to the questioning of relatives and in some cases to the public. Investing the extra time and effort might not stop the family from questioning the outcome, but it often does provide the necessary information to allow the family to move on with their grief.

If the investigation has reached this point, and it is still equivocal, and if there was previously a hesitancy to conduct such a search of digital evidence during the preliminary investigation; that hesitancy should evaporate at this stage. The absence of such information becomes crucially important when there is also an absence of risk factors or antemortem suicidal behaviors, found during the victimology assessment.

After reading the file, and reviewing all evidence collected, the next effort is to plan or map out the investigation. This involves forming a *theory of the crime* and then creating an *investigative plan*.

Theory of the Crime

The theory of the crime is basically what detectives believe happened and is an important step in all death investigations, because this forms the roadmap for the remainder of the investigation. There are two important concepts in forming a theory of any crime. First, no theory is ever *set in stone or is unchangeable*. Instead, detectives must be flexible and willing to adjust their theory as new information or evidence is discovered. An easy way to think of this concept is that any theory of a crime should be *written in sand, and not concrete*. A rigid nonflexible theory often leads to "*tunnel vision*," *confirmation bias*, or *cafeteria evidence*, all of which is defined as the tendency to accept information and evidence that *confirms* or supports one's theory of events but discounts or ignores evidence that does not agree with their theory. An example of the tunnel vision problem was found in Case Study 7.1.

When tunnel vision or confirmation bias is present, detectives tend to become focused on one suspect or one theory, to the exclusion of all others and may purposely or subconsciously prevent other ideas or evidence from being accepted or even considered. Geberth (2013) notes how these tendencies can start with the initial dispatch to the scene, wherein, detectives respond with an *assumption* they are looking at suicide and are almost programed to accept what they find.

The second concept in theory development is that theories must be based on the *evidence and information* that is present for each event, and not solely on a detective's personal experience, beliefs, or suspicion. Each event must be judged and evaluated based on the information and evidence that is present for that particular event. There may be similarities between events, but each must be judged and evaluated based on the unique circumstances and the particular individuals involved in the event. Many times, detectives will act and make important decisions based upon their "gut feeling" about the case because of their experience and how they previously handled other similar cases. However, *sometimes a gut feeling is just gas*. Meaning experience needs to be correctly applied to each situation based on the particular circumstances of that event rather than solely on past events. One of the best ways to develop and test a theory of the event is to use the *scientific method.*

Scientific Method

When investigating any crime of violence, one extremely important concept is the notion that all information obtained from witnesses, victims, or suspects must either be confirmed, corroborated, or refuted, to the greatest extent possible. A detective cannot simply accept the word of anyone. Adcock and Chancellor (2016) state this concept simply as "believe nothing and verify everything." As part of this concept, it is helpful to have a systematic approach to guide the steps of the investigation. One systematic approach is known as the *scientific method* and is basically an organized and standard way to respond to the facts and circumstances presented by the current event, not relying solely on past experiences.

Use of the scientific method underlies the basic goal to arrive at the best explanation of events based on the known evidence, and using a process and methods that are generally accepted and that can be independently evaluated or replicated by other experienced homicide investigators.

At the heart of the scientific method is the process of conducting hypothesis or theory testing with the ultimate goal of *disproving* various hypotheses or theories of the crime. Detectives should come up with various hypotheses or theories of the crime that are then tested against the evidence. Those theories that are disproven are set aside. If a theory cannot be disproven, it is likely to be the best explanation of what happened. This allows the detective

The Latent Investigation   137

to pursue and focus on obtaining additional evidence or information to strengthen that theory, or to obtain other evidence to disprove it.

The effort to disprove a theory seems counterintuitive, but actually it is the opposite of tunnel vision. To disprove a theory all the evidence and information must be included and considered instead of accepting only that evidence that validates a particular theory.

The scientific method is actually rather simple,

1. You define a problem. What question do you have to answer?
2. You gather what information is available (physical evidence, statements, and other information).
3. Develop multiple hypotheses or theories as to what may have occurred.
4. Then test the hypothesis or theory of the crime, with the intention to disprove the theory.
5. If the theory can be disproved then you collect additional information, develop another theory, or adjust a theory to include the new information and then set about trying to disprove it.
6. When you cannot disprove a theory, then you have identified what is most likely to have occurred.

But detectives have to be on guard to continue to contrast any new evidence or information with the theory of the crime to determine if the theory needs to be adjusted based on this new information.

Most detectives are already doing a version of this, without knowing they are actually using the **scientific method** to do so. The main problem, as mentioned before, and this is a big issue, one cannot simply discard or eliminate evidence or information, because it does not agree with the theory. If there is strong evidence that refutes or disproves the theory, then the theory is disproven and must be eliminated or adjusted. This is why theories are written in sand and not concrete so they may be easily adjusted.

Investigative Plan

Once a general theory of the crime or event is developed, the next step of the investigation is to establish the way forward for any investigation by creating an *investigative plan*. An investigative plan **(IP)** is basically a "road map" or "to do list" and consists of any investigative leads generated during the preliminary investigation or from questions or potential conflicts raised but not

138   Equivocal Death

yet answered. An IP is one of the more important investigative tools and acts as a reminder of things that need to be accomplished. It is not an investigative report per se; rather, it is the detective's notes on the case. It can be formalized by an agency and printed on a specialized form or can be completed on a piece of scrap paper. It should be considered as a "living document" designed to be added to, updated, or edited as the case progresses.

As the file is being organized and reviewed, identify those facts and evidence that needs to be corroborated or clarified, and determine what effort is needed to validate those facts. This is why sitting down and developing a theory if the crime is so important, because now, as the detective is formulating the plan for the investigation he can focus his attention on the theory of the crime, seeking out evidence that confirms or disproves the theory.

Since it is an informal document, the IP can be adjusted to the individual detective's own preference and be either handwritten or typed. Generally, a simple bullet, phrase, or comment format is all that is needed to identify the remaining leads. However, some detectives may need or want to write a detailed description narrative of what needs to be accomplished. Because it is an informal document, how it is created is usually up to the individual detective.

The IP is especially helpful when the detective is dealing with multiple cases to keep the various leads to the different cases straight. With an IP, the detective can quickly determine the remaining tasks that need to be accomplished, rather than go back through the entire file or try and recall from memory what needs to be done. It is also helpful if the case is transferred from one detective to another. The new detective has a chance to review how the investigation was going and what was the current plan. They may of course follow the current IP or create one of their own depending on the investigation and the individual detective.

The IP's form is only dependent on the detective's individual preference. Once initiated, it is easy to go through in regular intervals to edit the plan to take out those leads that have been completed or deemed no longer needed, and to add new leads as they are developed. The IP is likely to be edited and changed several times throughout the investigation as leads are followed up on and new information is added. The updating of the investigation plan is a continuing process and will help keep the investigation and the detective on the right path.

Box 7.1 is an example of a basic IP on a suspected suicide.

Box 7.1 presents an example of a basic investigative plan; it uses bullets or short statements to list the leads that need to be accomplished and keep the investigation on track. It also can document those leads already accomplished. As the leads are accomplished, they are checked or crossed off.

The Latent Investigation

139

BOX 7.1 INVESTIGATIVE PLAN.

1. Interview/statement John Smith (coworker).
2. Interview Nancy Smith (reference victim's fight with P. Johnson).
3. ~~Obtain copy of 911 recording~~ done (9/4/20).
4. Criminal background check of:
   - ~~Bob Jones (ex-boyfriend)~~ (done 9/2/2020).
   - Phil Johnson (boyfriend).
5. Determine ownership of gun?
6. Cellbrite phones (scheduled 9/5).
7. ~~Interview Sally Smith (friend)~~ (completed 9/4/20).
8. ~~Interview Sherry Johansson (best friend)~~ (completed 9/3/20).
9. P. Johnson check alibi (working, then to sister's house).
10. Interview B. Johnson (P. Johnson's sister).
11. Interview Mrs. Barbra Woodard (911 caller/discovered body).
12. Victimology interviews: Jean Kirk, Nancy Prichard (coworkers).
13. ~~Evidence to Crime Lab (gun/note)~~ (completed 9/3/20).
14. Obtain CS reports (CSI Garza).

Homicide Investigative Considerations

One of the first steps in the death investigative process was outlined in Chapter 2 to determine the type or category of homicide and thus identify potential motives for the death. In the *latent phase* of the investigation the type or category of homicide should be clear and investigative efforts are typically focused on identifying potential suspects. Thus, they are now looking for *M.O.M.* or those who have a *Motive, Opportunity*, and the *Means* to commit the homicide.

As previously noted, M.O.M. is a simple concept to apply when suspects or persons of interest have been identified. If your suspect has M.O.M., then you probably have a very good suspect. Conversely, if the identified suspect does not have all three elements, then you probably don't have the right suspect, or you have not found the right evidence. Trying to identify the motive behind the homicide or the potential suicide is one of the times when *tunnel vision or confirmational bias* begins and once started, it becomes difficult to change course. However, identifying the motive behind a homicide or a suicide is generally not complicated, this is where the concept of *Occam's Razor* may be applied. The basic definition of Occam's Razor *is that in nature usually*

140   Equivocal Death

the simplest explanation is correct and the more assumptions you have to make the less chance they are correct. Unfortunately, once the detectives become convinced of one theory of the crime the consideration of the importance of establishing M.O.M. is frequently discounted.

Suicide Investigative Considerations

In suicide investigations there is a slightly different concept that focuses attention more on the *victim and the event*, this is best explained using the acronym of **M.I.A.** or *Motive, Intent, and Ability.*

Motive

Motive, in the context of a homicide investigation, refers to the general reasons or why the offender killed the victim. In the case of suicides, we are concerned with identifying the reasons why the *victim* desires to kill themselves. Thus, the importance of the preliminary investigation and victimology assessment to identify motives behind a self-destructive act. Chapter 6 identified some of the various risk factors that may be present in someone's life and identify certain antemortem suicidal behaviors. These risk factors and behaviors can equate to the *motive(s)* that lead someone to self-destruction. In suicides, there may be multiple motives that combine to overwhelm the victim. However, if a clear **motive(s)** cannot be identified, and there are no antemortem suicidal behaviors, then a suicide determination should be questioned and another explanation, such as homicide or accidental death should be considered. This is when the *scientific method* as described previously becomes a key to understanding what may have occurred. If there is no evidence of a motive to kill yourself, there must be another motive or reason for the death.

Case Study 7.2 is an example of a reported suicide of a wife, but the husband is unable to provide a motive or reason behind the suicidal act.

CASE STUDY 7.2

In the early morning hours, a husband called 911 requesting medical assistance for his wife. The husband told the dispatcher he had been in the shower and when he came back into the bedroom, he found his wife had hanged herself with an electrical cord from the upper support

The Latent Investigation

bed board. When EMS arrived, they began performing advanced life support and also identified to deputies several ligature marks around the woman's neck. The wife was eventually transported to the hospital but was pronounced dead upon arrival. During their preliminary investigation, deputies noted the husband's explanation of events did not match the physical evidence at the scene. Also, during his initial interview he could not provide a reason or motive for his wife's suicide. At the wife's autopsy, the medical examiner determined the ligature marks around the victim's neck were actually horizontal and thus inconsistent with a hanging death. The cause of death was determined to be ligature strangulation and the manner of death was homicide. Confronted with these facts the husband admitted to strangling her and then staging the scene to resemble a suicide. (State of Tennessee v. Stanley v. Hill.)

As noted in the case study, the husband made a major mistake that is frequently found when a homicide is staged as suicide. He expressed complete shock over his wife's death and tried to show himself in the best possible light by insisting everything was fine within their life and marriage and could provide no *motive or logical reason* for her suicide. One of the markers Chancellor and Graham (2017) note in these cases is the husband or partner in staged suicide events always tends to *"paint themselves in the best possible light."* Meaning, it might be to his benefit to say they were having problems or provide motives for their wife's behavior, but they can't seem to do it. They are more concerned that they look like they had nothing to do with the act. However, as noted by Joiner (2010) no one just suddenly decides to commit suicide., so the husband's explanation of events was inconsistent with what he was attempting to portray at the scene.

When evaluating potential motives, it is critical to remember that the same stressful life situations that can be risk factors for suicide are also risk factors for homicide. For example, intimate partner and romantic problems leading to separation and divorce are high risk factors for suicide; yet these same issues also lead to domestic abuse and homicide (Brown & Seals 2019; Johnson & Hotton 2003).

Intent

When investigating suicide one must concentrate on the aspects of *intent*. Because as noted by Nolan (1988) the concept that defines suicide is *intention*. Suicidal intent can be defined as "understanding the physical nature and consequences of the act of self-destruction." Basically, that the deceased understood the consequences and finality of their actions and proceeded anyway. The problem of course is how can someone determine the intent of another person? The answer is to consider the totality of circumstances surrounding the event.

The *intent* to end one's life is different than the motive for suicide and can also be determined by how serious the victim was about killing themselves and if they truly understood the probable consequences of their actions. Intent cannot always be discerned by the victim's actions alone. There have been many occasions when the victim did something wrong, unsafe, or even stupid that resulted in their death, but they did not have any clear *intent* to end their life. Examples include a victim who was killed while trying to unload a newly purchased and unfamiliar weapon or someone who points a gun to their head to act stupid with their friends and pulls the trigger not knowing the gun is loaded. Although the death was the result of the victim's own actions, there was no clear *intent* to end their life and therefore should not be considered suicide.

Suicidal intent can be seen in several different ways including examining the lethality of the method chosen to end their life. This is one of the reasons that guns are often used to commit suicide because they are very lethal. It is also not unusual to see victims who may use multiple means to ensure their efforts are successful. Examples of using multiple means to commit suicide are known as *complex suicides* and are further discussed in the following.

Complex Suicides

The term *"complex suicide"* was coined by Bohert (2005) referring to those incidents in which more than one method to commit suicide is used. But it was Marcinkowski et al (1974), who first proposed two general categories for suicide events known as *simple or complex*. A simple suicide is basically when the deceased used one method or means to end their life. For instance, the person shot or hanged themselves resulting in their death. The second general category is *complex*, where the deceased used multiple methods or means to end their life. Complex suicides can be further classified as *planned or unplanned*.

The term *planned complex suicide* refers to the intentional use of more than one method to make sure that death will occur even if one method fails. Typically, two or more common methods of suicide are combined in the same event such as a victim who places a plastic bag over their head and then hangs themselves. Other examples of *planned complex suicide* are found in Case Studies 7.2 and 7.3.

The Latent Investigation

CASE STUDY 7.3

A young male was found hanging in his garage; the engine of his vehicle was running, and the garage was filled with car exhaust. Toxicology later determined shortly before his death he had also taken a combination of anti-depressant drugs and alcohol which would have likely resulted in his death from that combination alone. In this case three different methods of ending his life were used.

CASE STUDY 7.4

A young male was found hanging inside the laundry room of his apartment. He had sliced his wrists lengthwise multiple times on each arm, and then hanged himself. Toxicological results confirmed he had also consumed alcohol and antidepressants. In this case three different methods were used to end their life.

As noted in the previous two case studies, there is clear *intent* by each victim to end their life. This intent can be clearly seen by their use of multiple means.

An *unplanned complex suicide* is found when one method is attempted, but may be taking too long, has become too painful, or is insufficient to cause death, so another method is used to end their life. An example is ingesting a caustic liquid, but when death is not quick, the deceased then hangs themselves or uses a firearm. Other examples include using sharp force instruments to open their blood vessels, but the wounds were not deep enough, and the bleeding was stopped due to coagulation. So then so then they hang themselves or used another method that finally ends their life.

Although complex suicides only account for about 1–5% of all suicides (Bohnert 2005; Brown, & Seals 2019; Racette & Sauvageau 2007), they can be confusing to the responding police. Many times, when confronted with more than one method to end their life is used, homicide is often suspected. Homicide can be difficult to rule out in some cases, especially when the methods used are uncommon. Therefore, only a combination of scene examination, police investigation, and autopsy can reconstruct the circumstances of the death.

Frequently these scenes can be confusing when initially observed as noted in Case Study 7.5.

CASE STUDY 7.5

Police were called to a bloody scene by a sister who came to check on the brother who had not kept an appointment with her the previous day. When police entered the scene there was an extensive amount of blood throughout the house. Especially in the bathroom, on the floor, on the vanity, sink, and mirror and a razor blade found in the sink. There was also a blood trail out of the bathroom to the living room to an easy chair, where there was extensive bleeding on the floor adjacent to the chair. A blood trail then went out of the living room to the laundry room, where the deceased was found in the large laundry sink that was full of blood and water. His legs were sticking out of the sink and apparently, he "dove into" or went headfirst into the sink full of water. When the deceased was recovered, he was found clutching a plastic container of bleach. He was also found to have multiple cuts on both arms. The police were eventually able to discern he had cut himself in the bathroom with the razor blade and began to bleed. He then walked to his chair in the living room where he sat and remained for a while. But likely got frustrated at how long it was taking and filled up the laundry room sink with water, grabbed the full container of bleach, and then went headfirst into the sink. The bleach may have been used as a way to weigh him down and allow him to drown. At autopsy he was found to have water in his lungs, so the cause of death was actually drowning. The sister was aware her brother was having some difficulty over his marriage and financial situation, but she was not aware of any suicidal thoughts. The police conclusion the death was the result of suicide was consistent with other antemortem behaviors, and the scene examination could explain the blood in the different locations within the residence.

The next aspect of a suicide investigation is known as *ability* as described in the following.

Ability

Ability essentially refers to a couple of factors; first, the physical ability to commit suicide and second, having the means available to commit the suicidal act. One of the better examples of this was found in the previous Case Study 1.2 when the elderly female was found hanging in a shed, dead from an apparent suicide. The rope was tied tight to a truss that was over 10 feet off

The Latent Investigation

the ground. But there was no ladder found in the shed and friends reported that the victim was so arthritic in her hands that she could no longer sew or crochet. Thus, it was unlikely that she would have been able to first get high enough up into the rafters to tie the rope to the truss and second that she would be able to tie the rope itself.

Another example of *ability* was found in the previous Case Study 6.2 where the victim was reportedly operating a jet ski and jumping the wake of bigger boats and had an accident and felling to the water and drowned. However, the victim was born with a deformity to her hand that made the operation of the jet ski impossible. Therefore, she did not have the *ability* to do what the offender claimed.

The concept of ability also refers to the fact that the weapon or instrument causing the death is also present at the scene. The following Case Study 7.6 is an example of the police responding to the reported suicide but after looking at the scene and the victim, did not believe the victim had the *ability* to kill themselves in the manner depicted.

CASE STUDY 7.6

A woman reported to the police she had found her 81-year-old mother dead inside her apartment from an apparent suicide. The police arrived at the scene and found the woman face down on the floor with blood and vomit exuding from her mouth, and a necktie wrapped around her throat. Nearby was a note that read: "Tell the kids I love them. You don't need me anymore." The scene and the position of the victim on the floor just didn't look right to the police and they could not readily determine how the woman could strangle herself just using the necktie that was not somehow tied off. Not satisfied with the initial scene examination, the police initiated an investigation. They quickly discovered that prior to her mother's death, the daughter was engaged in a long term extra marital affair with another married man and was experiencing severe financial problems, including being over three months behind in her mortgage payments. They also noted that although her husband had received $30,000 from an inheritance, she had already spent the money shopping and enjoying herself. Her behavior following her mother's death was also questionable. This included within 24 hours of the mother's death, the daughter used her mother's credit card to pay off her electric bill, settle accounts with a collection agency, and even booked herself an out of state vacation. Then the daughter disappeared and was reported missing. She was later found walking the streets aimlessly by the police. She was brought to the police station and under additional

> questioning confessed to murdering her mother by strangling her and then staging the scene to make her death look like a suicide. She claimed to be over stressed because of her long-term affair with a local married man had ended and her mounting financial situation (Chancellor and Graham 2017).

In the previous case study, the responding officers immediately questioned the victim's *ability* to kill themselves using the method found at the scene. Whereas it's not impossible for someone to strangle themselves; it does take some effort because if the ligature around the neck is not somehow secured, the pressure is released once they lose consciousness.

Ability also refers to the fact that the weapon or instrument that caused the death is also present at the scene and this concept is often misunderstood and misapplied by those attempting to stage a scene. As noted previously in Chapter 4, the best example are those cases involving a firearm; particularly a handgun, when an offender murders the victim and attempts to stage the scene as a suicide by placing the weapon in the victim's hands. Placing the weapon into the victim's hand seems to the offender as the obvious place to put the weapon; thus, providing evidence of the victim's self-inflicted wound. However, in self-inflicted injuries the gun is not always found in the victim's hands. It is only important that the weapon or instrument used to cause the death is present at the scene and located in the general area near the victim.

As noted with homicides and the concept of M.O.M. being used to identify a potential offender, it is also the same with suicides and the acronym M.I.A. The police should be looking at the totality of information and evidence to see if the victim had the motive, intent, and ability to kill themselves. If M.I.A. is not present, the event should be carefully examined as a potential homicide.

Precipitating Event

As noted previously a person does not simply wake up one morning and decide to commit suicide. A precipitating event is something that may occur shortly before the suicidal act. This is interpreted as *"the last straw"* and coupled with other risk factors, leads the victim to follow through with their suicide. Examples may include: an arrest, losing their job, a significant personal confrontation with family or friends, loss of a significant other through death or divorce.

The Latent Investigation   147

However, in homicide cases there is also a precipitating event that leads to domestic homicide. For any interfamilial deaths detectives should be looking at events up to 96 hours from the time of death for such an event. This event could have led to a domestic murder or could have been the last straw in the decision to end the other person's life. So, looking for and recognizing this event is important in either case.

A precipitating event is not an absolute finding in either suicide or domestic homicide, but it's present enough that efforts should be made to look for such an incident.

Suicide Notes

As noted in Chapter 8, suicide notes are an important finding but are not always left behind by the deceased. Therefore, they may be significant if they are present, but does not necessarily negate a suicide finding if they are not present.

If such communications are found then every effort should be expended to validate them including forensic analysis such as fingerprint, handwriting, or even forensic linguistics are all possibilities. In any event, such writings if present should never be immediately accepted without some type of confirmation. Any electronic communications such as text messages or emails should always be viewed initially with skepticism until they can be validated.

If the communication provides reasons for their actions, then efforts should be made to confirm those reasons or motives. Additionally, if any last communications deal with the distribution of any valuable asset or personal property should also be carefully examined, as many times this might be the motive for homicide, and the scene staged as a suicide.

Recent Changes to Wills or Insurance

Depending on the circumstances of the event under investigation, it is necessary and proper to ask if the deceased had a prepared will and especially if there were any recent changes to their will. If there is a will and if there are new changes this might be an avenue of continued investigation. This is unlikely to come up in many cases, but it is important to remember that the will may provide a motive for homicide, especially if there were any recent changes and any changes to the will involve a large amount of money, other valuables, or a change to the recipients.

The same goes for any recent changes to life insurance policies such as an increase in the policy or change in beneficiaries. In both instances the date of the change and the knowledge of anyone to the change might be important to look at.

General Suicide Investigative Concepts

There may come a time in the investigation when the evidence, autopsy, victimology, crime scene, and other aspects of the event are all consistent with suicide. One of the things that may take place at this time is to provide a final briefing and the investigative findings to a family. As noted in Chapter 1 the family are likely not to be initially very receptive because everyone has their own ideas about suicide, and unfortunately no one wants to *accept* that their family member, especially children, committed suicide. This of course is the value and importance of conducting a thorough investigation.

To fully understand the concept of suicide Adcock and Chancellor (2016) provide two very important concepts.

1. You Cannot Rationalize an Irrational Act.

Basically, for those not suffering through personal troubles, depression, or feelings of hopelessness, we cannot always understand why a person could end their own lives; so, the act is often incomprehensible. Suicide, therefore, must be seen through the lens of the victim not our own. What is unthinkable from our perspective may be totally acceptable and even welcome relief for the victim. This is best explained by Shneidman (1996) who saw the main cause of suicide as what he described as *psychache* or psychological pain that the individual wishes to escape. In this sense, peace is what the person seeks and the "suicidal act" is both a moving away from the *psychache* they are experiencing and a move toward peace. In suicide, the two goals are merged as one: escape from pain is relief; and that is how peace is defined. The unbearable pain is transformed into peace and the suffering is taken away. At least this is what the suicidal person thinks and hopes to achieve.

In adolescents' suicide is seen as a way to gain relief from those pressures or problems confronting them, and as previously noted in Chapter 6, they unfortunately choose a permanent solution to what is generally a temporary problem. But again, suicide is what relieves them from all the pressures that they are feeling.

The second general concept is one that provides most of the difficulties in working suicide investigations and for family and friends to accept a

The Latent Investigation 149

determination of suicide because of their own background, personal beliefs, or feelings. This is especially important when the victim has used an unusual method to cause their death.

2. There Is No Such Thing as a Too Painful Way to Commit Suicide.

There are as many ways to commit suicide as there are motives for committing suicide. Some are rather painless, such as combining alcohol with other medications, resulting in basically falling asleep and never waking up. Other common methods include various firearms, sharp force instruments such as razors or knives. Other common methods include various forms of asphyxia including hanging, suffocation, or oxygen exchange such as carbon monoxide inhalation.

There are others however, who may choose more violent and certainly more painful methods, such as self-immolation, which is certainly a most painful death. Additional documented methods of committing suicide in what most would think are agonizing deaths include; drinking a caustic liquid; one young man that used a large book to literally hammer the blade of a hunting knife into his head; a wife who placed her husband's Sabre saw against her neck and turned it on, nearly severing her head from her body; or even a young man who walked into the woods with a chain saw, placed it on the ground, started it and then leaned into it, cutting his throat.

All of these are examples of some of the violent, painful, and unusual methods that people have used in the past to end their lives. The method used may actually have some special significance to the victim or it may simply be a case of using whatever means they have available. Regardless of what we might think about the infliction of pain on oneself; it is clear this is not always an issue with those who wish to kill themselves. Whenever these issues come up, sometimes the only possible response is to go back to the first concept: *You can't rationalize an irrational act.*

There are literally hundreds of ways to commit suicide and the person who wants to end their own life is only limited by their imagination and whatever materials or means they have available. Generally speaking, however, an offender is not likely to use a strange or unusual method of suicide to stage the scene because they want the event to be easily recognizable as a suicide. Using an unusual method may cause more of a police interest in the death, thus defeating the intent to stage the scene and misdirect the police.

These two concepts are particularly important when dealing with the surviving family who are seeking to understand what happened to their loved one. This again is the importance of identifying the motives, risk factors, and antemortem behaviors of the deceased that are consistent with suicide so the family can be presented with this information. Also, the more unusual or seemingly painful method used to end their life the more likely questions are going to come from the family.

When dealing with potential suicides, there are two general questions that should be asked and answered. These are:

1. **Does their death solve any problems for the "victim?"** This would include relationship issues, financial problems, or potential judicial punishments. In this instance, death may be seen by the victim as way to escape these problems. Remember that as noted in earlier chapters, sometimes people, especially adolescents or teens, will choose suicide as a solution if they become overwhelmed, embarrassed, or fearful of a pending event.
2. **Does the death of the victim benefit another person?** Generally, the benefit for another person is through financial gain in the form of an insurance policy or other business transactions. However, the death of the victim might also solve personal issues such as eliminating the need for a divorce, or other legal issues such as child custody.

As part of any death or murder investigation consideration must be given to whom would benefit from the death of the victim. The most common benefit is monetary based on insurance or inheritance. But other more intrinsic benefits could also include freedom from a failing or unsuccessful marriage without a divorce action, removal of the victim from a business partnership, revenge from some personal slight or other action by the victim. As stated, many times before in this text, there are as many motives as there are offenders. Generally, it is not difficult to determine who would most benefit from the death and much of this information can be obtained during the victimology assessment or other interviews with family and friends.

Suicides Staged to Resemble Homicides

Chancellor and Graham (2017) also provide a twist to suicide investigations such as Case Study 7.1, wherein someone commits suicide but then stages the scene to appear as a homicide. In these incidents, the intent is to misdirect a police investigation, to make their death appear to be the result of foul play rather than by their own hand. In these incidents the victim attempts to shift blame or responsibility for their deaths onto someone else rather than onto themselves and not necessarily trying to implicate a particular person.

The Latent Investigation   151

However, there are other instances wherein the victim clearly wants to implicate someone.

The following case study is another example of a premeditated homicide being staged as suicide; but this case is somewhat more complicated than other case studies because it was much better planned out. It involved multiple victims and multiple offenders working in concert with each other to create a credible scenario.

CASE STUDY 7.7

A schoolteacher and dentist in the United Kingdom were involved in a sexual affair and were convicted of murdering their respective spouses and staging both of their deaths to look like suicide. The couple had actually met at church and at the time both were unhappy in their current marriages. They began a sexual affair, which they covered by claiming he was going to her house when her husband was out of town to "teach her to play the guitar." During their affair, the woman got pregnant and then traveled to another city for an abortion. However, living in a small town it was impossible to keep the affair secret and eventually the dentist's wife learned of their relationship and was so devastated that she actually attempted suicide. She survived the attempt, but it gave her husband an idea how to solve both of their problems by murdering both husband and wife and then staging the scene to resemble a double suicide. The couple agreed to the double murder and when they were ready, the dentist gave his wife nitrous oxide as she napped on a sofa and then connected a hose from his car exhaust to where she slept, and she eventually died of carbon monoxide poisoning. At the same time the dentist was killing his wife, the woman had planned to place sleeping pills into her husband's food. The dentist arrived at the house and attempted the kill him in the same manner as his wife. He awoke during the process, but pair managed to hold him down until he finally died. The two lovers then put their respective spouse's bodies into a car and drove to an isolated building. The husband's body was placed behind the wheel and the wife's body into the passenger seat. The dentist placed a hose from the tail pipe into the passenger compartment and turned on the vehicle ignition. The victim's bodies were found a few hours later in the exhaust-filled building and the police concluded the two had made a suicide pact because of the affair and the case was closed without investigation. Almost 20 years later, the dentist, without prompting, came forward and told police what happened and then testified against his former lover. Both were convicted and sentenced to long prison terms.

The previous case is another example of the police being satisfied during their initial viewing of the scene and accepting what they had found as fact; and never actually initiating any criminal investigation. One of the differences in the previous case study is the staging effort was clearly more involved and premeditated. This scene is also a good example of the difference between an *ad hoc* and a *premeditated scene.* With a chance to prepare and plan the murders, a scene can be staged, and a believable scenario can be constructed that passes the initial police viewing of the scene.

Psychological Autopsy

There are some cases that even following a good crime scene examination, preliminary, and good follow up in the latent phase of the investigation, that the death is still considered as equivocal as to the manner of death. According to Ramsland (2019) between 10% and 20% of the deaths in the United States are considered equivocal or controversially determined. To help clarify some of the questions that arise in these situation, the detectives and coroners need to understand the potential *psychosocial* factors that may have influenced the death act.

In these instances, there is an additional step that might be taken to clear up any lingering questions, that effort is known as a *psychological autopsy or (PA)* (Tasu 2008). Leenaars (2017) describes a PA simply as "*a roadmap to uncover the baren bones of a suicidal mind.*" Although a PA may prove to be extremely helpful, this is traditionally one of the last leads to be accomplished, and generally only requested and performed when there are still questions remaining as to what happened after a thorough investigation.

The term *psychological autopsy* or *PA* is a detailed background investations conducted by *mental health professionasl* such as psychologists or psychiatrists, and is designed to understand the state of mind and what was going on in the last weeks and months of the deceased life. Gelles (1995) describes the psychological autopsy as essentially assisting the investigators in determining what role the deceased had in their own death and specifically identifying and understanding their intent. Tasu (2009) suscintly notes that the PA is a continuation and expansion of the *victimology assessment,* as detailed earlier in Chapter 6 but now reviewed by mental health professionals.

Ramsland (2019) identified some of the wide range of sources that the mental health professional seek out to obtain different aspects of the deceased background and what was going on in their life. These sources are found in Box 7.2.

The Latent Investigation

153

BOX 7.2 SOURCES OF INFORMATION.

First Responders interviews, other law enforcement personnel
- Autopsy and police reports
- Death Scene Photos and videos
- Forensic reports
- Suicide notes (video or other expressions)
- Social Media Posts
- Internet searches
- Journals, diaries, blogs, and webcams
- Correspondence
- Decedents artwork of poetry
- Family members
- Close friends and acquaintances
- Coworkers
- Former Spouses
- Records (school, military, work, medical, and prescriptions)
- Changes in behavior or life insurance policies
- Family history of mental illness or suicide

Box 7.2 is a wide range of sources the mental health professional can seek out for information on the background of the deceased and what was going on in their lives at the time of their death. Note that many of these sources are similar to the victimoogy assessment.

Perhaps the best example of the usage of a PA can be found in an actual criminal case where a psychological autopsy of a teen aged suicide victim was successfully introduced as evidence of child abuse against a mother. In Jackson v. State, 553 So. 2d 719 (Fla. Dist. Ct. App. 1989) the court described the expert witness's testimony about a psychological autopsy as:

> The expert psychologist specialized in suicidology and, for purposes of this trial, performed a psychological autopsy on appellant's seventeen-year-old daughter who had committed suicide in March of 1986. His testimony explained that a psychological autopsy is a retrospective look at an individual's suicide to try to determine what led that person to choose death over life.

Shneidman (1996) first coined the term *Psychological Autopsy* to refer to a procedure developed in the 1950s with the Los Angeles County Medical Examiner-Coroner's Office in conjunction the Los Angeles Suicide Prevention

Center (SPC). He defined the PA as "*A behavioral scientific impartial investigation of the psychological (motivational, intentional) aspects of a particular death.*" This coordinated effort originated from the ME's office asking for assistance in several recent equivocal deaths. The resulting inquires and analysis allowed the coroner to make the manner of death determinations in several cases. Typically, in questionable or equivocal cases, the manner of death typically lies between accidental and suicide. As noted in earlier chapters of this book, with efforts to stage the scene, homicide as a manner of death is also possible.

In developing the PA process, Schneidman (1996) identified three primary questions to answer when identifying suicide as the manner of death. These are:

1. Why did the person commit suicide?
2. Why did the person die at this time?
3. What was the most accurate mode of death in this case?

Outlines for Psychological Autopsy

The PA is basically a retrospective examination of a decedent's current and past life history, with the intent to get a better understanding of their *psychological intent*, using both the police investigative reports and their own interviews of relevant witnesses to reconstruct the behavior, personality, lifestyle, habits and history of the victim prior to death.

Like the victimology assessment, the psychological autopsy is based on a wide range of information concerning the victim and their background. This data is used to develop a victim's profile and background, and to better infer the interpersonal relationships, personality traits, and coping mechanisms. Shneidman (1981) developed a basic outline of topics to seek information for conducting a psychological autopsy. See Box 7.3

Box 7.3 is the basic list of topics Shneidman (1981) developed to produce a PA. Note how closely the topics match the victimology assessment as described in Chapter 6.

There is a caution when requesting a PA. The mental health professionals will require detailed information about the victim, the evidence, and circumstances surrounding their death, as well as those personality characteristics gathered during the victimology or during their later interviews. The goal of the PA however is not to establish the manner of death but to determine what is the *most likely* manner of death. The final decision for the manner of death will still remain with the coroner or ME. However,

The Latent Investigation

BOX 7.3   TOPICS FOR THE PA.

1. Identifying factors (name, age, occupation, marital status, and religion)
2. Death details (cause and mechanism).
3. Family history.
4. Family death history including illness types and suicides.
5. Personality and lifestyles.
6. Patters of reactions to stress and periods of disequilibrium.
7. Recent pressures, tensions of anticipation of trouble.
8. Role of substance in life or death.
9. Interpersonal relationships.
10. Fantasies, premonitions, dreams, and fears related to death or suicide.
11. Recent changes, such as eating habits, sleep issues, routines, and sexual patterns.
12. Information about successes and positive items.
13. Assessment of intention.
14. Lethality rating.
15. Reaction of informants to the death.

this information can provide an understanding of the deceased's *psychological state* based on the presence or absence of any stressors or risk factors and what was going on in their lives at the time of their death.

Value to the Investigation

The psychological autopsy is designed to assist in understanding the deceased's sense of mental health and well-being leading up to their death. This is especially important as previously noted in Chapters 1 and 3, (Chancellor & Graham 2017) Suicide is among the top four themes to stage a scene, so the real value comes from the analysis being completed by an independent mental health professional rather than another police officer. These reports are certainly helpful for the police investigation, but they can also be of value to family members that are struggling with the death of their loved one. The psychological report may identify significant mental health issues, increased high risk or antemortem behaviors experienced by the victim prior to their death and allow the family to accept the suicide determination.

156   Equivocal Death

From a detective's perspective, there is the potential for investigative usefulness of these reports. Particularly when the mental health professional can identify victim behavior that is either consistent or inconsistent with suicide.

Although in this chapter we have focused on using the PA in a potential suicide investigation, the PA is also useful in other death cases where the manner of death is still in question. Box 7.4 is an example of the different types of deaths that PA could be helpful.

Box 7.4 is other examples of equivocal death scenarios that a PA may provide additional information.

BOX 7.4   OTHER EQUIVOCAL DEATHS.

- Drug-related deaths
- Autoerotic asphyxia
- Self-induced asphyxia (e.g., the "choking game")
- Drownings
- Single vehicle deaths
- "Russian roulette"
- "Suicide by cop"
- Staged death scenes

Court Acceptance

Testimony by expert witnesses over their psychological autopsy findings has been used and accepted in civil courts, and in limited situations in criminal courts. In the United States vs. St. Jean,[1] the PA was used by the prosecution to assist in determining whether or not a suspected homicide victim was a likely candidate for suicide. In a very real sense this is what we attempt to determine when requesting a psychological autopsy.

Chapter Summary

The most important concept when conducting any death investigation, that after the initial response, the crime scene, autopsy, and preliminary the investigation is seldom complete. There is almost always more investigative steps that need to be accomplished. It's important at some time after the preliminary steps, to sit down and read the file and review all the information and

The Latent Investigation

evidence that has been developed thus far. Then organize the investigation and map out a "way to go" and create a road map or IP, of what needs to be done to complete the investigation. This is also a way to priorities the investigative leads if necessary.

Detectives need to be aware of how easy it is to develop *tunnel vision* or cognitive bias and ignore evidence that does not agree with their theory of the event. Using the *scientific method* to validate their theory of the crime is the best way to confirm or refute the various theories of the crime.

During the latent stage of the investigation efforts should focus on identifying either the M.O.M for homicide suspects or the M.I.A. for suspected suicide cases. When one of the elements is missing, then the theory needs further investigation as something is missing.

If there are any "suicide notes," changes to wills, or insurance policies, should all be looked at and confirmed through forensics analysis or other witness interviews. The key to remember is that such communications, changes in wills or insurance policies, may provide motives for murder as well as suicide.

A *psychological autopsy*, performed by mental health professionals, may prove beneficial if at the end of the investigation there are still unanswered questions. It is also beneficial for other equivocal deaths.

Note

1   The United States vs. St Jean United States Court of Appeals for the Armed Forces, No. 95-0756 Crim. App. No. 29942.

Bibliography

Adcock, J. M., & Chancellor, A. S. (2016). *Death Investigation* (2nd ed.). Amazon Press.
Bohnert, M. (2005). Complex Suicide. *Forensic Pathology Reviews*, 2, 127–143.
Brown, S., & Seals, J. (2019). Intimate Partner Problems and Suicide: Are We Missing the Violence? *Journal of Injury and Violence Research*, 11(1), 53–64. doi: 10.5249/jivr.v11i1.997. Epub 2019 Jan 13. PMID: 30636256; PMCID: PMC6420923
Chancellor, A.S., & Graham, G.D. (2017). *Crime Scene Staging, Investigating Suspect Misdirection of the Crime Scene*. Springfield, IL: Charles C. Thomas.
Craun, S. W., Tanner, L., Clausen, V., Merola, M. A., Opanashuk, L., and Keel, T. (2021). *Homicide or Suicide: How Nudity Factors into This Determination, Homicide Studies* (pp. 1–16). Thousand Oaks, CA: SAGE Publications.
Geberth, V. (2013). The Seven Major Mistakes in Suicide Investigation. *Law and Order Magazine*, 61(1), 54–56.

Gelles, M. G. (1995) Psychological Autopsy: An Investigative Tool. In Kurke, M. I. and Scrivner E. M. (eds.), Police Psychology into the 21st Century (pp 337–357). New York, NY: Psychology Press.

Joiner, T. E. (2010). *Myths about Suicide*. Cambridge, MA: First Harvard University Press.

Joiner, T. E. (2014). *The Perversion of Virtue*. New York, NY: Oxford Press.

Johnson, H. & Hotton, T.. (2003). Losing Control. Homicide Studies, 7, 58–84. 10.1177/1088767902239243.

La Fon, D. S. (1999). Psychological Autopsies for Equivocal Deaths. *International Journal of Emergency Mental Health*, 3, 183–188.

Leenaars, A. A., (2017). The Psychological Autopsy, A Roadmap for Uncovering the Barren Bones of the Suicide's Mind. New York, NY: Routledge.

Marcinkowski, T., Pukacka-Sokolowska, L., & Wojciechowski, T. (1974). Planned Complex Suicide. *Forensic Science International*, 3, 95–100.

Nolan, J. (1988). Suicide, Sane or Insane and Suicide Intent. In J. Nolan (Ed.), *The Suicide Case* (pp 51–65). Chicago, IL: American Bar Association.

Petherick, W. (2007). *Criminal Profiling: A Qualitative and Quantitative Analysis of Process and Content*. Queensland, Australia: Bond University.

Racette, S., & Sauvageau, A. (2007). Planned and Unplanned Complex Suicides: A 5 Year Study. *Journal of Forensic Science*, 52(2), 449–452.

Ramsland, K. (2019). *The Psychology of Death Investigations, Behavioral Analysis for Psychological Autopsy and Criminal Profiling*. Boca Raton, FL: CRC Press.

Sampath Kumar, P., et al. (2007). Psychological Autopsy: The Psychological Assessment of an Equivocal Death. *Sri Ramachandra Journal of Medicine*, 1(2), 41–43.

Shneidman, E. S. (1981). The Psychological Autopsy. *Suicide and Life-Threatening Behavior*, 11, 325–340.

Shneidman, E. S. (1993). *Suicide as Psychache: A Clinical Approach to Self-Destructive Behavior*. New York, NY: Roman & Littlefield Publishers, Inc.

Shneidman, E. S. (1994). The Psychological Autopsy. *American Psychologist*, 49, 75–76.

Shneidman, E. S. (1996). *The Suicidal Mind*. New York, NY: Oxford University Press.

State of Tennessee v. Stanley B. Hill. (2013). Tennessee Court of Criminal appeals No. E2012-00289-CCA-R3-CD, January 29, 2013.

Tasu, B. (2008). Forensic Techniques in Crime Scene Investigation – The Psychological Autopsy. Retrieved January 27, 2014 from http://researchgate.net/publication/49592815_Forensic_Techniques_in_Crime_Scene_Investigation_The_Psychological_Autopsy

Timmermans, S. (2005). Suicide Determination and the Professional Authority of Medical Examiners. *American Sociological Review*, 70, 311–333.

Notes or Last Communication

8

STEPHANIE C. DAVIES

How many times have words like this been stated at potential suicide scenes?

Well it must be a suicide because there is a suicide note.

Indeed, a *suicide note* found at the scene of a death in most cases, will point to a genuine suicide although such *last communications* are only left in a minority of suicide cases. Due to the myth that suicide notes are prevalent in most (or all) self-harm deaths, one attempting to stage a homicide as a suicide may well place emphasis on a note being left at the scene to reinforce the false narrative they are wanting to portray.

A suicide note can be defined as a message that has been authored by an individual when they decide to end their life. This message is an opportunity for them to explain why they are ending their life, to apportion blame to a person or situation for their decision, or to provide instructions that are to be carried out after their death (Gregory 1999). For the purposes of this chapter, the terms "suicide note" or "suicide letter" are used interchangeably with "last communication," in that it is a physical document, live stream, or recording, as opposed to a verbal statement made in front of a witness, which tends to be construed as *suicidal ideation.*

Suicide notes are believed to provide unique insight into suicide victims' thoughts, emotions, and motivations as to why they want to permanently end their lives (Shneidman 1969, 1981; Leenaars 1996). They assist with the formation of a victim profile to support a hypothesis of suicide, accident, or homicide (Darkes et al 1993), and they form a significant role in psychological autopsy investigations (Bhatia et al 2006). In addition, they are also important in the development of suicide prevention programs (Ho et al 1998).

Thus, any form of "last communication" left by a decedent is vital in an *equivocal death* investigation, as it can form crucial evidence when determining the precise manner of death.

DOI: 10.4324/9781003373865-8

Suicide Notes Are Important but Are Not Always Present

Contrary to popular belief, ongoing research demonstrates that suicide notes or last communications tend to be left in only a minority of suicide cases. Researchers (such as Carpenter et al 2016; Cerel et al 2014; Eynan et al 2018; Gunn et al 2012; Holmes & Holmes 2005; Shneidman 1969; to name but a few) have found that the proportion of notes left, broadly average between a quarter and a third of suicide cases. This dispels the myth that notes are left in all genuine suicides.

The absence of a note may be due to various factors, such as the non-desire by the decedent to express themselves in written form, or they lacked the opportunity or ability to write one. Those with a long history of mental illness and previous suicide attempts may feel a note explaining their actions is less required, due to loved ones already being aware of the reasons why they want to exit this life. Conversely, those without mental illness or prior attempts may feel an explanation is warranted so that loved ones can understand better why they have ended their life (Eynan et al 2018).

General Categories of Suicide Notes

So what characteristics are there that influence if a suicide victim leaves a note or last communication? This can depend on various factors such as age, gender, the location of suicide and background culture. Salib and Maixmous (2002) have suggested that characteristics unrelated to the suicide act itself may explain the propensity to leave a note, such as the decedent's education level and literary skills. So, for a lot of people, it can come down to factors such as having the means, opportunity and access to writing materials or technology such as cell phones or other devices such as video or audio to record their last communications. Illness, disability, and dexterity issues can hamper such efforts, as will technological naivety if the only thing available is a cell phone and the individual is unfamiliar with how to record voice memos or how to send a text message. It can also come down to simple practicalities, such as the desire to complete the act before family members return home.

Impulsivity refers (in this context) to suicidal acts that take place without any prior planning or forethought (Chalker et al 2015), where there is a very short (or non-existent) time between the decision to take one's life and carrying out the act itself. The longer the time between the two, the more time there is to plan and thus record or write a last communication.

Research into those who leave suicide notes or not has shown mixed results. Cerel et al (2014) found that out of nearly 3,000 suicides, 18% left a

Notes or Last Communication

note and that there were no significant differences between those that left notes and those that did not. Stack and Rockett (2018) found that note leavers varied in terms of demographics, life events, mental health backgrounds, and their chosen suicide methodology. However, they expressed concern at placing too much emphasis on overgeneralizing such characteristics in note writers as opposed to non-note writers. Callanan & Davis (2009) found the only difference between those who left notes and those that did not was that note-writers were more likely to have lived alone and had prior suicidal ideation.

Essentially, the meaning of suicide is unique to the individual that is carrying out the act, and there can be a myriad of reasons as to why they leave a note or not.

Box 8.1 Summarizes some factors that can influence if a note is left.

Due to the global variety in legal definitions as to what constitutes a suicide, in some areas importance is placed on a note having been left (or equivalent communication) before a manner of death can officially be assigned as a suicide (Shah 2008). Otherwise, the manner of death in those scenarios may well be misclassified as accidental or undetermined – skewing the true picture of suicide statistics. Take as an example in England and Wales, up until summer 2018, suicides were only recorded as such where the evidence met the criminal *standard of proof*, i.e., beyond reasonable doubt. These would

---

BOX 8.1   FACTORS THAT CAN INFLUENCE IF A NOTE IS LEFT.

- If the act is planned rather than impulsive.
- A slower suicide method (such as toxicity) rather than quick (i.e., gun).
- The location – i.e., indoors with writing media rather than out in the wilderness.
- The educational level/absence of a literary disability (such as dyslexia).
- Absence of illness/physical disability that could otherwise affect dexterity.
- Personality traits (i.e., ability to express oneself in written form, has ability to plan).
- Availability of writing materials/medium, i.e., pen, paper, phone, computer, printer.
- Motivation behind the act and if the reasons are not already known by loved ones.
- If there are previous suicide attempts and/or ideation.
- Dependent upon the nature of a triggering event.

be cases where the decedent had left a note or communication that clearly implied their intention to permanently end their life; or where there had been clear *suicidal ideation* expressed prior to their death. Post summer 2018, this standard of proof changed from *criminal* to the *civil* standard of proof (i.e., where it was more likely than not, and on the balance of probabilities) – so the probability threshold of a case being a suicide essentially dropped to 51%. This is specifically relevant considering that in the United Kingdom since 1961 suicide – i.e., "self-murder" (acts as well as attempts) – was no longer deemed to be a criminal offense. Equally suicide has long since been decriminalized in the United States, along with most countries worldwide.

Referencing the fact that most suicide decedents do not leave any form of communication stating their intention to end their lives, this means that those investigating potential suicides must consider the totality of the evidence before concluding that a case is indeed suicide. The takeaway message here is that the *presence* of a note does not prove it is a suicide, just like the *absence* of a note does not prove it was *not* a suicide.

The Format of the Note

Notes can be left in a variety of formats (Holmes & Holmes 2005) and with the ever-growing ubiquity of technology, the format is becoming increasingly varied as time goes on. Traditionally, they were handwritten on paper, walls, or mirrors but with the advent of more modern forms of communication, they are also being sent electronically by text message, email, or via social media (such as a status update or a live stream of the act itself). Notes sent electronically right before the suicide have been termed *e-suicide notes* which can be in an audio, textual, or video format (Behera et al 2014). It has been suggested that those that adopt this modern way of leaving last communications, could be in a separate sub-group of note-writers themselves in terms of their characteristics (Eynan et al, 2018). Barrett et al (2016) found that "new media" note-leavers tended to be younger and may have a history of substance misuse. However, one could argue that the instant sending, and receipt of e-suicide notes could provide a small window for the individual to be saved, and in this context, is the note actually a cry for help, rather than a legitimate last communication?

Duddin et al (2021) analyzed 75 suicide notes, where the majority (88%) were handwritten, and a small amount (12%) were electronic. In terms of recipients, 92% of notes were addressed to loved ones, whereas 8% were addressed to the police. One wonders if the type of recipient could depend upon the family and social network of the suicide victim, or who may be likely to find their body.

Notes or Last Communication 163

Box 8.2 lists the different formats of suicide notes.

In addition, there need not be just one note left by a suicide victim. There can be multiple notes left, where each one serves a separate purpose, such as being addressed to more than one recipient, or separating out instructions and explanations.

Box 8.3 summarizes why multiple notes may be left.

Research has shown there can be a multitude of themes that suicide notes can be categorized into. For the purposes of this chapter, there are three fundamental themes that suicide notes can fall into: *Explanatory, Accusatory, or Instructional* (Meyer et al 2017).

Explanatory notes are where the decedent is explaining to loved ones the reason(s) why they have chosen to end their life. It can refer to the need to escape from a chronic illness or mental health condition or being unable to live with a life change such as the loss of a job, the death of another, or the breakdown of a relationship. These types of notes may be left where loved ones are not aware of what exactly led to an individual choosing to end their life.

BOX 8.2   FORMATS OF SUICIDE NOTES.

- Handwritten on paper
- Typed on paper
- Emails
- Written on a wall, door, or mirror
- Text messages
- Voice recordings
- Social media messages or status updates
- Recording live on social media
- Inscribed on the skin (using pen or sharp implement)

BOX 8.3   PURPOSES OF LEAVING MULTIPLE NOTES.

- To cover all angles, i.e., one note instructional and one explanatory.
- To additionally provide instructions for the funeral/distribution of possessions.
- To provide contact details for the next-of-kin or representative should the finder be someone different.
- Different notes addressed to different recipients.

164 Equivocal Death

Accusatory notes are where the suicide victim apportions blame to a specific person, organization, or situation; and they felt that they were left with suicide as their only option. Notes in this category tend to express negative affect, such as the use of language such as *"hate," "deceit," "cheat," "it's your fault," "look at what you made me do,"* and *"I hope you are happy now."* There may also be swearwords expressed in these communications. These types of notes can be written following triggering events, where the individual chooses to express themselves in the heat of the moment, for example.

Instructional notes tend to be less emotional in nature, and they provide practical assistance in terms of funeral wishes and the distribution of possessions. These notes may be more apparent where the decedent has not formally written a will beforehand. Of note, a will should not be defined as a suicide note as such, unless it has been strategically placed by the decedent immediately prior to their death to show their intention.

Sinyor et al (2015) found in their study that just over 20% of their sample (285 suicides notes) contained "will content." The majority of these decedents had a history of mental ill health, and some also had substance misuse. However, such clinical findings may have a bearing on the legal processing of the decedent's affairs due to the question if they were indeed of "sound mind" when they made those instructional statements.

Case Study 8.1 describes how last communications left via social media can be perceived differently by the intended audience.

Social Media and Bystander Apathy

CASE STUDY 8.1

Simone Beck was a 42-year-old woman who at 10 p.m. on Christmas Day 2010 posted to over 1,000 Facebook friends this status update:

Took all my pills, be dead soon, bye bye everyone.

However, instead of calling emergency services or trying to help her, some of her online contacts taunted her calling her a liar, or that she "does this all the time," or that it was "her choice." Some of the contacts begged for her address or phone number, but of those that lived close by, no one thought to call round or call the police. Several posts were from people arguing with each other, and in total the post received over 150 responses.

Notes or Last Communication

It was only the following day when the police were contacted, when Simone's mother found out about the post. Simone was taken to hospital but died not long after arriving. Arguably she could have survived had help reached her earlier.

While last communications like this being made on social media can give the person attempting suicide a better chance of survival (especially as suicide prevention algorithms in social media continue to improve), there is the danger that with so many people being aware of the context of the statement, that *bystander apathy* sets in. This psychological phenomenon, which refers to the "diffusion of responsibility" describes how victims are less likely to be helped, the more bystanders that are present. The other issue with such communications being expressed via social media in this manner is that the audience may perceive that the individual is only doing it to get attention, and that they are not serious about taking their own life. It could be that Simone was literally crying out for help and because no one "heard" her, she tragically died as a consequence.

Other people have chosen to take their lives while using the live-streaming option on social media, such as that available on Facebook, Instagram, and TikTok. In these scenarios, the available window to save them is virtually nothing, especially for suicide methods that reach death quickly, such as hanging or using firearms. One such example is described in Case Study 8.2.

Live Streaming of a Suicide

CASE STUDY 8.2

In April 2022 in Greater Manchester, UK, 34-year-old David Hilton live-streamed his death on Facebook. He started the Facebook-Live broadcast and put his cell phone camera where his audience could view in real-time his suicide. Many of his contacts watched the stream where he proceeded to hang himself. The emergency services were contacted as soon a friend realized what was happening. An ambulance arrived at the property within six minutes of the call, and they were with David as soon as they were able to force entry. The live stream was still filming when paramedics broke in. But by that point, just ten minutes after the call was first made, David was sadly beyond resuscitation and died.

166   Equivocal Death

This is an emerging phenomenon in the evolution of suicide messages intertwined with the evolution of social media. Live streaming one's suicide is a wholly impactive and devastating final "announcement" that can inevitably shock and traumatize anyone who witnesses it. On the other hand, it can take away a lot of ambiguity in terms of the true manner of death.

Interpreting Suicide Notes

When it comes to suicide research one of the first steps is the inevitable interpretation and categorization of suicide notes, some of which was described earlier. Such communications can offer explanations to loved ones, assisting in their grieving process (Callanan & Davis 2009) or they can be useful for evidentiary purposes in death investigations (Koehler 2007). However, last communications can be debatably subjective, personal, and unique to the decedent (Ault et al 1994) and such interpretations must be used with caution rather than as definitive proof of suicide. Some notes classified as "suicide" notes may simply have been a means for a troubled mind to express oneself without the intention to actually end one's life (i.e., a "cry for help").

Case Study 8.3 describes how notes can be subjective and not provide definitive evidential proof of suicidal intent.

CASE STUDY 8.3

Between June 2015 and June 2016, a high number of neonatal baby deaths and collapses occurred in the same hospital unit in Chesire Hospital in the United Kingdom. The police were asked by the hospital to investigate these deaths and collapses, in the event they were suspicious. The one common denominator appeared to be a nurse, a woman in her thirties, working in the neonatal unit. The police eventually gathered enough evidence to arrest her for several deaths of children under her care. Her trial took well over six months due to the complexity of the case. When her house was searched two days after she was first arrested in 2018, a significant handwritten note was found among several notes. This note appeared to contain expressions of conflicting thoughts going through the writer's mind at the time. Phrases were written such as:

Notes or Last Communication

"NOT GOOD ENOUGH"

"I am an awful person."

"Kill myself right now."

"I'll never have children or marry."

"I haven't done anything wrong."

"Police Investigation."

"I feel very alone + scared."

"HATE"

"Hate myself so much."

"PANIC FEAR LOST."

"I DID THIS."

"I don't deserve to live."

"I killed them on purpose because I am not good enough to care for them + I am a horrible evil person."

"World is better off without me."

"I AM EVIL I DID THIS." [1]

This note was found at her home address among other notes said to contain numerous claims of innocence. During her trial in 2023, the Prosecution submitted it as significant evidence, but then, so did the Defense. The prosecution perspective was that it was a "confession" of sorts, whereas the defense perspective was that it detailed distress "ramblings" caused by being under investigation. She pleaded "Not Guilty" to all charges.

As can be seen in this note, it contains protestations of innocence, as well as guilt. To put it into context, numerous notes were found during the search, but it was this one that was focused on at the trial. Is it that being investigated by the police for doing her job has made her believe she *must* be guilty, even though she could be innocent? Or is this an outpouring of resentment from someone who *did* commit several murders and attempted murders, and she is distressed because she may now not get away with it? The take home message here is that this note arguably does not prove her guilt, nor her innocence. It is open to speculation and subjective interpretation, where each jury member will have had to consider how much this note points toward or away from guilt. It is interesting that it was submitted as "tangible" evidence in such a high-profile serial murder trial. One must exercise caution when relying on such evidence, especially in the absence of any confirmative forensic evidence. A similar principle could well apply to notes left behind by suicide victims, whereby the ambiguity expressed in some notes may not definitively conclude that

168   Equivocal Death

the decedent indeed intended to permanently end their life at the time that they wrote the note.

Suicide Notes and Equivocal Deaths

What role can suicide notes or last communications play when the death is equivocal? In other words, where the manner of death is ambiguous and could be attributed equally to a suicide, a homicide, or an accident? Sadly, there have been cases which *should* have been treated as potentially suspicious from the outset but were prematurely characterized as suicide due to the presence of a suicide note. Due to investigator *confirmation bias,* vital red flags were missed for these cases. One such example was a serial murder case in the United Kingdom (Case Study 8.4).

CASE STUDY 8.4

Between June 2014 and September 2015, Stephen Port murdered four young men in London, UK. He had met them through gay internet sites and after meeting, he gave them a fatal overdose of GHB (gamma-hydroxybutyrate – a central nervous system depressant also known as a "date-rape" drug). All four victims' bodies were (at separate times) left in close proximity to each other, just a short distance from Port's home address. The first and second cases were superficially investigated, as the Metropolitan Police concluded they were accidental "chemsex" and drug-related deaths. This was despite several concerns being raised early on by those that knew the victims. The third victim, a 21-year-old chef named Daniel, was found dead three weeks after the second victim was found, in the exact same place. A handwritten note was found with his body that described why he had taken his own life. It stated that he was responsible for the accidental death of the earlier victim and that he could not live with what he had done. Interestingly, the note also stated:

> BTW. Please do not blame the guy I was with last night, we only had sex then I left, he knows nothing of what I have done. I have taken what G I had left with sleeping pills, so if does kill me it's what I deserve. Feeling dizzy now as took 10 min ago so hoping you understand my writing.[2]

The police quickly decided that this case was also not suspicious and closed the investigation down. This was despite the handwriting not being confirmed by either the family or a handwriting expert. The police did their own (unqualified) "analysis" by comparing the writing in the note with that found in a diary at Daniel's home address. In addition, the phraseology used, plus the omission of loved ones' names and the way it was signed off, raised significant red flags for Daniel's family. Also, there was no evidence that Daniel had even known the earlier victim, and in any case, Daniel's demeanor had not once changed after he had supposedly killed this person. The concerns raised by the family were dismissed by the police.

A fourth victim was then killed in 2015, after Daniel's inquest was heard and the verdict reached by the coroner was an "open" verdict. It was only at the continued insistence of the victims' loved ones, did the police *finally* see a connection between the cases. In 2016, Port was found guilty of all four murders. A later inquiry determined that had the police properly investigated the first victim's death, the later victims most likely would still be alive today.

Case Study 8.4 gives all police forces considerable lessons to learn. The note written by Port was planted with Daniel's body simply as a means for Port to distance himself from the murders. A clear red flag that police should have spotted early on is the part stating that Port had "nothing to do" with the deaths. This was simply another tactic used by Port to distance himself from murders and frame an innocent person instead. This case has demonstrated how police are arguably not sufficiently trained or equipped to investigate equivocal deaths, or homicides that may have been staged to look like a suicide or an accident.

Suicide Note Investigation

Notes and communications that imply suicidal intent provide vital evidence during death investigations. Before such notes can be used to confirm that a death is a genuine suicide, the handwriting must be properly verified. Not only that, but the phraseology and contents of such communications must also be confirmed. If there are inconsistencies, further investigation must be done before the case is closed.

An example of a case where the authenticity of a suicide note caused division in professionals was seen in the Paula Gilfoyle case (Case Study 8.5).

170 Equivocal Death

CASE STUDY 8.5

Paula Gilfoyle was a married 32-year-old woman who was eight and a half months pregnant, living in Merseyside, UK. In June 1992, she was found hanging in the garage of the marital home by her husband, Eddie, when he returned from work. In the kitchen he found a two-page letter addressed to him. The note was handwritten and spanned two pages. Extracts from this note included:

"Dear Eddie. I've decided to put an end to everything and in doing so ended a chapter in my life that I can't face up to any longer. I don't want to have this baby that I'm carrying. I wish that I'd got rid of it ..."

"... Don't blame yourself Eddie it's not your fault, I've caused all your pain and heartache ..."

"... P.S. I apologize for all the pain and suffering I have caused by taking my own life. I don't mean to cause any problems for anyone, no-one is too blame except myself".[3]

Initially police did not regard the death as suspicious meaning that vital investigative opportunities were missed from the outset, such as the failure to take scene photographs, or taking the core temperature of the body, or preserving the ligature.

A few days after the death, some of Paula's friends and family approached police raising concerns that the death was not a suicide. Friends said that Paula had previously informed them a month or two before her death that her husband was doing a project at work on suicide, and that he asked her to write out suicide letters, which he dictated to her. Paula had also apparently informed her friends she was taken into the garage and shown how to put up a rope, and that this scared her. Eddie worked in a hospital as a technician, and there was no evidence such a project existed. Eddie denied all of this. He was then arrested, and Paula's death was treated as a murder. However, the court ruled that the evidence from her friends was inadmissible.

The prosecution made the case at trial that Eddie had tried to make a homicide appear to be suicide, and that he had fooled his wife into writing a suicide note and had managed to get her to simulate hanging herself.

Professor David Canter, a pioneer in Investigative Psychology in the United Kingdom, was asked to analyze the suicide note. He concluded that the letters could have been written by either Paula or Eddie, and he felt her death was *not* a suicide. However, after the trial (where Eddie was convicted of murder) Professor Canter was shown further notes written between Eddie and Paula and decided his initial opinion was wrong. He felt that Paula had indeed taken her own life and had written the note of her own free will.

Professor Canter's evidence was not considered as part of the trial nor any of the subsequent appeals. Likewise, the hearsay evidence from the friends that prompted the murder investigation did not form part of the evidence.

To this day this note causes division among many professionals and those that knew both Paula and Eddie. It can never be 100% confirmed if this note was a genuine or simulated note, especially due to the early loss of forensic opportunities. Professor Canter pointed out in 2005 the severe ramifications of incorrectly interpreting suicide notes, leading to potential *miscarriages of justice*. This case highlights the need to treat such evidence with extreme caution when determining the guilt or innocence of an individual, especially where there is no forensic evidence to back up such conclusions.

Another case that emphasizes the need to treat notes with evidential caution is that of Case Study 8.6.

CASE STUDY 8.6

Douglas and Jacqueline Patrick were husband and wife living in London, UK. On Christmas Day 2014, Jacqueline put anti-freeze in husband Douglas's glass of wine. Along with her daughter, they had planned to murder him and they went ahead with their plan for Christmas 2014. Anti-freeze, i.e., Ethylene Glycol, is odorless and sweet-tasting, meaning that this toxin can be disguised in sweet, brightly colored drinks. Jacqueline gave Douglas the drink in the evening of Christmas Day and then called an ambulance nine hours later on Boxing Day. In hospital she handed a typed note to medical staff which acted as an *"advance directive"*:

> I Douglas Patrick do not wish to be revived as i would like die with dignaty with my family by my side thank you.
>
> D. Patrick[4]

However, eagle-eyed doctors at the hospital were concerned that the directive had not been dated, or hand-signed, and they contacted the police. Mr. Patrick, then 72 years old, woke up and confirmed that he had not written the directive. Mrs. Patrick was found guilty of attempted murder, and her daughter was found guilty of encouraging or assisting her mother.

The above case demonstrates how for some deaths, there may be little or no police involvement until it is too late. Had Mr. Patrick died at home, the police would have attended to investigate the sudden death. However, had he then died in the hospital, there would have been the loss of forensic evidence as well as the lack of police involvement. In some jurisdictions, unnatural deaths such as suicides and accidents may not ever be reported to the police if the person was treated in hospital for a period of time first. Thankfully, not only did the doctors save Mr. Patrick's life, they also quickly raised concerns with the police. This meant that when the police investigated, they found ample evidence that the wife and daughter had planned and tried to execute the murder.

Given that those offenders that attempt to stage homicides as suicides are likely to be known to the victim, it could be argued that the risk of staging is even higher where the victims were known to have had prior suicidal or euthanasic predilections. So by the time the police investigate, the question surrounding prior suicidal intent is ticked off their own "'suicide checklist." Or indeed an offender can always use an "old" undated suicide note and "plant" that at the scene of a homicide victim's death so as to mislead the police investigation.

Suicide Note Authenticity

Analyzing suicide notes by handwriting comparison alone is often not enough, especially given the electronic formats of many suicide notes these days. In addition, a person can be coerced to write a note, or indeed it could be a note that they had authored at an earlier time, that is then found with their body.

Homicides where the deceased's phone has been used by the perpetrator to send messages to loved ones pretending the victim is alive and well is another example where there is no means to verify handwriting as such, but the terminology and content in the text message may be sufficient to raise inconsistencies or red flags. So, when considering the context, terminology and grammatical style within a last communication, the utilization of professional *Forensic Linguistic Analysis* may be required to probe further before the document can be used for evidential purposes.

Forensic Linguistic Analysis is the analysis of how terminology and grammar is expressed to determine the authenticity of a questioned document. The field of forensic linguistics is incredibly diverse and comprehensive, so with respect to suicide notes, it will only be briefly covered here.

There have been several studies looking into the linguistic themes in authentic and simulated suicide notes. It has been suggested that genuine notes differ to simulated ones in terms of sentence length and structure, where genuine notes had shorter, less lexically diverse sentence structure and the simulated notes did not. Researchers have suggested that the highly

Notes or Last Communication

173

emotional state of the suicide note writer limits the communicative range that they are able to express at the time. Likewise, the attention of the suicide note writer will focus on the most important aspects while discounting information that is deemed to be trivial or extraneous (Gregory 1999; Jones & Bennell 2007; Montgomery 2000; Osgood & Walker 1959). In addition, the shorter, simpler sentences seen in genuine notes understandably ensures that the intended recipient receives the key message that the author is trying to convey. Despite the negative context, genuine notes can still express positive affect and emotion (Stella et al 2022). In addition, Ioannou and Debowska (2014) found that authentic notes were more internally consistent and easier to understand than simulated ones.

The ability to discriminate between genuine and fake suicide notes also depends upon the practitioner doing the analysis and what level of relevant training they have received. Police officers receive little, if any, specific training in this forensic specialty, and they may rely on their experience to guide them rather than seek the expertise of a professional forensic linguist. Jones and Bennell (2007) utilized statistical prediction models to identify authenticity when considering average sentence length, and the expression of positive effect. They found that their computerized algorithm performed better than mental health professionals.

Essentially, when it comes to establishing authenticity, until a refined computer model is widely accepted, police officers and investigators would benefit from specialized training in this field when they investigate suicide notes in equivocal deaths.

The potential characteristics of authentic notes compared with simulated notes are suggested in Box 8.4.

BOX 8.4   AUTHENTIC VERSUS SIMULATED NOTES.

Authentic	Simulated
Shorter, less lexically diverse sentences	Longer, more lexically diverse sentences
Mentions of loved ones by names or nicknames	Little mention of loved ones by names or nicknames
Phraseology unique to decedent	Generic phraseology
Sign-off unique to the decedent	Generic sign-off
Expression of emotional/positive affect	Less expression of emotional/positive affect
Big-picture oriented	Inclusion of extraneous/trivial information

The text of most notes will include an apology to other family members or to God, expressing their action was "taking the easy way out," or admitting current family or relationship problems were their fault. They often express an unwillingness to continue living. There are often statements asking for forgiveness by family and God for their actions. Other comments include feeling tired, indicating they are not enjoying life, or their current living conditions. There may also be a sentence or two saying goodbye to specific family members and friends and expressing sadness over leaving them.

Case Study 8.7 describes the importance of utilizing professional forensic linguists.

CASE STUDY 8.7

In October 2019, 23-year-old Evie Adams was unknowingly given a fatal amount of tramadol and diazepam over a number of days, which her partner Jordan Monaghan had purchased on the black market. A typed letter – a "suicide" note – was found, but it turned out Monaghan had written this himself. He was found out due to:

Forensic Testing: The letter only had his fingerprints on it, and not hers.

Linguistic Analysis: The writing in the letter was inconsistent with Evie Adams' linguistic style but was highly consistent with Monaghan's unique style. This was despite Monaghan attempting to replicate the type of phraseology that Evie would use, in an attempt to make the letter look authentic.

Not Having the Means: In addition, Evie was very inexperienced with computers and printers, so the fact that the note was typed was a red flag in itself.

Monaghan had failed to stage Evie's death as suicide. He was later found guilty of her murder.

The case above demonstrates the importance of not only carrying out basic forensic tests, but also the utilization of professional linguists (rather than untrained police personnel). Evie Adams died from drug toxicity, which as a less "violent" means of death, overtly at the postmortem examination there may have been no signs of third-party involvement whatsoever. This case could easily have been misclassified as suicide for these reasons. Because the note was typed, handwriting analysis was not possible. But investigators

Notes or Last Communication

wisely went a step further and employed the professional services of a forensic linguist. It was the analysis of the writing style which still managed to demonstrate who the real author was and that it was not the deceased victim. It was this note that first raised alarm bells and prompted the investigators to delve deeper to establish how Evie had met her death.

Suicide Note Investigative Considerations

This final part reiterates the importance of dealing with suicide notes as potential evidence. When a note or last communication is found in relation to a death, investigators must take a number of steps before concluding a case is a genuine suicide. They must, without fail, preserve the forensic integrity of the note in the event further information comes to light later, and they then need to test the note for latent fingerprints or DNA. In addition, importance is placed not only on handwriting verification, but that the grammatical style, dialect, and content of the note is consistent with respect to its presumed author, as well as the document's authenticity.

A summary of the key investigative considerations are listed in Box 8.5.

BOX 8.5 SUICIDE NOTE INVESTIGATIVE CONSIDERATIONS.

- Photographing the note *in situ*.
- Securely seizing the note (to enable any future forensic testing).
- Obtaining a sample of handwriting from a neutral source (i.e., not from a potential suspect).
- Can loved ones verify that the handwriting is that of the deceased?
- Can loved ones verify that the phraseology in the note is consistent with what the decedent used?
- Consider formal handwriting comparison by a forensic handwriting expert.
- Consider analysis of the linguistic style by a professional forensic linguist.
- Consider analyzing computers/tablets/phones belonging to the deceased for any relevant messages/emails.
- Consider obtaining further information from the recipients of these notes or messages.
- Thus determine that the note is authentic.
- Determine that the decedent was indeed the author of the note and was not coerced by a third party.

176 Equivocal Death

Chapter Summation

This chapter corrects a popular belief, that suicide notes are present in most suicidal events. As noted, notes are only present in a minority of suicide cases. Notes when found are extremely important and can provide explanations into the motives of the suicidal act and can also be of evidential value in equivocal death investigations. Caution must be exercised when interpretating suicide notes, as they can only be validated through linguistic or forensic analysis. Before a conclusion of suicide can be reached, investigators must always consider the totality of the evidence and not rely on the singular fact that a note is present. In other words, the *presence* of a note does not prove it is a suicide, just like the *absence* of a note does not prove it was *not* a suicide.

Notes

1 The original note can be viewed here: www.independent.co.uk/news/uk/crime/lucy-letby-nurse-note-picture-b2202448.html
2 See www.independent.co.uk/news/uk/crime/stephen-port-grindr-killer-victim-fake-note-b1947849.html for an image of this suicide note
3 Original note and typed version can be found here: www.eddiegilfoyle.co.uk/suicide-letter
4 Original note can be seen here: www.standard.co.uk/news/crime/bus-driver-s-wife-tried-to-coverup-antifreeze-poison-plot-as-suicide-bid-a2945176.html

References

Ault, R. L., Hazelwood, R. R., & Reboussin, R. (1994). Epistemological Status of Equivocal Death Analysis. *American Psychologist*, 49, 72–73.

Barrett, J., Lee, W., Shetty, H., Broadbent, M., Cross, S., Hotopf, M., & Stewart, R. (2016). 'He left me a message on Facebook': Comparing the Risk Profiles of Self-Harming Patients Who Leave Paper Suicide Notes with Those Who Leave Messages on New Media. *BJPsych Open*, 2(3), 217–220.

Behera, C., Karthik, K., Dogra, T. D., Lalwani, S., Millo, T., & Singh, S. R. (2014). E-suicide Note: A Newer Trend and Its Medico-Legal Implications in India. *Medico-Legal Journal*, 82(2), 80–82.

Bhatia, M. S., Verma, S. K., & Murty, O. P. (2006). Suicide Notes: Psychological and Clinical Profile. *International Journal of Psychiatry in Medicine*, 36(2), 163–170.

Callanan, V. J., & Davis, M. S. (2009). A Comparison of Suicide Note Writers with Suicides Who Did Not Leave Notes. *Suicide and Life-threatening Behavior*, 39(5), 558–568.

Canter, D. V. (2005). Suicide or Murder: Implicit Narratives in the Eddie Gilfoyle Case. In Alison, L. J. (Ed.), *The Forensic Psychologist's Casebook* (pp. 315–332). Devon, UK: Willan.

Notes or Last Communication 177

Carpenter, B., Bond, C., Tait, G., Wilson, M., & White, K. (2016). Who Leaves Suicide Notes? An Exploration of Victim Characteristics and Suicide Method of Completed Suicides in Queensland. *Archives of Suicide Research*, 20(2), 176–190.

Cerel, J., Moore, M., Brown, M. M., van de Venne, J., & Brown, S. L. (2014). Who Leaves Suicide Notes? A Six-Year Population-Based Study. *Suicide and Life-threatening Behavior*, 45, 326–334.

Chalker, S. A., Comtois, K. A., & Kerbrat, A. H. (2015). Impulsivity and Suicidal Behavior: How You Define It Matters. *International Journal of Cognitive Therapy*, 8(2), 172–192.

Darkes, J., Otto, R., Poythress, N., & Starr, L. (1993). APA's Expert Panel in the Congressional Review of the USS Iowa Incident. *American Psychologist*, 48, 5–15.

Duddin, K. S. E., & Raynes, B. (2021). Why Choose the Railway? An Exploratory Analysis of Suicide Notes From a Sample of Those Who Died by Suicide on the Railway. *Crisis*, 43 (5), 419–425.

Eynan, R., Shah, E., Heisel, M. J., Eden, D., Jhirad, R., & Links, P. S. (2018). Last Words: Are There Differences in Psychosocial and Clinical Antecedents Among Suicide Decedents Who Leave E-Notes, Paper Notes, or No Note? *Suicide and Life-Threatening Behavior*, 49, 1379–1394.

Gregory, A. (1999). The Decision to Die: The Psychology of the Suicide Note. In Canter, D. & Alison, L. (Eds.), *Interviewing and Deception* (pp. 315–332). New York, NY: Routledge.

Gunn, J. F., Lester, D., Haines, J., & Williams, C. L. (2012). Thwarted Belongingness and Perceived Burdensomeness in Suicide Notes. *Crisis*, 33(3), 178–181.

Ho, T. P., Yip, P. S., Chiu, C. W, Halliday, P. (1998). Suicide Notes: What Do They Tell Us? *Acta Psychiatrica Scandinavica*, 98 (6), 467–473.

Holmes, R. M., & Holmes, S. T. (2005). *Suicide: Theory, Practice and Investigation*. Thousand Oaks, CA: : SAGE Publications.

Ioannou, M., & Debowska, A. (2014). Genuine and Simulated Suicide Notes: An Analysis of Content. *Forensic Science International*, 245, 151–160.

Jones, N. J., & Bennell, C. (2007). The Development and Validation of Statistical Prediction Rules for Discriminating Between Genuine and Simulated Suicide Notes. *Archives of Suicide Research*, 11(2), 219–233.

Koehler, S. A. (2007). The Role of Suicide Notes in Death Investigation. *Journal of Forensic Nursing*, 3(2), 87–89.

Leenaars, A. (1996). Suicide: A Multidimensional Malaise. *Suicide and Life-threatening Behavior*, 61, 221–235.

Meyer, C. L., Irani, T., Hermes, K. A., & Yung, B. (2017). *Explaining Suicide: Patterns, Motivations, and What Notes Reveal*. Cambridge, MA: Academic Press.

Montgomery, J. W. (2000). Relation of Working Memory to Offline and Online Time Sentence Processing in Children with Specific Language Impairments. *Applied Psycholinguistics*, 32, 117–148.

Osgood, C. E., & Walker, E. G. (1959). Motivation and Language Behavior: A Content Analysis of Suicide Notes. *Journal of Abnormal Psychology*, 59, 58–67.

Salib, E., & Maximous, J. (2002). Intimation of Intent in Elderly Fatal Self-Harm: Do The Elderly Who Leave Suicide Notes Differ from Those Who Do Not? *International Journal of Psychiatry in Clinical Practice*, 6(3), 155–161.

Shah, A. (2008). Pure Elderly Suicide Rates Versus Combined Pure Elderly Suicide, Accidental and Undetermined Death Rates: Methodological Issues in Cross-National Studies. *International Psychogeriatrics*, 20(2), 421–423.

Shneidman, E. S. (1969). Suicide, Lethality, and the Psychological Autopsy. *International Psychiatry Clinics*, 6, 225–250.

Shneidman, E. S. (1981). Suicide Notes and Tragic Lives. *Suicide and Life-Threatening Behavior*, 11(4), 286–299.

Sinyor, M., Schaffer, A., Hull, I., Peisah, C., & Shulman, K. (2015). Last Wills and Testaments in a Large Sample of Suicide Notes: Implications for Testamentary Capacity. *British Journal of Psychiatry*, 206(1), 72–76.

Stack, S., & Rockett, I. R. H. (2018). Are Suicide Note Writers Representative of All Suicides? Analysis of the National Violent Death Reporting System. *Suicide and Life-threatening Behavior*, 48, 12–20.

Stella, M., Swanson, T. J., Li, Y., Hills, T. T., & Teixeira, A. S. (2022). Cognitive Networks Detect Structural Patterns and Emotional Complexity in Suicide Notes. *Frontiers in Psychology*, 13, 1–16).

Atypical or Special Suicides 9

Introduction

Although the previous chapters on suicide focused on the equivocal nature of some reported suicides and emphasizes the need for a thorough investigation to validate that the death was indeed the result of an intentional act by the victim. This chapter focuses on actual suicides that are atypical or only occur infrequently and under unusual circumstances. But because of their nature, these events generate media attention and generally require additional investigation to determine what may have motivated the victim to engage in their behavior that led to their death. Examples of these types of suicide cases include, *Sacred Suicide, Suicide as s Staged Event, Suicide by Cop, and Murder/Suicide.*

The importance of working on these cases is being able to recognize and explain the irrational behavior of the deceased and hopefully identify through their background what led up to their final acts.

Sacred Suicides

There are both historical and modern examples of what Lewis and Cusack (2018) identify as *sacred suicides.* Such examples range from mass suicides as noted in the Jonestown Guyana in 1978, to the numerous suicide bombers that kill themselves while killing others to make a political statement. This aspect of suicide is generally thought of as being motivated by fanaticism (Lewis & Cusack 2018).

Perhaps the best historical example of a sacred suicide is the mass suicide of some 900 Jewish rebels that occupied the mountaintop Judean fortress of Masada in 73 AD. These rebels, known as the Sicarii, were a group of Jewish zealots that strongly opposed the Roman occupation of Israel. They were known as an early version of organized assassins, that would kill Romans or their supporters in a crowd or gathering and then escape. They had participated in the uprising against the Romans, but when unsuccessful they retreated to the mountain top fortress as a refuge. They then found themselves surrounded and under siege by three Roman legions. After a

DOI: 10.4324/9781003373865-9

long siege, they realized that they had reached the end of their resistance. Upon reflection, the men concluded they would likely be killed in a final Roman assault and any survivor including their women and children would be captured and enslaved. Therefore, they decided that death would be preferable to life as a slave. In this instance, suicide was in response to a defeat, but it has been turned into another narrative of resistance and has become a foundational myth for the state of Israel.

There are many other examples of mass suicides in more recent history. Lewis and Cusack (2018) termed these events as New Religious Movements (NRM) and they include the 1978 mass suicide of some 900 persons in Jonestown, Guyana, the 1997 mass suicide in Rancho Santa Fe, CA, of the Heaven's Gate community, and even the 1978 incident involving David Koresh and his followers the Branch Davidians in Waco, TX, could be looked at as mass suicide. Although all of these incidents are somewhat related to religion, there are actually diverse reasons behind such actions including sociological, political, and even legal reasons behind some of their actions.

Military Suicides

The history of the world is raft with examples of serving military who have willingly sacrificed their lives for their comrades or for their country. Militaries across the world recognize these sacrificial acts with awards and medals, an example in the United States is the Congressional Medal of Honor, the highest military award for valor in combat. The medal of Honor is frequently awarded to military members who have sacrificed their lives to save others, and examples include throwing themselves onto a hand grenade or other explosive device in order to protect other comrades from the blast. Other examples include exposing themselves to enemy fire to protect their comrades or to achieve their mission. Although their actions did result in their death, these events are not looked at as suicide but considered a heroic act and the ultimate personal sacrifice. But, in effect these are suicidal events.

In the same way Japanese Kamikaze pilots in the final days of World War II, intentionally flew their planes into American ships, willingly dying in an attempt to stop the enemy. They were initially seen by the allies as being brainwashed or fanatically unwilling to accept defeat, instead of being heroic. However, this willingness to die by diving panes into ships or participate in what was known as "banzai charges" was actually integrated into the Japanese military by the ideals of "bushido," or "the way of the samurai." This was a strict code of conduct that accepted an honorable death in combat but

Atypical or Special Suicides

considered surrender as dishonorable. Thus, suicide was considered honorable and acceptable by the Japanese, but surrender to an enemy, was not.

There are other examples of military and wartime events, but it is clear such intentional actions are examples of *sacred suicides* in that they were committed for a higher purpose and are seen as honorable or even valorous deaths and not just a self-destructive act. The US miliary does not consider these actions to be the result of suicide, but as deaths resulting from combat.

Suicides as a Dramatic Performance

Lester and Stack (2015) describe some suicidal events as *Dramatic Performance,* referring to events that are planned, and the timing, setting, method, and circumstances of the suicide are designed to heighten the impact on others. These suicides are the most well-known and impactful because they are almost always conducted in public and therefore are reported by the media. Thus, their deaths and messages they send are magnified.

One of the more graphic and certainly more dramatic singular forms of suicide is self-immolation or setting oneself on fire. This form of suicide is not intended to harm anyone else or inflicting any other material damage (Lewis & Cusack 2018). Instead, these acts are one of the more radical or extreme forms of protest. Such acts are traditionally done in public and often planned to ensure there is sufficient media coverage to document the act. There is often a statement provided to the media explaining the act as a protest at specific politicians or against a particular political or government policy. The purpose of the death therefore is to motivate the public to demand change to that policy as noted in Case Study 9.1.

CASE STUDY 9.1

In 1963, a South Vietnamese Buddhist monk *Thích Quảng Duc,* died by self-immolation at a busy Saigon intersection. He was protesting against the persecution of Buddhists by the South Vietnamese government that was then led by Ngo Dien Diem, a staunch Roman Catholic. Photographs of his self-immolation circulated around the world, drawing attention to the policies of the government. In response to the actions, President John F. Kennedy's made a very prolific statement, "No news picture in history has generated so much emotion around the world as that one." His comment succinctly defined the purpose of such personal sacrifices.

182 Equivocal Death

The self-immolation of the monk was in fact a purposeful suicide, and clearly the intent was to cause their death; but the motive behind the event was based on political issues. The public and horrific death was designed to create public awareness and to cause governmental change of policy. This death was not viewed simply as a suicide, but as a self-sacrificial act. Lewis and Cusack (2018) note how these suicides are different that other more common suicides stating, "... *individuals identified as religious-motivated suicide bomber or self-immolators are quickly categorized as people motivated by 'fanaticism.' In contrast. However, people who willingly sacrifice their lives for a national cause such as war are valorized as heroic.*"

CASE STUDY 9.2

A more recent example of self-immolation was a US air force service member in 2023, dressed in his military uniform, wanting to protest the war that was taking place in Gaza. He doused himself with a flammable liquid in front of the Israeli embassy and lit himself on fire. Prior to lighting the fire, he recorded his intentions and purpose on his cellular phone. However, there was no effort to notify the media earlier or effort made to call attention to his "sacrifice." There was no large media response so clearly this act of protest was unsuccessful. It is fortunate however, that the man recorded the entire event on his phone and police could confirm that this was a case of suicide and not homicide.

Case Study 9.2 is an example of a *dramatic performance*; however, there was clearly something missing from being effective. There was no media attention, so his death really had no impact and resulted in just a few paragraphs in the local newspaper.

In contrast to the previous case study is the infamous homicidal acts on September 11, 2001. When the US experienced its greatest terroristic act with the destruction of the Twin Towers in New York, the Pentagon, and United Airlines flight 93. In these incidents there was also no prior alert to the media, but it was the size of the event that garnered instantaneous worldwide media attention. These multiple events were actually a well-planned murder suicide and was purposely designed to kill as many Americans as possible. The 19 perpetrators accepted their own deaths to carry out the plan. Again, this action was clearly a *political statement*, although it could also be seen as having a religious bases since all of the attackers were Moslem who apparently believed their deaths as martyrs would result in a reward in their afterlife. Like other examples, their actions certainly achieved their main political

Atypical or Special Suicides

goal of gaining media attention, but the end results of their action were actually catastrophic for their organization.

As horrible as the September 11th attacks were, they were clearly a *dramatic performance*, because it did gain media attention and literally caused a worldwide reaction to the events.

There are other such events that take place in normal or routine situations that are clearly designed to be dramatic performances, as noted in Case Studies 9.3, 9.4, and 9.5.

CASE STUDY 9.3

On January 22, 1987, the Pennsylvania State Treasurer Budd Dwyer, called a news conference ostensibly to comment on his recent conviction of bribery. The conference was called the day prior to his sentencing and the media was expecting to hear his resignation speech. Instead, Dwyer began speaking and handing out envelopes to his coworkers and friends. Then suddenly, he withdrew a pistol from a paper bag and was likely going to say something, but friends started to press him to take the gun away and he quickly put the gun in his mouth and pulled the trigger. His suicide was clearly intended to be witnessed and reported by the media.

CASE STUDY 9.4

On July 15, 1974, 29-year-old Christine Chubbuck, as television reporter for a Florida TV station began her daily broadcast like any other. But a technical problem led to a brief moment of dead air before she could continue with her script. When she began again, Chubbuck went off script stating, "In keeping with the WXLT practice of presenting the most immediate and complete reports of local blood and guts news. TV 40 presents what is believed to be a television first: in living color, an exclusive coverage of an attempted suicide." She retrieved a pistol from her bag and fired a bullet into her head while the cameras were still rolling.

CASE STUDY 9.5

A soldier deployed to Iraq was experiencing a lot of marital difficulties with the wife expressing her desire to divorce the soldier. The soldier was able to engage his wife online in a video chat room. The soldier began to express some suicidal thoughts and demanded his wife look into the camera. The wife sensed what was going to happen, so she refused his demands to look at him. Instead, his wife moved to turn off the camera and suddenly the soldier raised his weapon and shot himself. Likely the soldier's intent was to cause her pain over the divorce, by watching him commit suicide.

Case Study 9.5 is a little different in that the dramatic effect sought by the soldier was not for the world to see, but rather for his wife and was probably intended to inflict some pain onto her. But again, he was attempting a dramatic performance but committing suicide while his wife watched.

Suicide by Cop (SbC)

There is one event that is sure to be thoroughly investigated by police, when during a confrontation with someone, the police resort to using deadly force. Many times, the police are literally forced into using deadly force by the actions of the deceased person to prevent harm to others or to themselves. The ensuing investigation is typically centered around whether the use of force was justified. In most incidents the police response is a bifurcation of investigative effort between the agency's Internal Affairs Unit, solely concerned with the officer's training and their adherence with departmental policy on the use of force. Other detectives are responsible for conducting a death investigation into the event. It is important to remember that such deaths are considered, and should be investigated as homicides, because the death was caused by another. The main difference, the death was caused by a police officer and may involve self-defense or other justification for the use of deadly force.

These instances are often intentionally precipitated by the deceased, in a manner that caused or sometimes forced the police to respond using deadly force. These events are known as *suicide by cop* (SbC). Unlike other suicide events noted earlier in this text, these events are typically thoroughly and aggressively investigated by police. There is always great media and public attention given to any incident when the police have used deadly force, thus the police have reason to aggressively investigate and hopefully validate or justify the use of force to avoid community outrage or condemnation.

Atypical or Special Suicides 185

During these investigations, there are often aggressive efforts made to identify what was going on in the deceased life prior to their death. It is in these situations that the detectives will develop a *victimology assessment* on the deceased and look for any of the risk factors or antemortem suicidal behaviors as previously covered in this text. Sadly, it is in these tragic incidences that involve the police that information on the deceased's background, and what was going on in their life, is considered important. It is typically only in these incidents that the police try to conduct an actual victimology assessment. So, they can understand and perhaps explain the motivation of the deceased.

When looking at SbC events, Lord (2015) notes there are different indicators of suicidal intent exhibited by the deceased which can be divided into categories identified as: *primary, secondary, evidence of irrational thought and minimal evidence of suicidal intentions.*

Primary Indicators of Suicidal Intent

These are the individuals that have clearly expressed their suicidal intention to others before or during the incident. These indicators may be verbal or nonverbally demonstrated by their behavior such as use or display of a weapon in a threatening manner. Other indicators may be verbal statements to the police demanding they kill them, threatening to harm others if he were not stopped, and even conversations held with hostages or others expressing their intent or desire to end their lives. In these situations, the individual often intentionally initiates contact with police by either telephoning them themselves, or as Lord (2015) notes *committing an outrageous act* causing someone else to notify the police. This intentional effort to summon the police shows a clear *intention* to provoke a response or cause the police to end their lives.

Secondary Indicators of Suicidal Intent

Secondary indicators would include any previous suicide attempts and exhibiting threatening behavior at officers after committing a criminal act or their response after being served an arrest warrant for some unrelated incident. These actions may include confronting the police with verbal abuse or threats, banishing a firearm or other weapon, or other intentional actions to provoke a police response. Police are often surprised at what seems to be an overreaction to the event, especially verbal behavior such as "*I'd rather die than go back to jail*," or other similar statements. In these events the individual may seem to decide if there is no escape to their situation, they want to *go out in a blaze of glory*. Perhaps they desire suicide but may not have the courage to self-inflict an injury but in this situation the police are forced to kill them. Therefore, being killed by an officer can be seen as a more macho or manly death than taking their own life.

Evidence of Irrational Thought

Most of the irrational thought process is the result of alcohol or drug intoxication, coupled with a history of other mental health problems or other events that have recently occurred in their life. Such examples would include those high-risk factors of a recent arrest or other legal action, suffering a financial loss, or experiencing relationship issues. Particularly if there were any domestic conflicts, separation, or divorce that have taken place recently. An increase in alcohol or drugs combined with irrational thoughts may lead to efforts of self-mutilate or self-injury in front of the police. The irrational thoughts based on mental health issues or alcohol and drugs, make communicating with the individual difficult.

In some instances, there are no other persons involved in the incident but rather the individual has self-barricaded themselves in their residence or other location and may not only threaten self-harm but also threaten the police.

Minimal Evidence of Suicidal Intentions

This individual may not have expressed any previous suicidal thoughts but may have had a criminal past, particularly violent crimes, and even served time in prison. The situation develops when they are confronted by police, even for a minor reason, they immediately refuse to surrender, and then seek some escape from the situation. The response is often confusing to the police as there is often a limited opportunity to escape the situation and the police contact may be for a minor issue.

These indicators are generally identified as police conduct a background or victimology on the deceased. The importance in these situations is to identify those high-risk factors or other suicidal behaviors. Lord (2015) notes that one of the major differences between SbC and other self-inflicted suicides revolves around criminal activity related to the incident, possession of weapons, and their unwillingness to surrender to police. Basically, without other options, they simply prefer to die rather than return to prison.

There are other behaviors that can be seen as the individual *precipitating* or acting in such a manner that it almost forces the police to act and use

Atypical or Special Suicides 187

deadly force. Perhaps the most direct behavior is banishing a weapon, advancing toward the police, and refusing to follow any orders to stop or drop the weapon. Police response may increase if the individual actually points the weapon at the police or at someone else. Again, the police are put into a position where they may have no choice but to defend themselves or someone else. It's also possible that even after being wounded, the individual may continue advancing or pointing a weapon and again forcing the police to defend themselves. In the previous examples this behavior leaves no doubt that the intent of the individual was to make the police use deadly force (Leenaars 2010).

It is interesting that in these situations where there is an officer involved in the death the police will use the very techniques described in this text such as background information and victimology to determine what was going on in the deceased life prior to the incident, but seldom if ever use these same techniques when conducting other suspected suicide cases.

Murder-Suicide

There is another "suicide" event that is almost certainly to be further investigated; this is a suicide following a homicide that may include the murder of family members, another person, or even multiple victims. It is sometimes difficult to understand the suicide and someone taking their own life, but the idea of first killing someone else and then taking their own life is sometimes even more difficult to grasp. Because there does not always seem to be any logic or reasoning behind these actions, especially in those instances when multiple people are murdered, many of which were not even known to the offender before they take their own lives. Joiner (2014) notes that only about 2% of all suicides in the United States fall into this category, but the horror of these events, particularly those involving multiple victims, has always loomed large in the public consciousness.

Murder/Suicide events are typically reported by the media and well documented by the police during a subsequent investigation. Unfortunately, any subsequent investigation is almost always focused on the homicide aspects of the event with little attention paid to the offender and what motivated them to commit such egregious actions. There are many examples of these events ranging from the Virginia Tech and Columbine High School multiple murders followed by the perpetrator's suicide to intrafamilial homicides when a husband kills wife and sometimes other family members, and then kills himself.

One of the more common occurrences is interfamilial homicide wherein a husband or wife kills their spouse, and sometimes their children, and then takes their own life. Most murder/suicides involve a domestic or intimate partner relationship. More often it is the man that kills his wife or girlfriend, then takes their own life. Such events are often the result of a history of domestic violence and a breakdown in their relationship that may have occurred over time.

Eliason (2009) notes that these events occur across all demographics, so who are committing these acts? Meaning is there some way to identify or categorize the offenders to better understand these events? Marzuk et al (1992) proposed a set of typologies based on the *relationship* between the *perpetrator and the victim.* These typologies seem to include the majority of murder-suicides that take place within a family or interpersonal relationships. These offender types are *amorous jealousy, declining health, filicide-suicide, familicide, and extrafamilial.*

Marzuk et al (1992) also identified one triggering event for the many of the spousal or intimate partner events as the "female's rejection of her lover and her immediate threat of withdrawal or estrangement." Often these events take place while the male is confronted while female is in the process of moving out or shortly after separating and moving into a new residence. Coupled with estrangement is a threat of divorce or the ending of the relationship. A divorce for a married couple is the *ultimate rejection.* Closely related to the concept of rejection, Belfrage and Rying (2004) and Campbell et al (2003) also noted in separate studies of police investigative files, *jealousy* was identified as a as one of the key *motives* behind the murder of a spouse or intimate partner. Closely following is the egotistical and selfish concept of "*If I can't have you then no one else can.*"

Cohen et al (1998) also found some distinct and important differences between murder-suicides committed by younger and older people. For example, older couples were more likely to have medical issues and murder suicide was an attempt to end the suffering of one, and subsequent suicide was a way to join the deceased partner. However, as noted above, younger people were more likely to have a history of domestic issues that preceded the event.

It is important to consider that instances when an elderly couple are nearing the end of their life and a decide to end their suffering, normally they choose something that is peaceful like taking certain drugs with alcohol and simply going to sleep, or in some cases where a quicker and lethal method is used such as a firearm. However, instances where there is extreme violence noted at the scene or upon the victim should be questioned, especially if there was never a history of domestic violence. Case Study 9.6 is an example. Police, however, concluded after a minimal investigation that this was a case of murder suicide, and the husband murdered his wife and then took his own life.

Atypical or Special Suicides

189

CASE STUDY 9.6

Police were called to the residence of an elderly couple that were found deceased in the marital bed, with the bedcovers pulled all the way down, to the foot of the bed. The wife was found to have suffered extreme blunt force trauma to her head probably from a hammer that was located in a sink at the scene and appeared to be washed off. The woman also suffered from multiple sharp force incised wounds to her head and one stab wound in her forehead from a kitchen knife that went full into her brain and was still in place with only the handle exposed. The husband was found next to her with a plastic bag over his head but did not appear to have any injuries. One important fact, the husband did not have significant bloodstains on his pajamas or on his hands that was expected if he had inflicted the various blunt force or stab wound injuries to the wife. Investigation noted that the couple had been married for nearly 60 years and according to family and friends had never experienced any domestic violence. Subsequent police investigation discovered that the couple believed in euthanasia and had told their family that when the time came, they intended to take their own lives rather than suffer through medical or other issues. Their plan was to take pills and alcohol and then place a plastic bag over their head and simply go to sleep in the manner recommended in the book Final Exit.[1] However, the scene was far from a peaceful and respectful end to their lives. It was extremely violent. Also observed was the wife's night shirt was actually pulled up toward her waist, she was not wearing underwear, and this exposed her pubic area, which would have been terribly embarrassing to any female. The police responded properly to the scene but quickly decided without a lot of evidence, that this was a case of murder/suicide wherein the husband killed his wife as part of their euthanasia plan and then took his own life. The question of why it was necessary for the husband to use such violent means and leave his wife in such a condition with a knife protruding from her head and her night shirt pulled up to expose her pubic area. Especially when they had an agreement on a plan of action that was more planned out and more peaceful.

Like other cases described in this text, when confronted with the unexplained facts found at the scene and other background information that was never explored, the police steadfastly declined to further investigate. What makes this case study so important is the fact that only three years later, and only a short distance away, another similar event took place. That event is noted in Case Study 9.7.

CASE STUDY 9.7

In this event an elderly couple, married for over 60 years with no prior history of domestic violence, were found deceased in their marital bed. It was a very bloody scene, and police immediately suspected it to be a homicide. Police found the wife had received several blunt force injuries to her head and multiple stab and incised wounds across her throat. At autopsy, the examiner found several blunt force and sharp force defensive wounds on her hands, consistent with her attempts to ward off the attack. The husband had also received multiple sharp force injuries, including a cut left wrist, a gapping cut across his throat, and a knife was found fully impaled into his chest. He also appeared to have sharp force defensive wounds on his hands. Police also noted two punctures to the mattress consistent with a stabbing action. When the couple was found, the bed covers were pulled up to their waists, but when they were recovered the husband was found to have a large amount of blood on his right pajama leg, so if this was a murder/suicide, this meant the husband would have to murder his wife, then get into bed, pull the covers up and then self-inflict these massive injuries on himself. Another important factor, once the covers were removed, the wife was found to have her night shirt pulled up toward her waist. She was not wearing underwear, and her pubic area was exposed in the same general fashion as the victim in Case Study 9.6. The police did substantially more investigative work than on the previous case but eventually the case went cold, and they concluded that this was another murder/suicide. Although it is unclear how they could conclude the gaping injuries to the husband's neck and the deep penetrating stab to his chest could have been self-inflicted.

The similarities between the two events screamed out for further investigation as the chances that two similar events took place by chance within the same general area have to be astronomical. But even when they were pressed about both cases and the similarities, the police steadfastly refused to conduct any further investigation. In these cases, the police were satisfied to conclude in each was the result of murder/suicide, rather than search for other possibilities.

Atypical or Special Suicides

Certainly, these types of cases deserve full investigative effort, again to determine the motive for the homicide and to further look at aspects of the suicide. According to Joiner (2014) one of the most important factors to consider when investigating these events is that like other suicide events, the murder/suicide type events are not *impulsive acts*. Many of these events are well planned including the final suicidal act. Therefore, murder/suicide events are not typically the spur of the moment's reactions to some other event, but are premeditated. Joiner (2014) further identifies perhaps the most important concept when investigating these events, that the offender has decided on *suicide* first; and plans for murder or homicide are developed later. Therefore, to fully understand these events, it is necessary to identify what was going on in the offender's life immediately prior to the event, including the presence of any risk factors, suicidal behaviors, any relationship issues, or any history of domestic violence.

Therefore, in both Case Studies 9.6 and 9.7, there should have been efforts to look at each husband and document the motives behind their suicide. Failing to find such a motive or risk factors, then the theory of murder/suicide should be very closely examined or abandoned as inconsistent with the case facts.

Joiner (2014) in an effort to fully understand these events, identified different categories of murder/suicides based on the *motives behind the act*. He describes the "true" murder-suicides and the motive behind them as a *perversion* of *interpersonal virtues;* he identifies these virtues as *mercy, justice, duty, and glory*. Joiner (2014) contends that all murder suicides can be placed into one of these categories with *justice and mercy* as the two most common events.

Mercy

The dictionary definition of mercy is *the compassionate treatment of those in distress, especially when it is within one's power to punish or harm*. Perhaps the best example of the concept of the *virtue of mercy* can be seen when someone is suffering or in pain and seeks relief through suicide, and they are assisted by a medical doctor, or others close to them. Certainly, the intent to relieve someone of their pain can be viewed through the lens of mercy, pity, feeling sorry, or sympathy for their situation. A typical example would be as noted above in older people that husbands may end the life of their wives, to end the pain of their disease. In many instances they may also commit suicide so as to not live without them.

Other examples are a little more complicated, such as parents who are suffering deep economic problems that they do not feel able to recover decide to end their lives, but do not want their children to be left by themselves or become wards of the state decide the *merciful* thing to do to is to first kill the children and then take their own lives as exampled in Case Study 9.8.

CASE STUDY 9.8

One of the more famous examples of these incidents is the well documented case that took place in Berlin in 1945, when Joseph Goebbels, Adolf Hitler's propaganda minister, and his wife Magda, both diehard Nazis, knew the end of the war was at hand and they did not want to subject their children to the retribution that was certain to follow. So, they gave them each of their six children a lethal dose of poison and then they killed themselves. Again, the thought process in murdering the children was based on mercy and saving them from whatever was to come after the war and becoming orphans after their parent's death.

It is uncertain why any parents deciding to end their children's lives, so as to not being left alone, is really a mercy. It is also important to note that the children in these cases are not part of any suicide pact with the parents or had agreed to end their lives. They were murdered.

Justice

The definition of justice is the concept that individuals are to be treated in a manner of equitable and fair manner. Basically, for each person to get what they deserve or is due. The real meaning however may vary based upon each individuals' personal beliefs and values.

Pointer (2014) identified some workplace violence incidents as examples of the virtue of *justice.* In these incidents an employee feels they have been wronged and without any other way to seek redress they enter the workplace and begin to murder their supervisors and coworkers. In most of these incidents the killing is only stopped when the disgruntled employee runs out of ammunition, the other employees escape, or the police arrive and then they commit suicide. Certainly, if they had the chance or ability to do so, they would have killed more.

In these cases, it is easy to see the employee's perception of how they were treated or how some conflict, disagreement, or situation affected them, is far more important than anything they are going to inflict on anyone else.

Atypical or Special Suicides 193

In these situations, others must suffer for them to achieve any satisfaction or justification for their actions. What is important to note is that suicide was the original thought, but assaulting the company and employees was a way to get some *justice* for the perceived wrongdoing and these events are not spur of the moment but rather planned events.

An example of this concept is found in Case Study 9.9.

CASE STUDY 9.9

A husband and wife were estranged and living apart after the wife had filed for a divorce. They were married for 10 years and had one child. The wife finally left her husband over some rising domestic conflict that caused her to fear for her safety. They were in the last stages of their divorce and the wife had begun dating again. The husband had tried repeatedly to reconcile, but the wife refused. The husband found out who she was seeing and confronted his wife and her new boyfriend at the boyfriend's house. The husband immediately shot and killed the boyfriend and his 10-year-old son who was also at the house and then turned to his wife and shot her nine times, including three times in the head. He then fled from the house and went to his mother-in-law's house, but she was not home. He then drove away and along the way using his cell phone he made a full confession as to why he had murdered his wife and the man she was seeing. He only briefly expressed bad feelings about killing the 10-year-old boy but essentially brushed the death off as unplanned "collateral damage" to his intent. He also noted his original intent was to also murder his mother-in-law, but she was not at her house. He then went on to express his feelings about the divorce and how it was affecting him and how he did not want to go on living without his wife. After a 45-minute audio statement, that altered between blaming his wife for his actions and his own feelings about living without her love, he turned the pistol on himself and committed suicide. From his audio statement it is clear he had decided to take his own life, but then thought his wife also deserved to die for bringing him to that point.

In this case, the husband certainly was *jealous* and affected by the separation and his wife beginning a life without him. In his mind, killing his wife, and her new boyfriend were justified because of what her ending their marriage had done to him. The other man was basically considered a co-conspirator and therefore his death was also "justified." The husband's

Duty

Duty is defined in the dictionary as a moral or legal obligation, or responsibility to someone or something. In murder/suicides the virtue of duty is twisted or perverted by the offender to believe they have some duty, obligation, or responsibility to kill another. Joiner (2014) explains that in their mind, they are acting to protect them or take care of them by relieving them of some obligation and thus not leaving them behind to suffer an even worse fate. A cited example is an elderly man decides to commit suicide, but not wanting his wife to suffer or go through the pangs of his death, decides to killer her first, and then kill himself. Thus, his death and obligations are not passed onto his wife.

In many ways this category of murder/suicide is similar to the aspects of mercy, in that the offender thinks that ending another's life will spare them from any pain and suffering, after they take their own lives. It is important to note again that it is the planned *suicide* that precipitates or is the motive for the murder.

Heroic Glory

The basic definition of *heroic glory* is to be brave and to praise or give honor for some deed or act and implies a positive reaction. However, Joiner (2014) noted that in this category the concept of honor and glory are meant only for the perpetrator and not for the general public. Examples are those instances when after deciding upon suicide, the offender then seeks to kill as many others as possible, to essentially go out in a blaze of "glory" and thus be remembered.

The best example cited by Joiner (2014) is the 1996 Columbine High School murders that took place in Colorado. Many experts attempting to dissect the motive behind the murders, claimed the outburst and murders of their fellow students were the result of the two shooters being social outcasts and subject to bullying. Thus, the shootings were seen as a way to extract revenge from those engaged in tormenting them. However, later research concluded that neither of the shooters were social outcasts and neither were bullied, in fact they had engaged in bullying younger students. What was also not widely reported was the contents of their journals and videos that explained their motive was based on glory and to be famous. Before they

Atypical or Special Suicides   195

took their own lives, which was always a part of their plan, their goal was to kill more people than Timothy McVey, the Oklahoma City Bomber and thus become famous for killing the most people.

As repeated throughout the chapter, their suicide was always planned and accepted first, and then other aspects of the "murder" were planned out. Many times, the perpetrators of these types of situations have attempted suicide in the past but were unsuccessful. This aspect is frequently lost in the overwhelming nature of the other murders that also have taken place. But to have a clear understanding of these events, it is critical to take an intense look at the background of the offenders.

This same concept may be found in terroristic suicidal bombers. When looking at these events a more correct title should be murder/suicidal bombers because the intent is to kill as many others as possible while they kill themselves. During these events the bomber may look at their acts as either religious or political but see their deaths as achieving martyrdom. Basically, their death, and the lives of others, will somehow achieve some special significance in whatever struggle they are engaged. Thereby their death is heroic and glorious.

It is important to remember that there are some suicides that take place after murders that should not be considered murder/suicides because they are much different. For instance, a man murders his family or others and then flees. However, for some reason his escape plan is thwarted, and the police arrive intending to take him into custody, but he then kills himself. This is not a murder/suicide, because as previously noted, there was no previous plan to kill themselves or it was not the primary motive behind all of the other deaths. Their actual plan or intent was to kill others, and then escape. He only resorted to suicide when their plan failed, and he did not want to face the legal consequences of his actions. This is a subtle but importance difference.

Chapter Summary

This chapter focused on actual suicides that may occur infrequently but tend to stand out because they are completed under unusual circumstances. Also, there are some suicides that by their nature, require additional police investigations to determine what happened. Some suicides can be especially problematic because they use the police as the instruments of their own demise, by forcing the police to use deadly force against them. Lastly there are other instances known as murder/suicides that are often investigated but frequently there is more attention paid to the actual murder than the subsequent suicide. However, as noted throughout this chapter, it is suicide that is the primary motive behind all of these actions. Therefore, it is imperative that police spend time and conduct the victimology assessment of the "suicide" victim to understand the motive behind their other actions. Unfortunately, it is only in these situations that any great investigative effort is spent trying to identify any antemortem behaviors or risk factors that would cause the deceased to act in any of these situations in this chapter.

Note

1 *Final Exit* is a 1991 book written by Derek Humphry, a British-born American journalist, author, and assisted suicide advocate.

Bibliography

Belfrage, H., & Rying, M. (2004). Characteristics of Spousal Homicide Perpetrators: Study of All Cases of Spousal Homicide in Sweden 1990–1999. *Criminal Behaviour and Mental Health*, 14, 121–133.

Campbell, J. C., Webster, D., Koziol-McLain, J., et al. (2003). Risk Factors for Femicide in Abusive Relationships: Results from a Multisite Case Control Study. *American Journal of Public Health*, 93, 1089–1097.

Cohen, D., Llorente, M., & Eisdorfer, C. (1998). Homicide-Suicide in Older Persons. *American Journal of Psychiatry*, 155, 390–396.

Eliason, S. (2009). Murder-Suicide: A Review of the Recent Literature. *Journal of the American Academy of Psychiatry and the Law*, 37, 371–376.

Joiner, T. (2014). *The Perversion of Virtue: Understanding Murder Suicide*. New York, NY: Oxford University Press.

Langley, M. (2020). *American Roulette: Murder Suicide in the United States* (7th ed.). Washington, DC: Violence Policy Center.

Leenaars, A. A. (2010). *Suicide and Homicide-Suicide Among Police*. New York, NY: Routledge Publishing.

Lester, D., & Stack, S. (2015). *Suicide as a Dramatic Performance*. New Brunswick, NJ: Transaction Publishers.

Lewis, J. R., & Cusack, C. M. (2018). *Sacred Suicide*. New York, NY: Routledge Publishing.

Lord, V. B. (2015). *Suicide by Cop, Comprehensive Examination of the Phenomenon and its Aftermath*. Flushing, NY: Looseleaf Law Publications.

Marzuk, P., Tardiff, K., & Hirsch, C. (1992). The Epidemiology of Murder-Suicide. *JAMA*, 267, 3179–3183.

Accidental Deaths 10

Introduction to Accidental Deaths

An accidental death refers to a sudden, and unintended event, that takes place without one's foresight or expectation. This brief definition covers a wide range of possibilities.

According to the CDC in 2021, there were approximately 3,458,697 deaths reported in the United States, with accidental deaths totaling approximately 224,935 (Ahmad et al 2023; NHSA 2021). Clearly accidental deaths and unintentional injuries occur thousands of times a day, every single day throughout the country. According to the National Center for Health Statistics (2023), accidental deaths are now the fourth leading causes of death in the United States. For those between 5 and 24 years old, accidents are the *leading cause* of death, with almost a third of those deaths resulting from a drug overdose. According to NIDA (2021), more than 106,000 persons in the United States died from drug-involved overdoses in 2021, including illicit drugs and prescription opioids.

Accidents are also among the leading causes of death for people aged 25–44. (USA Facts 2023). These incidents account for the vast numbers of deaths that typically confront first responders. Therefore, it is not unusual, especially in large urban areas, for experienced officers to arrive at a scene and make a quick judgment as to the cause of death and determine that no other investigation is necessary.

However, as previously noted this response is what the offender staging a scene is counting on, that the scene and explanation provided will be close enough to be accepted by the first responder. If the scene is accepted no further investigation is going to occur and the case will be quickly closed.

Responding to Accidental Deaths

Based on the statistics as provided previously, first responders are far more likely to be confronted by an accidental death than a suicide or a homicide. Yet, as noted in previous chapters, every reported death should be initially looked at as a potential homicide. This should especially include reported

DOI: 10.4324/9781003373865-10

accidental deaths because as noted by Chancellor and Graham (2017), *accidental deaths* are one of the top four themes used to stage a homicide. From an offender's perspective an accident provides a good explanation for a death, because in their mind it causes no suspicion to fall upon themselves. Because, unless there is some type of negligence involved, accidents are not criminal events. If there is no criminal event, then there is no reason for the police to initiate an investigation.

Like staged suicide events discussed earlier, the offender is counting on the first responder arriving at the scene of a reported accidental death, and not seeing an obvious criminal act, to quickly determine there is no need for further investigation. The staging of a scene to resemble an accident is frequently found in *interfamilial* and *personal conflict* types of homicides that occur within the home. Since many accidental deaths also occur in the home, a person attempting to stage a homicide to look like an accident, the home might be the perfect place. A normal house often presents potentially hazardous areas that are common locations for an accident. These locations include, but are not limited to stairs or ladders, swimming pools, bathtubs, hot tubs, spas, or other bodies of water.

Other possibilities are dependent on the house or residence, or general location where the death took place. This might include operating farm implements, interactions with animals, industrial accidents, and even traffic accidents.

So, like other situations previously described, the offender needing to misdirect a police investigation is only limited to what is available and their imagination as to which method they may use to stage the scene.

Therefore, first responders and detectives should arrive at all death scenes with a bit of skepticism. Meaning the explanation and scene should not be automatically accepted without taking some basic investigative steps to ensure the death is indeed a result of an accident. In most incidents the facts and circumstances surrounding an accidental death can be validated rather quickly, based on consistency of the scene, the explanation of events, and injuries suffered by the deceased.

Altering a homicide scene to resemble an accident is often more successful than other themes for a couple of reasons. First, because the typical accidental death does not necessarily involve firearms, physical violence, or any clear intent to purposely harm the victim. Instead, they are portrayed as *unintended* events. Second, most of these events require little imagination, preparation, or any special equipment outside normal household items. Third, in many instances the offender's explanation of events includes that they were away from the residence at the time of the "accident" therefore they were not aware of the event and thus could not render any first aid. However, police

Accidental Deaths 199

must remember that being out of the area at the time of the accident is an example of a *coincidence*, frequently found in staged events.

According to NCS (2023) the six most common causes of accidental deaths are identified in the following:

1. Traffic Accidents
2. Falls
3. Poisoning
4. Choking
5. Fires
6. Drowning

A deeper dive into the statistics, by the NSC (2023) found that poisoning, traffic accidents, and falls typically account for over 85% of the *preventable* accidental deaths. No other *preventable* cause of death including fires, suffocation, drowning, choking, firearms, natural, or environmental disasters accounted for more than 5% of the total.

Preliminary Investigation of Accidental Deaths

As stated earlier, the preliminary investigation is the initial stages of an investigation to determine and verify the explanation of events offered by witnesses, combined with a scene examination, and injuries to the victim. Case Study 10.1 is an example of a quick preliminary investigation that confirmed the accidental nature of the death. The importance is the consistency of information relative to the explanation, the scene, and injuries to the victim.

CASE STUDY 10.1

On a mid-morning Saturday, Police were called to the scene of a reported accidental death. Arriving they noted a 60-year-old man was reportedly working on the roof of his house when he fell off a ladder and struck his head on a stone retaining wall of a flower bed. The wife was present and was not only distraught but also mildly angry stating that she warned her husband not to go up on the roof, but he insisted. Looking onto the roof the police could see tools and repair items on the roof, and there was an extension ladder on the ground nearby. Police interviewed the neighbor across the street who had called 911 to report the accident. The neighbor stated that he had observed the man beginning to climb down the ladder and then he turned away to do something. Suddenly he heard a loud noise or crash, he turned around to see the ladder on the ground and the deceased on his back on the lawn. Police observed that when he fell his head struck a small stone retaining wall that was part of the flower bed. There was blood on the stones consistent with impact and the man had received a severe blunt force trauma injury to the side of his head. Based on the lighting consideration and fair weather, the police were able to conclude the man must have lost his balance coming down the ladder and fell striking his head on the retaining wall. They concluded the death was the result of an accidental fall.

In the previous short case study, the explanation of events, the scene, and the injuries were all consistent, and the preliminary investigation lasted but a few minutes. One additional step not mentioned in the police report would be to examine the ladder to determine if there was any damage that could have contributed to the incident. Most accidental deaths are going to be confirmed with such minimal investigative effort, but it is vital that such efforts are expended because of the efforts in some instances to stage the event to hide criminal conduct which should always be a consideration.

Vehicle Accidents

Traffic accidents are the most common of all accidental deaths. What is different in traffic accidents, however, is if a death has occurred, it is typically investigated by specially trained officers such as state patrol officers or a traffic accident reconstructionist. Typically, this involves an inspection of the vehicle and thorough scene examination to determine the speed, efforts to brake, and unsafe road conditions, then determined what happened or what caused the accident.

Staging a homicide to resemble a traffic accident is not really that common; but does occur. There are different types of staging involving vehicles. One type takes place after an actual fatal traffic accident has taken place and the offender, who was likely driving the vehicle, moves the deceased, likely a passenger, to the driver's seat. Thus, attempting to establish it was the deceased that was driving the vehicle at the time of the accident. Many of these attempts can be quickly identified during the autopsy based on the location of injuries. Such injuries include abrasions and contusions from seat belts for the driver found across the left shoulder and for passengers across the right shoulder. There are also classic blunt force injuries to the chest and the forehead from hitting the steering wheel, generally occurring when seatbelts are not used, or

Accidental Deaths

from blood on the airbags if deployed. This of course depends on the specific vehicle that was involved in the accident.

The other type of accident involves efforts by the offender to stage a homicide to look as if the victim was in a traffic accident that caused their death. Many times, this effort follows a planned or unplanned homicide of the victim who has sustained blunt force trauma; therefore, the car accident was used to explain the victim's sometimes severe injuries. Case Study 10.2 is an example of a traffic accident used to explain an unplanned homicide.

CASE STUDY 10.2

Police were summoned to the scene of a car crash on an inter-city freeway, and upon arrival the police assisted in the removal of the injured female driver who was taken to a local hospital but was pronounced dead upon arrival. The initial viewing of the scene appeared to be consistent with an alcohol related accident after a late-night drinking session. The other occupant of the vehicle was her boyfriend who claimed to be riding in the front passenger seat at the time of the accident. The boyfriend seemed to be genuinely distraught but was otherwise uninjured. During his initial statement to the responding police, the boyfriend stated that both were drinking and were falling asleep as they drove away from the club. However, upon closer observation of the scene and vehicle, detectives noted the victim's injuries and other evidence observed in the vehicle's interior, did not appear to be consistent with the reported accident. For instance, the location of some bloodstains was inconsistent with the victim's position in the vehicle when found. Later coordination with medical authorities revealed that although she had hit the windshield during the accident, her injuries were not serious enough to cause any life-threatening problems. However, there were other injuries that were *inconsistent* with the traffic accident and unexplained such as contusions around her temple and upper right cheek and hemorrhages on her face and eyes that were consistent with being strangled. Later toxicology showed the victim had no drugs in her system and her blood alcohol level was just over the legal limit. Medical authorities also opined that the victim was probably dead by strangulation before the accident. During their investigation, detectives soon discovered the boyfriend was married to another woman and had begun the relationship with the deceased without telling her he was married. When she found out he was married, she accepted his explanation that it was only a marriage of convenience, and he was going to get a divorce. Detectives also discovered their relationship included constant fighting, break ups, and then reconciliation. According to her friends, the confrontations with the boyfriend were getting more physical and violent. On at least one occasion, he physically assaulted her, and he was arrested. Later the victim dropped the charges. Close friends noted that on the night of the accident, the boyfriend became enraged when the deceased joined other members of her girl's football team and stripped naked, for a photo shoot. The girls had all covered up their genitalia for the photo but seeing her disrobed in front of other people was *"more than he could stand."* They were at a club when the photo was taken, and they continued drinking until they finally left several hours later. Several hours after they left the club, their vehicle slammed into a parked car and the girlfriend was "killed." As part of their investigation, detectives contacted the estranged wife and learned her husband had confessed to killing the victim. As he told his wife what happened, the wife was recording the conversation on her cell phone. During this conversation, the husband admitted to becoming angry as they drove away from the club and he began to punch her in the head, grabbed the steering wheel and the vehicle left the highway. Once the car stopped, he continued with a physical assault. He had considered taking her to the hospital, but decided against it because it would get him into trouble. So instead, he placed his forearm across her throat and strangled her. He then pushed her back to the driver's seat, unbuckled her seat belt and while steering from the passenger seat, caused the vehicle to accelerate, and intentionally crashed into the parked car. The husband was later tried and convicted of murder (Chancellor & Graham 2017).

The incident described in Case Study 10.2 is an example of what Chancellor and Graham (2017) describe as an *ad hoc* type of primary staged event. Ad hoc staging refers to efforts to alter the scene *after* another event has already taken place. Now the scene and event must be staged in order to misdirect the police investigation. In this case, the man assaulted then strangled the victim and then had to come up with a story to explain her death. However, because the event was not planned, he was extremely limited with possible explanations since he was away from his residence at the time of death. Since he was in a car, and away from other opportunities, he attempted to stage her death as the result of a traffic accident. In the previous case, the initial responding accidental reconstructionist noted the inconsistency of the blood within the interior of the vehicle. Based on their initial findings they correctly contacted detectives immediately to respond to the scene and take a closer look at the incident.

Accidental Deaths

Case Study 10.2 is an example of the importance of being observant of such details and not just accepting what is being portrayed. Because the police were observant of the inconsistencies between the explanation, the scene, and the injuries they were able to prevent a murderer from getting away with the crime.

For fatal traffic incidents, Chancellor and Graham (2017) have identified several factors that should be considered whenever confronted with a traffic fatality. These include:

- Are the victim's and other passenger's injuries consistent with the vehicle damage and their stated location within the vehicle?
- Are there disparaging differences between the injuries of the driver and victim involved in the same event?
- Was the victim wearing a seat belt or did the seat belt fail?
- Was the victim generally known to use seatbelts?
- Is there a logical explanation if seat belts were not used?
- If airbags are available, did they deploy? If not, were they disabled?
- Does the vehicle damage and description of events prior to the accident match the explanation provided by surviving passengers?
- Are bloodstain patterns found on the vehicle interior consistent with the reported incident and the deceased's placement in the vehicle?
- Are bloodstain patterns found on the deceased or their clothing consistent with the reported incident?
- If skid marks are present at the scene, do they match the reported speed of the vehicle?
- The vehicle should always be safety inspected including steering, brakes, signals, and tires and exploitation of vehicle computers.
- If a vehicle defect is reported by survivors, is there evidence at the scene to validate the defect?

Accidental Falls

According to the National Safety Council (2015), accidental falls are the second-leading cause of unintentional death in homes in the United States and is only surpassed by traffic accidents as the leading cause of non-intentional deaths. Falls were responsible for more than 25,000 fatalities and approximately 8.9 million visits to the emergency room. Accidental falls are especially problematic in the elderly, young children, or the intoxicated.

Possible physical injuries are also varied and can be found on many different parts of the body. The unusual disposition of injuries is due to the body in movement, striking different objects or surfaces, as it travels down the stairs. For instance, as it falls down a flight of stairs, the body could impact against different parts of the steps, the walls, or railings.

There are many examples of falls being used to explain a death and one of the more common scenarios particularly in an interfamilial incident, that involves a fall downstairs in the home. Case Studies 10.3 and 10.4 are examples of reported accidental falls that were really staged events.

CASE STUDY 10.3

A husband reported that he had found his wife dead at the bottom of the stairs in their home. When the police and EMT's responded just minutes later, they noted the victim was already cold to the touch and the early stages of rigor mortis were evident, and thus more consistent with the wife's death occurring several hours prior to the police notification. A child's skipping rope was found next to her body and the husband speculated she must have tripped on it and fell down the stairs. During his formal interview, the husband reported he had been sleeping on the sofa downstairs and did not hear the fall and only found his wife after he woke up. However, during a police canvass, neighbors reported the previous night they heard a very loud scream from the victim's apartment, followed by a "bang" as if something had hit the floor hard. The neighbors described the sound as being so loud that they first thought it came from their own apartment. During the subsequent preliminary investigation, the police learned the couple was experiencing marital problems because the husband was engaged in an extra marital affair and despite his assurances and promises to his wife to stop; he was continuing the relationship. The husband even began discussing with his girlfriend a future life together. At autopsy, the medical examiner (ME) found several injuries to the victim's face that were more consistent with a physical assault from a fist or a kick rather than falling down the stairs. The ME also opined the fall down the stairs did not cause her death, but rather she died of asphyxia most likely caused by suffocation. The husband was later tried and convicted for his wife's murder (Chancellor & Graham 2017).

CASE STUDY 10.4

A husband called 911 reporting he had just discovered his wife had fallen down the stairs and was unresponsive and not breathing. EMTs arrived and as they began their victim assessment, they noted the woman was lying on her back at the bottom of a flight of stairs, her arms slack at her sides with the palms facing up. There was dried blood on one of her nostrils and there were scrapes and dark purple bruises covering her knees. Resuscitation efforts continued for over an hour as she was evacuated to the hospital where she was eventually declared deceased. The husband reported to the police he had left the house to get some breakfast and when he returned, he found her at the bottom of the stairs. During his initial interview, police observed scratches on his face and neck. The man explained his wife had experienced some severe abdominal cramping that morning and she'd accidentally scratched him in the face during a spasm of pain. During the initial medical examination, the wife was noted to have sustained contusions and abrasions on several locations on her body, including her neck. A black eye was forming on her face, and cartilage in her neck was broken and petechial hemorrhages were present in her eyes. Later the ME determined her injuries were consistent with being forcefully throttled, and the ME concluded the cause of death was strangulation, not the fall downstairs, and ruled the manner of death as homicide. The police then initiated their investigation, and quickly discovered that unlike the husband's assertion of a good marriage with no problems, the couple were in serious financial problems and argued frequently over the husband's lack of employment and their debt. These arguments also included numerous text messages and threats by the wife to divorce her husband. In one exchange of text messages sent the night before her death, she had text her husband, "I hate my life, I hate the man I married, and I wish I could erase the past three years." One of the more interesting pieces of evidence was internet searches found on the husband's iPhone and laptop computer on whether it is possible to break someone's neck with your bare hands, or if falling downstairs could break your neck. The husband was later tried and convicted of murder (Chancellor & Graham 2017).

The previous case presents the best argument for conducting a preliminary investigation when initially responding to a reported death. If the medical persons did not note the unusual injuries, which caused the coroner to request an autopsy it is possible the explanation of accidental death would have been accepted.

Case Studies 10.3 and 10.4 are good examples of how an accidental fall can be used to stage a scene and present an explanation for a death. In these case studies we see a few of the common red flags that alert us to possible staging. First, in Case Study 10.4, there is another example of a *coincidence*; wherein the husband leaves home for a short period of time and returns to find a tragic event that had taken place in his absence. As noted by Chancellor and Graham (2017) a *coincidence* is one of the most common red flags when staging an event. Second, in both case studies, based on the appearance of the victim, that their death took place much earlier than reported. Third, in Case Study 10.4, we see another instance where the husband attempted to portray himself in the best possible light, that he was happily married with no problems, and he was being a good husband by getting them breakfast in the morning. However, this directly conflicts with the phone texts where his wife had threatened him with divorce over their financial problems. Fourth, in Case Study 10.4, the husband's internet searches relating to injuries from falling downstairs made just days before his wife's death should be looked at as not just circumstantial evidence but also as another example of premeditation. Fifth, in both cases, the injuries sustained by both victims were inconsistent with an accidental fall down the stairs.

Chancellor and Graham (2017) have identified several factors to consider when evaluating a death resulting from household falls. These are:

- Age and medical history of the victim should be considered including any chronic conditions, such as heart disease and high or low blood pressure.
- Any medication that could cause dizziness or brief loss of consciousness?
- In the elderly, was there any indication of dementia?
- Are there any repetitive injuries in the same location of the head?
- Are there injuries to the hands consistent with trying to brace or break their fall?
- Evaluate the physical ability for the victim to have climbed the ladder or to ascend or descend the stairs.
- Review the complete autopsy including toxicology to determine the presence of alcohol or drugs in the victim's system.

If the death was a result of falling down a flight of stairs, a physical examination of the stairs should be conducted, to include the following observations:

- Are there any defects or damage to the steps or the risers?
- Are there any hairs, fibers, blood or other physical evidence within the defects, damage, or other location along the falling pathway?

Accidental Deaths

- Are risers of uniform height?
- Are they level?
- Are the stairs carpeted or bare?
- If the stairs are carpeted is the carpet secure?
- Condition of the floor at the top of stairs or on landings (check for any uneven walking surface or missing tiles).
- What are the lighting conditions in the stairwell?
- Are the handrails defective, damaged, or improperly placed?
- Are the stairs wet or recently polished?
- Was the deceased wearing footwear? Could footwear or lack of footwear have contributed to the fall?
- In cases involving a ladder is there any apparent damage to the steps or rungs?
- Does the ladder have rubber footpads?
- For outdoor stairs:

- What are the general lighting conditions?
- Are there any recent weather hazards – rain, sleet, ice, snow, hail, frost?
- Are there any obstructions such as leaves, pine needles, clothing, toys, exposed cables or electrical cords, or any other objects or obstructions on the steps or around the stairway?

Although most of the case studies in this chapter are focused on incidents that take place in the home, there are also other examples of deaths resulting from falls that have occurred outdoors and were reported as accidental. These accidental falls in the workplace, or during leisure events such as rock climbing or hiking also occur as Case Studies 10.5 and 10.6 demonstrate.

CASE STUDY 10.5

A wife reported her husband of eight days was missing after leaving their house with unknown friends. Just days later, the wife called police again reporting that she had found her husband's body below a steep hiking path. However, her friends noted she showed no emotion after discovering the body and made a comment that she could now have a funeral and words to the effect of the cops were no longer needed. Police were correctly suspicious when the wife was the one who found his body, at a place she said he expressed wanting to see before he died. Police investigation revealed that the wife was having second thoughts about her marriage and texted a friend that she was going to talk to him about the marriage the day he disappeared. The wife was eventually confronted with surveillance tape that showed both arriving together at the hiking trail. The wife then admitted confronting him about their marriage and arguing. He then grabbed her arm, she broke free and pushed him away, causing him to fall over the cliff to his death. She then drove back to her residence and later made the missing person report. The wife later plead guilty to second degree murder and was sentenced to 30 years in prison.

CASE STUDY 10.6

A husband was vacationing with his wife to celebrate their 12th year anniversary by visiting a state park and hiking. The husband initially notified police that his wife had fallen some 130 feet off a cliff when she slipped while taking a photograph. Police were suspicious of the event as explained by the husband and later discovered a map in his vehicle with an X marked where the wife's body was located. Further investigation revealed the husband had a four-million-dollar insurance policy taken out on his wife, without her knowledge. When investigating his background, police discovered that the husband's first wife was also killed in a tragic accident when they were both changing a tire, and the car slipped off the car jack, crushing her under the vehicle.

Accidental Fires

Accidental fires are responsible for a number of deaths and millions of dollars' worth of property damage in the United States and across the world. Arson, the intentional setting of a fire, is also a very popular method used to cover up crimes by destroying evidence or the murder of someone with the same concept that any evidence of foul play would be consumed in the fire. The following case study is a good example where arson was used to stage a murder to resemble an accidental fire and at the same time cause significant property damage to obtain an insurance settlement for the loss.

CASE STUDY 10.7

A businessman was deeply in debt due to high living and some bad business ventures, so he planned to eliminate his financial obligations and rekindle his lavish lifestyle by intentionally torching his $700,000 dollar house for the insurance money. This particular case was a little more complicated because the offender also decided to take care of another problem, his elderly mother, who was living with his family. As part of his plan, he brought his 90-year-old mother down to the basement, where he then spread lacquer thinner as an accelerant around one of the walls and lit a match. He then left his house with his children and took them to the movies attempting to create an alibi that he was not at home when the fire started. Initially, his plan seemed to work, and the preliminary investigation indicated the elderly woman walked downstairs to the basement, intentionally spread the accelerant on the walls and committed suicide by setting the fire. Toxicology revealed the mother had Risperdal (used for treating schizophrenia and bipolar disorder), Valium and alcohol in her system. The ME concluded she died of smoke inhalation and carbon monoxide poisoning, ruling the death a suicide. Further information initially unknown to investigators and the ME was later discovered that would shed a different light on the case. During later questioning, the businessman stated he left the home for the movie at about 6:15 p.m., with an approximate 15-minute travel time, arriving at the theater for a 7:05 p.m. showing. However, the youngest son stated they arrived about eight minutes into the movie; accounting for the previews, making their arrival at the theater at about 7:30 p.m. Interestingly, neighbors saw the businessman and his sons leave at about 7:00 p.m. and noticed smoke coming from the home at about 7:10 p.m. The businessman further stated his mother sometimes acted in a psychotic manner was taking medications, had previously burned herself, and had talked about committing suicide in the past. Through additional interviews, detectives discovered he told his housekeeper his mother had said she wanted to burn the house down. When checking on the mother's medications, investigators learned the businessman had obtained the Risperdal prescription for his mother without her being examined by a doctor and the Valium had been prescribed for him, but not his mother. Moreover, the stairs leading down to the basement were steep and the mother had physical disabilities limiting her mobility. It was also learned that seven days prior to the fire a codicil had been added to the mother's will stating in the event of her death, she did not want an autopsy to be conducted, and she wished to be cremated immediately, although the attorney who drafted the original will was not aware of the change. The businessman's background revealed he had previously collected on a $50,000 insurance claim that burglars had broken into his home and stole numerous personal effects. They also discovered he had moved his mother from out of state to his home, arranged to sell her house, but placed the proceeds into his own account where he then spent most of the money. Then, about eight months before the fire, he increased the amount on his homeowner's insurance policy. The police also discovered the businessman had contacted his insurance company to start his claim for the damage to his house the night of the fire but waited until the next morning to contact his sister and inform her of their mother's death. The man was eventually tried for premeditated murder of his mother, arson, and insurance fraud and was convicted (Chancellor & Graham 2017).

In the previous case study, the first major red flag is again a *coincidence* wherein the businessman takes his kids to the movies, leaving his mother at the house alone and then something tragic happens while they are gone. Another key aspect to this case is in the pre and post incident behaviors of the businessman, including his current financial situation, his previous insurance claim, and what appeared to be the diversion of funds from the sale of his mother's house. Likewise, the mother's toxicology results especially since the Risperdal being prescribed without a doctor's examination and the Valium being prescribed to the businessman rather than the mother. Additionally, there seemed to be no history of suicidal tendencies on the part of the mother, only claims of such on the part of the businessman.

Another important factor is the mother's physical disabilities, making it unlikely she could walk down the steep basement stairs without assistance. Finally, the post crime behavior that is most significant was calling his insurance company about the damage to his property even before he contacted his sister to inform her of their mother's death. Although these factors taken individually may be explainable; when they are combined together, they are consistent with a premeditated plan.

The following case study is another example where arson was used to destroy evidence of a crime and staged to resemble a residential burglary.

CASE STUDY 10.8

A police officer was involved in a long term extra marital affair with another woman in his town. Eventually the woman became frustrated when he would not leave his wife as he had led her to believe was his intention and decided to try and force them to divorce by sending the wife several anonymous notes informing her of the affair. The notes created problems in the officer's marriage and when confronted, by his wife, promised he would end the affair. Instead, he continued to see the woman, even stopping by her house before or after his regular patrol shift. This continued for over a year before the wife discovered the affair was still ongoing. Confronting her husband again, the officer once again promised to end the affair and he went to the woman and tried to end the relationship and returned her house key. Shortly thereafter, the woman sent several very angry emails to his official police email account about his abrupt ending of their relationship and threatened to tell his wife they were continuing their affair. The officer continued to stop by her house before or after his shift, although he had told his patrol partner he was having problems with the woman. In the early morning hours, the officer was on routine patrol alone, when he left his own patrol area and drove by her house where he claimed to observe smoke coming from the residence. The officer later said he stopped to check it out and called the dispatcher claiming he was at the scene and reported a fatality inside the house. When other officers arrived, they were met by the other police officer who reported that the occupant was inside, but she was already dead, although he admitted he had not been able to get inside the house because of the smoke and fire. He later told another officer he had indeed been able to get inside the house and had found the woman on the bed, but the bed was on fire, and he was unable to reach her. He then told yet another officer he had gone inside by crawling through a window and tried to remove her but was unable to because of the fire and smoke. After the fire was extinguished, the woman's body was found lying in bed on her back. She had been repeatedly stabbed and her body partially burned. The ME would later determine at autopsy the woman had had been stabbed or slashed 21 times in the back, right shoulder, neck, and cheek. Several stab wounds had penetrated her heart, left lung, right lung, and her carotid artery was also slashed. Crime scene investigators also found the woman's dog, a small poodle was found dead from a stab wound in another part of the house. They also noted evidence of an apparent break-in, including a kitchen window with the screen cut out, and an open gate in the backyard. But, upon closer examination they noted the window screen appeared to have been cut from the inside. One of the investigators tried to enter the house through the kitchen window, but he could not do it by himself because he needed a ladder to reach it. But entering the home that way would have been difficult because the sink was located under the window and was full of dishes. Further, looking outside at the ground underneath the window there was no evidence that a ladder or other object had been placed there to assist in climbing into the house. Detectives also discovered the back door to the house was still locked from the inside and the victim's telephone line had been manipulated to allow calls out, but anyone calling her number would have received a busy signal. Finally, there was no evidence the victim was sexually assaulted and nothing of value was missing. Thus, there did not seem to be a motive for the murder. Fire investigators later were able to determine the fire was intentionally set and the offender had poured gasoline on the mattress where the woman's body lay and, on the floor, leading to the bedroom door and then ignited the gasoline while standing in the doorway. An empty container of gasoline was also found in the bedroom. The investigators quickly concluded the scene was staged to resemble a burglary and then arson was initiated as a way to further misdirect the investigation and eliminate evidence. The detectives quickly turned their attention to the police officer who was involved in the extra marital affair with the victim and had *coincidentally* reported the fire *and* was the first to arrive at the scene. When the police officer was unable to establish his whereabouts at the time of the incident he was indicted, tried, and later convicted of the murder and arson (Chancellor & Graham 2017).

As in other cases, when we review the facts of this case study and look at the various *red flags*, it is clear this was a staged event. The first and perhaps most blatant red flag was the police officer who reported the fire was *coincidentally* the one that was engaged in an extra marital affair with the victim, and who just *happened* to drive by the house that was out of his patrol area, at the very time the fire was observed. Also note the offender's changing story to different people and his attempts to place himself in the best possible light, that he managed to get into the house but could not rescue her because of the flames and smoke. The staged entry point was also inconsistent and unlikely as the window screen was cut from the inside, and there were no indentations on the ground under the window for a ladder or anything else that would

Accidental Deaths

allow entry into the window. The difficulty of entering through the kitchen window does not match what we know of burglars who seek the easiest way into a residence.

This case study is also a good example of the concept of *exaggeration*, wherein the offender leaves too much or conflicting evidence. We see this in not just the effort to show forced entry into the house, but also in the manipulation of the telephone. Cutting the line would be acceptable and consistent with an attempt to limit the victim from alerting anyone else but taking the time to actually rewire the phone to allow outgoing calls, but deny incoming calls, does not make any sense and is inconsistent with typical offender behavior. What criminal would really take the time to manipulate the phone in this manner? Even more illogical, if they went into the scene to murder the victim then why did they have to worry about them making a call or anyone calling in?

Lastly, there is no clear motive for the incident. There was no evidence of theft of personal property and there was no evidence of a sexual assault. As with other staged homicides we have discussed in this text, the only real crime that was committed was the murder of the victim and the arson set to destroy evidence or further stage the scene.

Drowning

In the United States, about ten people die every day from unintentional drowning, and two of them are children aged 14 or younger. According to the CDC (2021) drowning ranks fifth among the leading causes of unintentional injury death in the United States. Because drowning occurs frequently across the country it is also used as a theme for a staged scene and again does not require a lot of preparation or scene alterations.

One of the more well-known murder cases over the last few years was the Drew Peterson case from Illinois. Peterson was a police officer that claimed his fourth wife Stacy Peterson was missing under rather unusual circumstances. (This case happened to coincide with the Scott Peterson case from California about a missing wife that had disappeared under unusual circumstances.) It was while police were engaged in looking for his fourth wife and investigating those unusual circumstances, they became aware of the death of his third wife Kathleen Savio, who reportedly died from accidentally drowning in the bathtub some years before. At the time, her death was determined to be an accidental death, even though she was found in a dry bathtub and there was no water on the bathroom floor. The coroner's inquest heard from another police officer who *assured them that Peterson would never hurt his wife*. Ironically, it was the missing fourth wife that caused police to take

214　　Equivocal Death

another look at the accidental death of the third wife. The subsequent inquiry led to the third wife's exhumation and second autopsy, which concluded her death was no accident, but the result of homicide following a struggle and she had been placed in the bathtub to stage the scene. Interesting in this case, it was his missing fourth wife Stacy that had provided Peterson's alibi when his third wife died. Peterson was later convicted of Savio's death.

CASE STUDY 10.9

The hotel management was summoned to a room when other hotel occupants complained of a ceiling leak. When they entered the room, they discovered the bathtub was running over and the bathroom had flooded. Floating dead in the tub was the body of a young female, dressed in her panties and a turtleneck sweater. Sometime later, the woman's boyfriend returned to the hotel to find the police inside his room. When questioned, the boyfriend stated he left the room earlier to go drinking and his girlfriend was still sleeping in the bed. The boyfriend surmised she must have gotten up and wanted to take a bath but passed out due to medication she was taking. Police began to look closer at the boyfriend when they talked to the other hotel occupants and learned they had observed the leaking ceiling almost 10 minutes before the boyfriend said he left the room. A preliminary investigation revealed the couple had a turbulent relationship and were constantly fighting, breaking up, then reconciling, and the girlfriend had recently decided to finally leave him. The boyfriend was later tried and convicted of murder (Chancellor & Graham 2017).

In the previous case, the offender left the hotel room to try and establish an alibi, but he was unaware the tub had already started to run over and flood the bathroom thus causing the leak. His departure is another example of a *coincidence*, wherein he left the hotel and for a short period of time, only to return to find a tragic accident had taken place in his absence.

CASE STUDY 10.10

A man called 911 reporting he came home from work and found his wife unconscious in the bathtub. He said he had tried, but failed to get her out of the water and he needed help. The responding EMT found the wife nude and still submerged on her back with her face directly

Accidental Deaths   215

under the nozzle. Although unconscious she was still alive and was transported to the hospital. When initially questioned, the husband maintained that his wife must have accidentally slipped in the bathtub and hit her head then fell unconscious into the water. He denied being home when she started the bath or any involvement in the accident. However, the following day his wife's condition was critical and there were indications she might recover, so the husband went to the police and tried to change his story. During police questioning, the husband admitted they had been fighting because his wife had asked him for a divorce. Becoming upset he held her under the water for a few minutes. He then admitted that afterwards he tried make her death look like an accidental drowning, so he removed her wet clothing and put them in his car to make it appear she was taking a bath. The wife later died in the hospital without ever regaining consciousness and during pretrial motions the husband's confession was later ruled inadmissible. But when he was in the throes of drowning his wife his then 8-year-old daughter happened to walk in and saw what was happening. She was able to testify against her father. He was convicted and sentenced to a very lengthy prison term (Chancellor & Graham 2017).

CASE STUDY 10.11

An ex-husband reported that he went to visit his ex-wife at her apartment complex and while they were talking near the apartment's pool, she had a sudden seizure and fell into the water. The husband said he could not swim so it took a few minutes for him to be able to reach his wife and remove her from the pool. EMT arrived at the scene and the woman was still alive but was dead upon arrival at the emergency room. The police treated the incident as an accidental death and there was no follow-up investigation. The victim was later autopsied, and the ME reported that the injuries and death were inconsistent with the ex-husband's explanation of events. However, for some reason this was never reported to the police or if so, they never took any action. The ME's comments were found during another unrelated death investigation when detectives from another jurisdiction were talking to the ME about another case. The detectives from the other jurisdiction coordinated with the responsible department but there was no interest in following up on the case as they had already closed their response to the scene as an accidental death.

It is both tragic and shameful that the death described in Case Study 10.11 was not further investigated. Sadly, the initial first responder's impression of the scene seemed to generally match the ex-husband's explanation of events and was therefore believed. There was not even an effort to determine if the victim had a history of seizures. The investigation was simply closed even before an autopsy was conducted. Then following the autopsy that was inconsistent with the ex-husband's explanation, the police never responded.

The following are some common factors or red flags identified by Chancellor and Graham (2017) in cases involving suspected drowning accidental deaths:

- Are there unexplained injuries to the victim (i.e., trauma to the head or defensive injuries to the hands)?
- Was water found in the lungs of the victim consistent with drowning?
- Does the water in lungs match the body of water where found?
- Are there any alcohol or drug levels found at autopsy which could be a contributing factor?
- Were any drugs found at the scene prescribed?
- For bathtub drowning, is the victim wearing any clothing?
- Is there water in the tub or spa or is it wet and consistent with being recently drained?
- Is there water on the floor of the bathroom or surrounding the hot tub?
- Is the victim appropriately dressed for the body of water involved in their death (i.e., bathing suit, for swimming activities, naked in the bathtub or spa, life jacket in boating incidents)?
- For swimming incidents, are towels and other such items present at the scene, consistent with someone swimming?
- Is the victim's clothing in place and properly worn?
- Were there any efforts at administering lifesaving first aid?
- Is the clothing of the person who found the body wet? (Consistent with helping or removing the victim or performing lifesaving efforts.)

Firearm Accidental Deaths

There are many accidental deaths that involve firearms from mishandling or unfamiliarity with a firearm to hunting accidents. Some of these events are misclassified as suicides because the coroner reasons that the deceased

Accidental Deaths 217

cased their own death. But as noted in previous chapters this is incorrect. An example is found in Case Study 10.12.

CASE STUDY 10.12

An 18-year-old soldier was home on Christmas leave after basic training. He came into his mother's house very excited because he had just bought his first pistol. His mother was less excited and was concerned with a loaded pistol in the house with younger children, and she ordered her son to unload the weapon and put it away. The young man sat down in a lazy boy recliner in the living room with younger kids watching TV and his mother reading a magazine in another chair next to him. However, he was unfamiliar with how the pistol operated and as he was trying to remove the magazine and unload the chambered round, the weapon unexpectedly discharged, striking him in the chest and penetrating his heart. The young man died almost instantaneously. The police and coroner were called to the scene and conducted a brief investigation but found no evidence of criminality or any behavior consistent with suicide. Everyone in the house agreed that the young man was excited to be in the army and about buying his first pistol. Furthermore, he had a good relationship with his family and was looking forward to his military career. The police were satisfied that the event was a tragic accident, probably the result of being unfamiliar with the weapon. However, the coroner listed the death as suicide because the death was "caused by the victim." This of course is a misapplication of the suicide concept, Although he was pressed on this issue, he refused to change his mind and the death certificate listed suicide as the manner of death.

As noted previously, the coroner's decision does not make sense in that there was no evidence that the event was planned, or the deceased intended to kill themselves. This was just a tragic accident, but the emotional pain was increased to the family by the coroner's suicide determination.

There are also fatal hunting accidents that take place nearly every year. Some because of unsafe acts by either the deceased or the shooter. Case Study 10.13 is an example of a tragic hunting accident.

CASE STUDY 10.13

Two very experienced hunters were observing a deer about 100 meters distance from them. The buck was at the edge of a small dirt trail but was still in the foliage that would not allow them to take a shot. Slowly the buck walked into the center of the dirt road and paused. At this time both hunters aimed and took a shot. However, the buck sprinted away, the hunters advanced as each thought he had struck the deer. As they came to the spot in the road where the deer was last seen they heard a voice call out. They followed the sound and found another man, lying on his back, he was wearing an orange vest but had a severe gunshot wound to his left thigh above the knee. The hunters acted quickly and attempted to stop the bleeding by using a tourniquet. The men had their ATV's parked nearby and they quickly picked the man up and moved him to their ATVs and then quickly drove out to a clear area. When they were clear of the trees, they were able to obtain a cellphone signal. They called 911 and were able to identify their exact location on a map. At this same time the local emergency Air Ambulance crew were performing their pre-flight checks and had already started up the aircraft engines. They received the message to respond to the clearing and were in the air in a matter of minutes. They were able to find the men very quickly and the injured hunter was placed into the aircraft and was at the hospital in less than 15 minutes. At the hospital, a surgery team was already present, having just finished treating a traffic accident injury. The injured man was literally brought into the surgery almost immediately upon his arrival at the hospital with a full surgical team present. Unfortunately, the large caliber projectile had ruptured two major blood vessels in his leg and even with everything seemingly in his favor, the man expired from loss of blood and shock. The police responded after the reported death and returned to the site in the woods accompanied by the two other hunters. The police noted the location where the hunters were located by the expended rounds and disturbance of the area. Walking along the road, they discovered fresh deer tracks in the mud at the location where the hunters stated the deer had emerged from the brush. They then went behind the fallen tree where the victim had been sitting. Police found an orange cap, normally worn by hunters as a safety precaution, a thermos of coffee and a half full coffee cup on the fallen tree. By line of sight the fallen tree lined up with the deer tracks and the other hunter's position. In a re-creation effort, police went back to the scene

Accidental Deaths

219

and while standing where the hunters were positioned, they could not see someone sitting on the fallen log, where the victim was found, even when wearing the orange safety vest. However, when the orange cap was worn, it could be clearly seen through the foliage. Therefore, by removing his orange cap, the victim inadvertently contributed to his own death.

The actions of the police in Case Study 10.13 were correct in that after interviewing the hunters the police immediately went to the scene and verified their stories. When they found clear evidence consistent with their stories, the police were able to conclude the death was the result of an accident. Because of the effort by the police to immediately substantiate the explanation of the two hunters, the deceased hunter's family accepted the accident determination.

Chapter Summary

Because normal accidental deaths are so common and generally do not involve any weapons or special equipment, staging a homicide to resemble an accident is a very prevalent event. Especially those incidents that occur at home or between family members. Therefore, it is critically important that every death, even what initially appears to be an obvious accident, be initially treated as a homicide. Unless a careful look at the scene is conducted by responding officers it is quite possible that an actual murder may be overlooked or written off as an accident. It is imperative that the scene is carefully examined for any inconsistencies or any unusual behaviors by anyone present at the scene.

Out of all the various staged events, if an offender has ever staged a death and was not challenged or the death was accepted, it is not unusual for them to repeat the staging effort again. Therefore, discovering a previous accidental death, particularly if the circumstances are similar, should be considered as a big red flag that demands additional attention and investigation.

Bibliography

Ahmad, F. B., Cisewski, J. A., & Anderson, R. N. (2023). Provisional Mortality Data – United States, 2021. *MMWR Morb Mortal Wkly Rep*, 72, 488–492. DOI: http://dx.doi.org/10.15585/mmwr.mm7218a3

Centers for Disease Control and Prevention, National Center for Injury Prevention and Control. (2021). *Web-Based Injury Statistics Query and Reporting System (WISQARS)*. Available from www.cdc.gov/injury/wisqars

Chancellor, A. S., & Graham, G. D. (2017). *Crime Scene Staging, Investigating Suspect Misdirection of the Crime Scene*. Springfield, IL: Charles C. Thomas.

National Center for Health Statistics (NCHS). (2022). Obtained online from www.cdc.gov/mmwr/volumes/71/wr/mm7117e1.htm

National Center for Health Statistics (NCHS). (2023). *FastStats – Accidents or Unintentional Injuries*. www.cdc.gov/nchs/fastats/accidental-injury.htm

National Institute on Drug Abuse (NIDA). (2021). *Drug Overdose Rates*. www.nida.nih.gov/research-topics/trends-statistics/overdose-death-rates

National Safety Council (NSC). (2023). *Injury Facts - National Safety Council*. www.injuryfacts.nsc.orginjuries/death-by-demographics/top-10-preventable-injuries/

Slips, Trips and Falls. (2015). Itasca, IL: National Safety Council.

USA Facts. (2023). *Most Common Causes of Death in the US*. www.usafacts.org/americans-causes-of-death-by-age-cdc-data/

Accidental Death Latent Investigation

11

Introduction

Most accidental deaths can be easily determined based on the explanation of events and the crime scene examination. But there are some events that may require additional investigation needed to answer questions based on the *explanation of events, scene examination, and injuries to the victim*. Thus, the investigation must continue but there is no exact protocol for conducting a follow-up investigation as the circumstances of every scene and event is going to be slightly different. This is true as the response to an accidental death is going to be slightly different than a suspected suicide, or a homicide. But there are many similarities to all death investigations but maybe slightly different based on the circumstances.

For instance, one of the important tasks in all death investigations is the conduct of a *victimology assessment*.

Victimology and Accidental Deaths

Chapter 6 of this text covered the general concepts of a *victimology assessment* in conjunction with a suspected suicide; however, it should be considered in *all* death investigations including accidental deaths. The depth and detail of the assessment is case specific, meaning there are some events that may not require as in depth assessment as other cases. The information for a victimology in an accidental death is the same as with other assessments and consists of the collection of *factual and subjective criteria* about the deceased and then compare these factors to the explanation of events and the scene examination.

The basic premise for an assessment in an accidental death is to determine if the circumstances of the death are consistent or inconsistent with how the victim led their normal life. For example, if someone was known to be a non-swimmer and was afraid of large bodies of water such as lakes or the ocean, but allegedly drowned while swimming in a lake, this would clearly be inconsistent

DOI: 10.4324/9781003373865-11

221

with their normal life. That would be significant change in their behavior and should be addressed. Another example would be the victim who is alleged to have done something that is beyond their normal physical abilities.

Limiting Physical Abilities

Perhaps the best example of limiting physical abilities were already discussed in Case Studies 6.1 and 6.2 in Chapter 6. In both of these cases the reported circumstance behind an accidental death was inconsistent either with the physical abilities of the victim to perform or the reported activity or was inconsistent with the victim's character. In both cases this victimology assessment was inconsistent with the information provided about their deaths.

Along the same lines in cases of traffic accidents when one victim was killed and was not wearing a belt, one question to ask or establish would be the normal use of seatbelts. Would not using seat belts be out of character?

Antemortem Behaviors and Events

Similar to suspected suicide cases, an important part of the preliminary and subsequent latent investigation an effort should be made to identify any antemortem behaviors and what was going on in the victim's life immediately preceding the event. The importance of learning what was going on in a victim's life preceding event is best explained in the following case.

CASE STUDY 11.1

Police and EMT's were called to a reported all-terrain vehicle (ATV) accident. The husband reported he was driving an ATV after dark, with his wife riding on the back, when he claimed to lose control and the ATM went over a 6-foot embankment and into a creek. Upon EMT's arrival, the wife was unresponsive but still evacuated to the local hospital where she was pronounced dead upon arrival. Police suspicions were initially raised when after the wife was evacuated, they noted the husband, who was supposedly driving the ATV, did not have any visible injuries and refused medical treatment at the scene by EMT's, but his wife died during the same event. The following day the police received autopsy results that determined the cause of death was downing but unlike the husband, the wife had sustained numerous contusions, abrasions, and blunt force trauma. This seemed inconsistent and the police began looking at the incident more closely and expanded their investigation. As part of their investigation, they visited the wife's workplace and discovered a handwritten note within the victim's day planner at her workplace that stated: *"If something happens to me ... Joe"* (her husband's name is Joseph.) The police dug a little deeper and when checking the victim's email, they discovered the victim had written an email to herself with a subject line of: "If something happens to me." The text of the email then stated, "Joe and I are having marital problems. Last night we almost had an accident where a huge log fell on me. Joe was on top of the pile and he had me untying a tarp directly below." The police also discovered two very important factors; first, the husband had recently taken out a 1.7-million-dollar insurance policy on his wife; and second, the husband was actively involved in an extra marital affair at the time of his wife's death. The woman he was seeing stated they had met several months before and the husband was planning to leave his wife but had no idea about any plan to kill her. The husband was later convicted of premeditated murder (Chancellor & Graham 2017).

When reviewing such accidents, it is important to note the disparity of injuries that might be present with people involved in the same accident. Whereas such disparity is not impossible, it should be looked at carefully to make sure what appears to have occurred is really what happened.

In the previous case study, it was the difference in injuries between the husband and wife that caused the police to take a deeper look into the accident. It was then they discovered the extra marital affair, the recent insurance policies, and the motive for killing his wife. But was finding the note and email that described what was going on in their lives immediately prior to the wife's death. The fact that she specifically wrote "If anything happens to me" type of comment makes it apparent that the wife was concerned for her safety. The email describing another potentially fatal accident was also a critical finding.

By examining the victim's workplace and computer, the police were actually engaging in a victimology assessment, as they were concerned with her background and what was going on in her life leading up to her death. Finding the email on her work computer that noted marital problems and describing a previous "accident" led to the discovery of the life insurance policy and the husband's extra marital affair. This is perhaps the best example of how conducting a *victimology assessment* and inquiry into the background of the victim can potentially lead to finding important evidence of a criminal act.

The following case study is an example of the importance of the follow-up latent investigation and being able to think out of the box when conducting a death investigation.

CASE STUDY 11.2

The couple had been married for over 50 years and were enjoying their retirement in a very well-maintained and furnished lakefront property. They were financially stable and were solidly in the upper middle class, despite their retirement status. One day the husband called the police reporting a tragic accident had taken place in his residence. He reported that he had observed a beaver outside in the lake and he decided to kill the raccoon because of the damage they were causing to the lake as well as residences in the area. He stated that he was walking through the house to go outside but tripped and accidentally shot his wife with a shotgun and she was dead. The couple lived in a rural area, and it was taking a Sherriff's patrols a long time to get from one part of the county to another and after 15 minutes, the husband called back to 911 to again report the death of his wife. He seemed impatient that the police had not yet arrived. When the police finally arrived the husband again explained what happened emphasizing how he accidentally shot his wife while walking through the house. He led the officer to where he had placed the shotgun. It was found on a kitchen counter (Photos 11.1 and 11.2).

The husband then showed the detectives the body of his wife located in a small alcove at the end of a hallway. The husband stated that he was walking down the hallway when he stumbled over the carpet, he later changed his

Photo 11.1 This figure depicts the living room area of the residence. The entire residence was extremely neat, orderly, and well maintained. Thus, it was easy to observe any disturbance or if anything was out of place. This was an important factor in this case.

Accidental Death Latent Investigation

Photo 11.2 This figure depicts the shotgun on the kitchen counter, placed there by the husband. The gun was unloaded by the husband with expended shell casing also on the counter.

Photo 11.3 This figure depicts the victim sitting in her chair as viewed from the living room.

story to say he tripped over the dog. As he lost his balance, he accidentally shot his wife who was sitting in the chair (Photos 11.3 and 11.4).

Photo 11.4 This is the hallway the husband was walking down with the loaded shotgun, when he supposedly stumbled and accidentally fired his weapon. The victim is seen at the end of this hallway still sitting in her chair.

The husband was initially cooperative with the responding sheriff's patrol and deputies and provided an oral statement as to the events leading up to the "accident." However, when asked to go to the Sheriff department for a full statement he declined because he had to attend his AA meeting scheduled for that date. He did agree to make a statement at a later time. Upon initial viewing of the scene the responding CSI almost immediately noted no marks or scratches on the walls of the hallway consistent with coming into contact with the shotgun as the husband lost balance. Further, even the carpet runner down the center of the hallway did not appear to be disturbed.

There were also some unusual and inconsistent behaviors exhibited by the husband that really drew attention to this event. Figure 11.5 depicts the victim still in her chair after being shot. But note, she was

Accidental Death Latent Investigation

Figure 11.5 This figure depicts how the victim was found upon police arrival at the scene. She had not been touched by the police or her husband. The victim is still in her chair after being shot, leaning over in what can be described as an uncomfortable position. But there was no effort to "make her comfortable." Also note again no disturbance of the carpet running in the hallway.

not moved by her husband after the event. There was no attempt at first aid and no evidence that she was touched or moved after she was shot. What would be expected in such accidental events would be the efforts to administer first aid, attempts to make her comfortable, by removing her from the chair and onto the floor, putting a pillow under her head, even covering her with a blanket. These efforts are consistent and almost expected occurrences in similar accidental events, even when there is convincing evidence that the victim is already deceased. Such behaviors are often seen as the husband trying to "apologize" for hurting his wife. However, in this situation, her husband of 50 years reaction to his "accidental shooting" was to simply leave her in this position. These behaviors did not match what was being claimed by the husband.

The lack of empathy or concern for his wife seemed inconsistent and the event appeared to be more than just an accident. When viewed as a potential staging effort, the husband believed he must show the police the position his wife was in when he accidentally shot her. Clearly, he wanted to leave no doubt as to what happened. This is an example of the mistakes an offender makes when staging an event. Since they did not really feel the loss of the person, or because the act was intentional, they don't show any emotions or feelings toward the victim that is present in other accidental events. Their main goal is to provide a scene for the police, that establishes their version of events. The problem in this case was other than a lack of disturbance and improper emotions shown by the husband, there was no physical or forensic evidence available at the scene. The CSI had to think out of the box to "find" evidence that is inconsistent with the explanation of events. One thing the CSI had in their favor was the fact the scene had not been disturbed by the husband or first responders. The CSI therefore decided to use the computer program *Poser*, that would enable them to produce a scale diagram and allow them to perhaps reconstruct the event. To use the program, it was necessary to obtain the exact measurements of the entire scene. In this case this included the walls of the alcove and hallway and height of the desk chair seat where the victim was sitting (Figure 11.6).

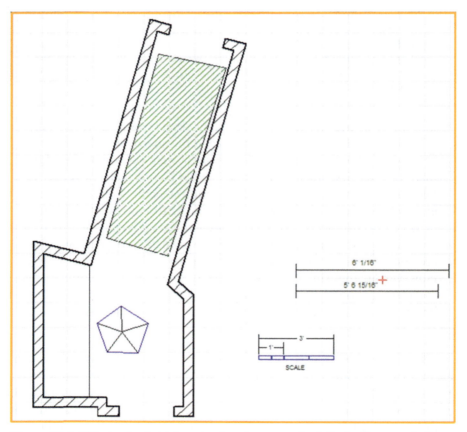

Figure 11.6 This is the initial scale sketch prepared of the hallway and alcove where the victim was found.

Accidental Death Latent Investigation

The height and weights of both victim and husband were also used as well as the measurements of the shotgun. Laboratory analysis of the victim's shirt and the shot pattern found at autopsy determined that the weapon was approximately 3–4 feet distance from the victim when fired. The pathologist was also able to determine the trajectory angle of entry wounds found at autopsy. All of this information was placed into the Poser program resulting in the diagrams found in Figures 11.7 and 11.8.

Figures 11.7, 11.8, and 11.9 are images from the Poser program. It was created by first placing the victim in her chair in the same position she was sitting when she was shot. Then the shotgun was added at a distance of four feet and tilted in the trajectory of the entrance wound as noted by the medical examiner. (The yellow line was added representing the trajectory of the projectiles.) Then a figure was created that was the same size and weight as the husband and he was placed up against the butt of the shotgun and it matched. Thus, the CSI circumstantially could show that it was more likely the husband shot his wife, rather than losing his balance and accidentally firing the gun.

There was also one witness that provided specific details concerning the husband's experience with firearms. The witness was his daughter who testified that she was familiar with weapons, having shot and hunted with

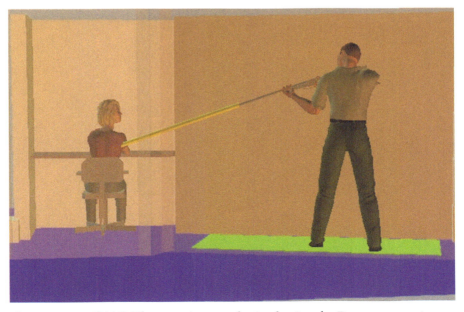

Figures 11.7 and 11.8 These are images obtained using the Poser program to recreate the event.

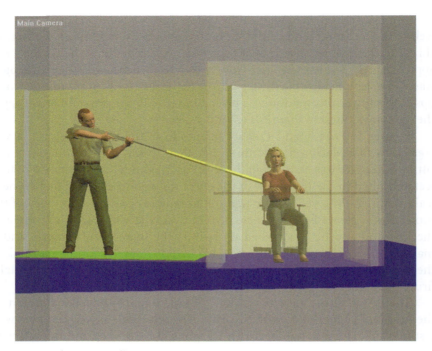

Figure 11.8 (Continued)

Figure 11.9 This is the Poser sketch depicting the event from above to get another perspective of the event.

Accidental Death Latent Investigation

her father throughout her life. She stated unequivocally that her father had one rule that he enforced without question, that is you never load your weapon inside the house or walk through the house with a loaded weapon. *Coincidentally*, in this case he broke that one rule he had instilled in his children. However, he had violated his own long standing safety rule, by carrying a loaded weapon inside the when the accident allegedly took place. The police were also able to determine that the husband had been having an extramarital affair with another woman and had told the woman that he planned to divorce his wife and marry her. The husband was eventually indicted and convicted of murder.

Multiple "Accidents"

Case Studies 11.3 and 11.4 highlight a very important *red flag* to note when responding to an accidental death. That is multiple accidental deaths associated with the same family or spouse. The discovery of previously reported accidental or suicidal deaths, involving spouses or children from the same family should be automatically considered suspicious. Unfortunately, when an offender escapes detection from their first staging attempt, they frequently are involved in a second attempt. Many times, they use the same method to stage the scene *because it worked the first time*.

CASE STUDY 11.3

A husband came home from jogging and discovered his wife at the bottom of the basement stairs with her head lying in a pool of blood and an electrical cord from a vacuum cleaner was wrapped around one leg. The police and EMT's responded to the scene and transported the victim to the hospital where she died the following day. There was a limited preliminary investigation completed, but because the death appeared to be the result of an accidental fall, a more thorough investigation was not pursued. Nine years later, the husband and his second wife were involved in another tragic event. In this case, a passerby observed a vehicle crashed into the guard rail. The other driver stopped to check on the occupants and observed a woman in the passenger seat, alive but unconscious, bleeding from a head wound, with difficulty breathing. Her husband was sitting in the driver's seat but was seemingly uninjured; and although he had a working cell phone within easy access, it was the passerby who actually called the police and EMT's for help. The woman was eventually transported by responding

EMT's to the hospital where she later died of her injuries. When police responded to the accident, the husband reported that he was traveling at about 55 mph when a deer suddenly crossed the road, and he was forced to swerve to avoid hitting the deer. He apparently over corrected and struck the guardrail. Police looking at the scene were concerned, because there was only minimal damage to the vehicle and the air bags had not even been deployed. This did not appear to be consistent with the husband's stated traveling speed and there was no evidence of emergency breaking or maneuvering in the roadway. There were also questions raised based on bloodstains found on the passenger side of the vehicle which did not appear to be consistent with the reported traffic accident. At autopsy the wife was found to have sustained a laceration and contusions to the right side of her head and fractures to her face, which were inconsistent with bloodstains observed within the vehicle's interior. The police observed that the blood stains within the vehicle were consistent with the victim already bleeding prior to the accident. Police obtained a search warrant on the husband's house and found numerous dried bloodstains in his garage area and were consistent with the passenger side of the vehicle if parked in the garage. The police surmised the second wife was assaulted at the house and her blood fell to the concrete garage floor as she was being placed into the car. The husband then staged the scene by driving the vehicle into the guardrail causing his wife, while she was probably unconscious, to strike the dashboard since she was not wearing a seatbelt. Police eventually conducted a reconstruction of the event and were able to determine the vehicle's impact to the guardrail was more consistent with a speed of about 20 mph, again confirming the injuries were unlikely caused during the accident. The husband had also given several contradicting statements concerning why his wife's seatbelt was unsecured; telling the coroner she had removed her seatbelt to make herself more comfortable; but telling friends her seatbelt had just come undone, and to others he claimed she was playing games to determine how long she could unbuckle the belt before the seatbelt light would come on in the dashboard. However, as they conducted their investigation into the traffic accident, the police learned of the first wife's accidental death from a fall inside their residence. As they inquired into the first wife's death, the police re-contacted the pathologist who performed the autopsy of the first wife. They learned her injuries of skull fracture and lacerations were inconsistent with a passive fall downstairs and believed they were more likely caused by an object striking her head. According to the first

Accidental Death Latent Investigation

wife's autopsy report, she had sustained 14 different impact injuries to her face and head with numerous abrasions and contusions located on her upper body and arms that were questionable injuries resulting from a fall. The pathologist believed the case was suspicious and indicated this information was passed onto the police following the autopsy. According to the police they were not appraised of this finding, and it is not clear if they ever received the autopsy report. The husband was later tried and convicted for the murder of his second wife. He later plead no contest to the murder of his first wife (Chancellor & Graham 2017).

CASE STUDY 11.4

A husband summoned paramedics and police to his home after finding his wife unconscious in their hot tub. The first responding police officers observed the husband attempting to revive his wife. The responding officers assisted in removing the victim from the hot tub, and continued resuscitation efforts. EMT's arrived and the husband insisted that she be transported to a specific hospital for treatment and not the closest hospital. Upon arrival at the hospital, she was pronounced dead. An autopsy revealed that the woman's death was not from drowning but from asphyxiation, further she had also had blunt force trauma to her neck, body, and scalp inconsistent with any attempts to revive her. Toxicology did show the blood alcohol level at the time of her death was 0.22%. An examination of the husband revealed fresh scratch marks on his arms, sides, and hands. In addition, the husband without prompting, told police: "I hope they don't try to put this on me." During their investigation the police learned that the husband was the beneficiary of a $100,000 life insurance policy and in the months preceding her death, the husband had attempted to portray her to friends as an alcoholic. However, the victim's longtime friends, noted that they had rarely seen the woman intoxicated. The police also discovered that a former wife in another state had also reportedly drowned in a bathtub. In that case interestingly, the responding EMT's and police noted that the tub was dry and there was no water on the floor of the bathroom consistent with the victim being removed from the bathtub. The facts and circumstances of his first wife's death closely resembled circumstances surrounding the second wife's death in that: Both women were in their thirties and in good health, and in each instances the victims had been drinking prior to the "accident." The husband also admitted in both cases that he had an argument with the victim the evening prior to their death. In both cases police noticed fresh scratch marks on the husband's arms, hands, and torso. More importantly, the autopsies of both women revealed that they had died from asphyxiation, not drowning. It is unclear why the police were not further involved in the death of his first wife. It is likely they looked at the scene and concluded it was an accident and it was quickly closed without additional investigation. The husband was later arrested and later made incriminating statements to fellow inmates while in the County Jail, admitting his culpability for both deaths (Chancellor & Graham 2017).

In these seemingly unrelated incidents, there are several common *red flags* that are present that could have alerted the police. In Case Study 11.3, in the death of wife #1, there is another example of a *coincidence*; wherein the husband left home for a short period of time and returns to find his wife has suffered a tragic accident. As noted previously, *coincidences* are claimed so frequently in staged scenes that whenever one is encountered as part of the explanation of events, the event should receive greater scrutiny. Another important element is the husband's post incident behavior in both events. In Case Study 11.3, although his wife was transported to the hospital, he did not accompany her, nor did he immediately go to the hospital to be with her. Instead, he remained at his house to "clean up the scene." There is also unusual behavior displayed after the traffic accident and the death of wife #2. The husband is uninjured, has a working cell phone, yet it is a passerby that stops and reports the accident. Although everyone reacts differently to such incidents, some behavior is so unusual or out of place, that it requires additional inquiry. Lastly, the injuries noted to both victims at autopsy were inconsistent with the circumstances of their reported deaths. It is unclear why this discrepancy was not caught during the first wife's death investigation, but it is likely the police were initially satisfied with the preliminary findings of accidental death and did not spend the necessary time to fully verify the circumstances.

A careful look at the evidence of the traffic accident as noted in Case Study 11.4, noted the damage to the vehicle was inconsistent with the husband's story and the injuries to the victim were also inconsistent with the other case facts. We also see another example of a *coincidence* wherein the accident supposedly takes place at the same time when the second wife was not wearing her seat belt. It is also interesting to note that the husband provided varied explanations to different people as to why her seatbelt was not buckled properly.

Accidental Death Latent Investigation

The main point in these last case studies is tragic events do happen, but two tragic events that involve the same person or family should be looked at in much greater detail. As with all incidents, the explanation of events is critical during the preliminary investigation and that explanation needs to be compared to the physical or forensic evidence discovered at the scene or in the vehicle.

Case Studies 11.3 and 11.4 are examples of why even accidental deaths have to be initially looked at seriously. The sad fact is that if an offender is successful in staging an event and misdirecting the police away from the true facts, they often will often commit a second murder. Often, they are likely to use the same theme even the same explanation and cause of death because it worked the previous time. Again, this is why it is important to at least check if there were any previous accidents involving the spouse or the family.

The previous case studies highlight many of the issues discussed throughout the text. In accidental events, the police often seem to be satisfied upon their initial viewing of the scene that there was nothing suspicious in the deaths. Because falls downstairs and traffic accidents are rather common occurrences, it is likely the police were already desensitized to these events and responded with a sense of *complacency*. It is also likely that in Case Study 11.3 the status of the husband as a respected member of the community added to that complacency.

Chapter Summary

Note that in all of the case studies found in Chapters 10 and 11 the reported accidental events are examples of a staged scene designed by the offender to get through the initial police viewing of the scene and hopefully avoid a thorough investigation. These examples are why it is important to at least take a critical look at all death investigations including accidental deaths. Even in cases that may appear clearly accidental, it only takes a few minutes extra to carefully examine the scene and listen to the explanation of the accident. Responding officers should be viewing the scene listening for any of the Red Flags such as *coincidences*, or explanations that are unlikely because of their physical or psychological problems. It is also important to check and determine if there were multiple accidental deaths from the same family or spouse. Multiple accidental deaths should always be challenged whenever they are found.

Reference

Chancellor, A. S., & Graham, G. D. (2017). *Crime Scene Staging, Investigating Suspect Misdirection of the Crime Scene*. Springfield, IL: Charles C. Thomas.

Common Investigative Mistakes

12

After participating in or reviewing literally thousands of investigations over 50 years, it is not hard to identify some of the more common investigative mistakes or failures that are found in many different types of investigations. There may be subtle differences because of the type of crime being investigated, but the same basic errors are present. Most, if not all, of the investigative mistakes or failures can be overcome through discipline and reliance on some of the more traditional investigative methods that have been emphasized throughout this book. In many cases, these mistakes are a result of a lack of training and in other cases it is just bad habits that detectives have developed over their careers and that have become part of their normal routine.

These mistakes may become more pronounced and aggravated when the detective and others have immediately determined the death is a suicide without conducting a proper preliminary investigation.

Complacency and Routine Cases

Perhaps the biggest failing and most common investigative error occurs when detectives respond to a death scene, and within minutes of viewing the scene they immediately determine the death is just a "routine case." This is especially problematic in suspected or reported "suicides" and accidental deaths. Many times, this thought process begins when they are dispatched to a scene for a reported "suicide," and they arrive with a preconceived notion of what they are going to find. As noted in the text there should be no such thing as a *routine death investigation*. Whenever a detective begins to look at suicides as being just another *routine case*, they show signs of *complacency*. This is an alluring trap for detectives who do not want to spend their time on what they see as a non-criminal event.

As noted in the text, this is exactly what offenders that stage a homicide to resemble a suicide or accidental death are counting on. They are counting on the police to respond to the scene and if it is close enough to what they have seen before, there is a good chance that there will be no other investigation. Thus, they can get away with murder. *The cure for this problem is to treat every death as a homicide until you can prove it's another manner of death.*

236 DOI: 10.4324/9781003373865-12

Assuming a Suicide Posture

As noted by Geberth (2013) one of the major failings and mistakes that detectives make when responding to a reported suicide is to immediately accept that the death is a suicide. This affects their entire response and often how the scene is examined and often limits their investigative effort. This of course is one of the most common and major failings of detectives. It is basically an example of police complacency and making an initial assessment of the scene and making an instant decision, that is often very difficult to overcome if the facts are changed in the future.

Improper Scene Documentation

Closely related to the concept of *complacency and routine cases* and assuming the suicidal posture is the failure to properly conduct and document a scene examination. Many times, when a detective or coroner determines that the death is a suicide or accidental, they also determine there is no need to document the scene or collect any evidence. The problem of course comes when days, months, or even years later, new evidence comes in that shows that the death was the result of a homicide. Now trying to initiate a homicide investigation becomes problematic because there was no proper scene examination and many times the scene was not even photographed.

As noted in many texts on homicide investigation and crime scene examination, there is only one chance to examine the scene correctly and that is the first time. Regardless of the circumstances of the death, the scene should be examined and documented properly. *There is an old saying that it is better to have the evidence and not need it, then need the evidence and not have it.*

Failing to Believe or Listen to the Family

There is a natural tendency for detectives to view each newly reported death from the prism of their past experiences and training, they almost automatically assume they understand or can determine what happened upon initially viewing the scene. This tends to be particularly true in suicide and many accidental death events. Therefore, they are reluctant, sometimes even resistant to discussing aspects of the investigation or listening to the concerns of family members or close friends of the deceased. Especially if they challenge their determination of the case.

There are several important reasons to take some time and listen to the family. As stressed in the text, the family is one of the better sources of information about the victim and what was going on in their lives antemortem. This may prove to be especially important if there were any personal conflicts with someone, especially domestic issues. The second is to provide them with information and assist them through the tragic event of the death of their loved one. Failure to talk to or listen to what the family is trying to tell the police could not only lead to mistrust and damage the long-term relationship with the family but might also cause the loss of valuable information and evidence.

Failure to Request or Conduct an Autopsy

A forensic autopsy is critical in every death investigation and without it the cause of death is really based on the "*best guess*" made after observing the scene. There is a misunderstanding of some detectives concerning the need for an autopsy. An autopsy is needed not just to determine the *cause of death* or identify any injuries, that can usually be established at the scene when viewing the body. A gunshot wound, a stab, or ligature strangulation all leave identifiable injuries. One of the main reasons to request an autopsy is to identify or eliminate *any other trauma* to the victim that is inconsistent with self-inflicted injuries.

Failing to conduct an autopsy and toxicology during the preliminary investigation of a suspected suicide becomes critical when later information alleges the death was the result of homicide. This is especially problematic if the victim was cremated.

Failure to Obtain Toxicological Samples

As part of any autopsy, toxicology samples should be requested and submitted for analysis. Such analysis is part of every forensic autopsy for both the detective and the family it is important to note if there were any drugs or alcohol present in the body of the deceased at the time of death. Failure to conduct such an analysis can cause mistrust with the family. In one case detectives told the family that the deceased had drank alcohol and taken pills which contributed to their death. Unbeknownst to the detectives, toxicology was never conducted and their statement could not be verified, leading to the family to conclude the detective was either lying, or incompetent.

Common Investigative Mistakes

Failure to Look for also and Validate Risk Factors

As noted throughout the text, no one suddenly wakes up and decides to end their life. There is no such thing as spontaneous suicide.

Although this is one of the easiest steps in a suspected suicide, it is seldom accomplished with any vigor. As noted, no one just wakes up one day and decides to commit suicide. Therefore, it is necessary to establish what was going on in their life prior to their death – specifically what risk factors are present. If no risk factors or suicidal behaviors are present, then there is something wrong and additional information and investigation is necessary.

Failure to Conduct Victimology Assessment

One of the more critical investigative steps in any crime of violence is a *victimology assessment*, or a detailed background investigation of the deceased. Detectives are either not familiar with the concept or the benefits of such an effort or they determine they don't have time to collect the necessary information. In most crimes of violence, victimology is designed to identify the various risk factors for the victim to become a victim. Unfortunately, in most crimes of violence the only "victimology" that is conducted is a criminal history name check As noted by Roy Hazelwood, one of the original members of the FBI's Behavioral Analysis Unit, in his training classes and talking about the importance and understanding the victim said, "*Tell me about your victim and I'll tell you about the offender.*"

However, in cases of suicide, victimology is used to determine and identify any risk factors or suicidal behaviors that could confirm or refute the death as a possible suicide. When risk factors are not present, then the death needs a closer examination.

Interviews with Next of Kin and Family

When investigating other crimes of violence, interviews with the next of kin and family members are fairly standard and expected. Unfortunately, this is not always the case in suspected suicide cases. In suspected suicides, if interviews are conducted, they tend to be superficial and often limited to spouses or significant others. The major exception is incidents involving adolescents or teenagers when parents would naturally be interviewed, because they are the logical next of kin to the deceased.

240   Equivocal Death

However, in cases of adults, typically the main focus is on the spouse or significant other, but efforts to interview siblings or parents is not always conducted. Failure to interview family members is a critical mistake, since in the majority of instances the family is familiar with what has been happening recently in the deceased's life, or if there were any other historical problems. This becomes critical because many homicides are the result of domestic violence incidents. As noted in this text, staging a homicide to look like a suicide is a common occurrence, therefore, it is important in both homicides and suicide cases to interview family members to gain the recent or historical background of the deceased on their living situation. Many instances family members are knowledgeable about potential domestic violence incidents and may in fact have evidence of such violence or other problems within the marriage. It is important to remember that the same motives that may be present and lead to suicide are also present and motives for homicide.

Failure to Interview Significant Witnesses

In the same manner as with family, friends, and perhaps coworkers, should be included in the preliminary investigation. This is true in both homicide and in suspected suicide cases. This is to ensure you get the full picture about the deceased and not a one sides distorted version offered by just the family or spouse. These interviews are also important because they are good sources of victimology because they have seen or interacted with the deceased outside their family. There are many instances when they may have more information about the deceased's current life situation and potential problems than the family.

The effort to locate and interview friends and coworkers does not always happen in many instances of a reported suicide. Again, this is a way to confirm or refute information provided by others.

Failure to Seek Corroborating Evidence

When investigating any criminal offense, corroborating evidence is essential for a successful prosecution, and juries are going to want to see it in some fashion. Corroboration can take on many forms including witness testimony, physical evidence, forensic evidence, and testimonial evidence. Even when working a suspected suicide, efforts should be made to obtain corroboration or confirmation to all to the information about the deceased that was provided by the spouse or family members. Such information, when true, is

Common Investigative Mistakes   241

generally easy to confirm but in all investigations, nothing should be automatically accepted. All information should be verified as much as possible.

Developing Tunnel Vision

Tunnel vision is perhaps one of the most prevalent common errors we find in most unresolved cases, regardless of the crime. It is essentially a dogged insistence to focus on one aspect of the case or one suspect regardless of whether the evidence points in another direction or to other people. Tunnel vision can best be understood through the adage: "don't confuse me with the facts," wherein detectives are determined to have the outcome they want regardless of the evidence that is presented to them. Another term that is frequently used to describe this concept is known as *cognitive or confirmation bias* or "*cafeteria evidence*," wherein the detective accepts as truthful and viable any evidence or facts fitting into their particular theory of the crime and points toward their particular suspect, but discounts or completely ignores anything that disagrees with their theory.

Failure to Consider Motive, Intent, and Ability (MIA) When Considering Suicide

If detectives are looking at the death as a suspected suicide, then they should be looking at MIA – the Motive, Intent, and Ability. Thus, identifying those risk factors or other information that provides the motive for suicide. Remember no one wakes up one morning and just decides to commit suicide, meaning there are motives or reasons for the suicide. The absence of such motives should lead to further investigation. The intent comes from the method that was chosen to end their life, the more lethal the means, the more serious the intent for the victim to end their life. The ability includes the means or method to end their life is present at the scene and the deceased had the physical ability to use that particular method or means.

Conducting an Incomplete Investigation

One of the major failures in suicide or accidental death investigations is conducting an incomplete investigation. This is seen many times when a detective believes a manner of death can be determined by a visual inspection of the scene and one or two minor interviews. If witnesses are identified by the victim or suspect, then they are interviewed but otherwise these detectives feel they are done. It is unclear how this approach can be successful in any criminal investigation, but it is certainly not possible in death investigations. One key question to ask while conducting an accidental or suicide investigation is to determine if there were any other similar deaths in the same family. A second or third "accidental" or suicidal death in the same family bares additional investigation. Although not necessarily unheard or, it is uncommon, especially if any previous family member died in the same general circumstances as the current investigation. Detectives should be looking for any pattern of similar "accidents" or suicides.

Not asking these questions is another aspect of tunnel vision, wherein the detective tries to remain totally and singularly focused on the current investigation and has no intention to widen the scope of the inquiry. Unfortunately, this is how we end up with multiple murder victims that are discovered years later, when some detective finally asks.

Failure to Properly Document Police Activity

Perhaps one of the biggest critiques of the modern detective is the lack of proper documentation and written reports detailing the results of their investigative efforts. Many times, this comes from the general nature of police officers who love to investigate and do all the action orientated things associated with being a detective but seem to avoid putting anything down on paper. This is not because they don't know how to write or prepare a report, but because it is time-consuming and takes away from the "fun" of investigations, of picking up evidence, conducting interrogations, or identifying witnesses. One of the prosecutor's biggest complaints is that investigations are not fully documented. The reluctance to make a written report or to properly document investigative activity can have severe ramifications in the life of the investigation.

There is an adage used to explain the importance of documentation that says: if it's important enough to do; then it's important enough to write a report about it. If it's not important enough to write a report about it, then why did you do it?

There is another investigative adage that applies to this same concept, if it isn't written down, then it didn't happen. The point is that we cannot rely on our memory and often it becomes just as important to document what we were unsuccessful with as it is to document finding a particularly useful piece of evidence. This is especially true when dealing with interviews and testimonial evidence. The best example is conducting an interview with a witness such as a neighbor or close friend without documenting it, and later finding his name on the defense list for court and discovering he made a statement

Common Investigative Mistakes 243

that is favorable to the defense. These situations are avoided by making sure we have conducted those interviews and thoroughly documented the results. Police work, particularly detective work, is all about documentation and report writing. It is part of the job and those unwilling to make their reports are in the wrong profession.

It is critical for the detective to collect all reports and documentation from everyone participating in the investigation. The greater the number of personnel or agencies participating in the process, the greater the chance of missing some reports. As exampled in the previous case study, the suspect was identified within the preliminary investigation and solid evidence linking him to the incident was collected within two months. But because the detectives from different agencies were not talking to each other, they did not share their reports. Thus, the case went cold, and the suspect was involved in another murder.

Any omissions or mistakes within the case file only serve to give defense attorneys fodder for cross-examination and can cause mistrust of the entire investigation by the family. However, it is difficult to criticize the investigation when it was conducted in accordance with established agency protocol, and such efforts were clearly documented.

Failure to Follow Logical Leads

Many times, clear and logical leads for some reason are never pursued. There are always innumerable reasons or excuses for not completing identified leads, but generally the real reason they were never completed is not because the lead wasn't recognized, but rather the detective just didn't want to follow the lead or didn't think it would be beneficial. The traditional thought process has always been that it is always better to run the lead and discover it was not beneficial than to ignore it and find out later that the defense completed the lead themselves and discovered other evidence. Now not only did the defense discover potential evidence catching you off guard, but it can be argued the investigation must be deficient; the defense might then try to make you seem incompetent, biased, untrained, or unprofessional. Once the family receives a copy of the police reports, they will also be able to spot obvious leads that were not followed and thus be able to question the results of the police investigation.

Experience has shown it is almost always easier to do the lead and document the results than to try to find a reason or excuse not to run it. Case Study 12.1 illustrates this failure. Although it involves robbery and homicide, the teaching point is the same for all investigations.

244   Equivocal Death

CASE STUDY 12.1

An armed robbery of a business was committed by two unknown black males driving a small green car. During the robbery, the business owner was shot and killed for not moving fast enough and the off enders fled the scene. There were two witnesses who were slightly roughed up and provided a brief description of the men. The homicide was unresolved and became a cold case. During review of the cold case file, a document used to record information obtained from the TIPS line for the city police department was found. This TIPS line was established so that the public could call the police anonymously with "tips," or information on crimes occurring within the city. The TIPS line call sheet documented a call from an unknown female who identified the two suspects as Tyrone (and last name) along with another male she only knew as Tyrone's cousin (no name provided), and that the car they used belonged to Tyrone's sister (no name given). The caller did not provide any other information. The call came just two days after the robbery and seemed like a very promising lead. The very next document found in the case file was a second TIPS line call sheet reporting a second call two days later (four days after the robbery) by an unidentified male who identified the robbery suspects as Tyrone (last name) and Robert (last name provided) using Tyrone's sister's vehicle. Looking through the remainder of the file, there was no other information about Tyrone, Robert, Tyrone's sister, or the green car. There had been no effort to do any type of background check, or to locate or interview or validate any information on either of the TIPS line information sheets. The case detective was questioned about the TIPS and confirmed knowledge of both Tyrone and Robert confirming that they were cousins and were well-known basic street thugs. The possibility of Tyrone's sister having a green car like the one used in the robbery and reported by the TIPS line was also not pursued. In the detective's opinion, he didn't think they had enough information to even talk with them about the incident, so they continued looking in other directions for the suspect. The detective had never considered even looking at either of the two men as suspects or as a person of interest. Although the tip was not real evidence per se, it could at least provide a starting point.

Months after it was pointed out to the detective the importance of at least trying to locate and interview Tyrone and Robert, the detective still did not think there was enough information to question them and had not further

Common Investigative Mistakes

pursued the investigative lead. Such obvious issues like this in suicide or accidental cases call into question the detective's capabilities and competency.

Investigation Stopped Too Early

The next two common errors are related and go hand in hand with each other. While the police are responsible for investigating the case, it is ultimately the prosecutor that is going to present the case to a jury. Therefore, it is imperative that detectives and prosecutors work closely together. As stated earlier in the book, it is often better when the prosecutor is brought into the case early on to get them involved and interested in the case. This helps to develop ownership of and a personal interest in the case. Even when the prosecutors become involved later, the police must realize the case or investigation is not over until the offender has been convicted. There are many occasions when detectives can expect to be actively pursuing leads and interviewing additional witnesses who have surfaced even during the trial. Unfortunately, there is sometimes a serious disconnect between the police and the prosecutor over duties and responsibilities. The following case study demonstrates these problems.

Failure to Fully Exploit Digital Evidence

Although many times police have seized or collected various digital devices, they are not always exploited. Meaning they are not examined for any chats, internet searches, texts, and phone calls. Additionally, there are many times when detectives have submitted digital devices for examination; however, when the results are returned to them, they do not actually read the results. Therefore, they have no idea what is contained within the device.

Overdependence on Forensic Evidence

Detectives can expect several instances when they must investigate a crime where there is little, if any, physical evidence, or any eyewitnesses that can point them in the right direction. Additionally, the evidence they do recover might not necessarily point to a particular person. Therefore, it is incumbent upon detectives to develop these other skills to locate additional evidence needed to resolve the case. While forensic evidence is a vital part of criminal investigations, there tends to be an overdependence on forensics. An example is in a new case if forensic evidence is present, then detectives know exactly what to do. If it is not present, many detectives are lost. They have become so overly dependent on forensics that if it is not available, they are lost. This is a weakness of the modern detective. We see this demonstrated many times when talking with detectives who report the case is paused "pending lab results." The best guidance in all instances of the investigation is to immediately submit all evidence to the laboratory for analysis, but then proceed as if the lab report will not be helpful. If the laboratory analysis later proves helpful, then it is a bonus. If the analysis is not helpful, then the case has not gone cold as it was still being pursued while "pending lab."

Misunderstanding Forensic Analysis

Along the same lines as overdependence on forensic evidence, a second aspect of forensic examination presents another problem: the misunderstanding of forensic results from the crime lab. We have found repeatedly that the police have correctly identified, collected, and forwarded the items of physical evidence to the laboratory for examination. But, once the report was received, detectives frequently just place it into the file as if they are checking off a box on a checklist, but they never take the time to really understand the report itself or what exactly the examination revealed. Even worse, they misinterpret the lab report. The following case study is an example.

CASE STUDY 12.2

When reviewing a cold case, the case detectives reported a negative laboratory analysis for evidence submitted on the case. However, when the file was reviewed, the crime scene examination was well documented. This included scene photography and evidence collected. Therefore, the negative lab analysis did not seem right when compared to the type of evidence that, according to the crime scene report, was recovered. Several lab reports dealing with DNA analysis were found and carefully examined. The first was a lab report that acknowledged request for DNA analysis in one paragraph and in the next paragraph advised the agency the lab had conducted a preliminary screening of the evidence and noted the presence of blood. The third paragraph, however, advised the agency if they still wanted the DNA analysis to be completed, they needed to reconfirm the request with the crime lab. The second lab report simply stated that since the agency had not *reconfirmed* their DNA request, the evidence was being returned to the agency. The case detective had misinterpreted the two reports as a negative finding. However, because of the expense of completing the DNA analysis, the crime lab had established a protocol requiring the agency to reconfirm the necessity of the analysis after the initial screening. Essentially, the crime lab was requiring the same analysis request to be made twice. In this case when the agency did not respond, the evidence was repackaged and sent back to the agency. The detective, not having totally understood the laboratory report, was under the impression that no offender DNA was identified from the evidence submitted. Unfortunately, as stated earlier, the detectives were also so convinced the forensic evidence was going to identify their offender, they had paused the investigation pending the results of the crime lab examination. Now, some 18 months later they discovered it was never examined.

In another example, detectives believed the latent prints from the crime scene were unidentifiable or did not match their suspect. However, the lab report indicated the recovered latent print was a palm print, but the detectives only submitted known fingerprint cards and not *major case prints* which would include the palms of the suspect's hands. The answer was simply to obtain the palm prints of the suspect and resubmit for analysis.

Another example dealt with Questioned Documents, wherein the detective believed the examiner was not able to match the handwriting of the suspect to a document. In reality, the report stated the examination was limited due to insufficient standards or known writing of the suspect submitted for comparison and the exemplars taken from the suspect were not correctly done.

The detective wrongly interpreted this as a non-match, but again the problem was simply that the detective did not take the time to completely read and understand the report. The only way to stop this problem is to encourage detectives to pick up the phone when they receive a negative report and talk personally to the lab examiner or talk to their supervisors to make sure they understand exactly what the report says and what it means to the rest of the investigation.

Failure to Send Evidence to the Lab

Perhaps the most common investigative mistake is the failure to send the evidence to the crime laboratory in the first place. There are literally thousands

248   Equivocal Death

of rape kits that were collected from victims during their physical examination that were collected by the police and logged into their evidence room but were never submitted for laboratory examination. There are many reasons behind not submitting these kits but very few of these reasons are valid. There was a time when the thought process was if we don't have a suspect, there is no reason to send in the kits for examination. With the advent of the Combined DNA Index System (CODIS) this should no longer be a consideration. Evidence, especially rape kits, should be submitted automatically to the lab for analysis.

Lack of Supervisory Oversight

Supervising a detective unit is not just about monitoring schedules, assigning cases, and monitoring training, supplies, and equipment. These tasks are all part of the responsibility of any supervisor. However, a detective supervisor has another important function, and it is one of the weakest points in US policing today. This major function is the review and oversight of individual cases to make certain the detectives are staying on track. Much of what has been written in this chapter about mistakes and investigative failures in the investigative process could be avoided if proper oversight was conducted by a supervisor who is monitoring the work of their assigned detectives. But this is not a widely held belief among US detectives. In fact, whenever we talk about this aspect of investigations to detectives during service training classes, there is often an open and loud hostility and attitude of rejection of the concept of someone reviewing or supervising their work. This is probably based on the type of personality of the individuals attracted to detective work in the first place – the independent self-starters and logical thinkers. They tend to place themselves in a category of being the exclusive determiner of what is important and what is not important in their cases and therefore guard their case file as if it were some sort of top secret, not yet copyrighted collection of their genius.

Unfortunately, this creates those situations and investigative failures as described in the various case studies in this chapter and throughout the book. An example of how these concepts might influence an investigation is noted in Case Study 12.3.

CASE STUDY 12.3

A state police agency had no centralized repository for any criminal investigations conducted by their detectives. It was the agency's policy that the original case file, whether it resulted in an arrest and conviction

Common Investigative Mistakes

or closed as unsolved, would be retained by the case detective. When they retired, they literally kept their files, including photographs, negatives, interview recordings, and all reports and notes at their residence. The concept was that it was their investigation, so they should keep their files. Years later when working cold cases, one of the first steps was to go find the original detective or in some cases his widow and try to locate and obtain the original file so that it could be worked again. When the file could not be located, there was no follow-up for an unsolved cold case homicide. This 50-year-old policy was finally changed in 2005 when a centralized repository for the original case files was created.

For individual case supervision, what exactly is important is usually case or event dependent, but it is certainly necessary to ensure that basic investigative steps are being taken in a timely manner. Such steps include making sure that evidence is sent to the lab, witnesses are interviewed on a timely basis, alibis are properly checked out, other investigative leads are completed, and the detective is still engaged throughout the investigation, even after an arrest is made.

Chapter Summary

If detectives were perfect and did not require any supervision, then there would be no need for a chapter on investigative failures. It is both sad and frustrating to even have to write this chapter because these mistakes could so easily be avoided. There are also very few instances where one single error or mistake causes a case to go unresolved. Most of the time failure to resolve a case is the result of a combination of events or series of mistakes that cause the case to bog down, frustration sets in, and the detective becomes inundated with newer cases, or simply loses interest.

Understanding the most common errors hopefully will spark awareness in detectives and their supervisors and help keep them on track and lead to more successful case resolutions. Victims, their families, and our communities are all depending on us to do the right thing, find the bad guys, and bring them to justice.

Reference

Geberth, V. J. (2013). The Seven Mistakes in Suicide Investigation. *Law & Order Magazine*, 61, 1.

Appendix
Homicide Staged as a Suicide

This case study is an example of an agency's protocol calling for a complete investigation into every death and the results. This case study is an example that when the investigation is completed correctly with proper crime scene examination, laboratory analysis of evidence, and follow-up investigative effort a wrong conclusion can be initially made.

In March of 1991, the police responded to a residence following a 911 call from a neighbor of an injured person in the house next door. A new detective was in the area and was the first one on the scene. He met a distraught husband in front of the house who reported his wife was inside and apparently had shot herself. The man led the detective into the house and to the master bedroom. The detective observed the woman lying flat on her back, pillows under her head, but with blood streaming from an injury to her head. He observed a small caliber pistol in her right hand, that was lying across her abdomen. The detective checked for signs of life and be believed he could feel a pulse and believed the woman was still breathing. He removed the gun from her hand and began CPR in the bed but was hampered because as he pushed down on her chest the mattress also was pushed down. By this time EMTs arrived and assisted the detective moving the woman into the living room of the house where she was placed onto the floor, and they began CPR again. A second EMT arrived with a stretcher, and she was moved onto the stretched and transported to the ambulance and then to the local hospital's emergency room. However, the woman was pronounced dead upon arrival at the hospital emergency room. Doctors were then able to determine she had suffered a penetrating gunshot wound to the right temple but did not appear to have suffered any other trauma.

Based on agency protocol, detectives and crime scene personnel were summoned to the scene and began to conduct a crime scene examination and preliminary investigation. The scene was documented by video and crime scene photographs. As the scene was being examined, detectives found three envelopes and three separate letters on the bed or on the floor at the foot of the bed. Based on their content, they were consistent with suicide notes. Two other pages of notebook paper with writing that seemed to be a list of complaints such as: "Won't help with the kids. Doesn't pay attention to me anymore. Makes me do everything. Tired of being told I'm not a good mother. Coming down too hard on the kids. Telling me I'm depressed or have mental issues." Detectives also found a .22 caliber revolver on the bed where it has been tossed by the responding detective after removing it from the deceased hand.

The detectives also discovered that there were two children a 5-year-old and 3-year-old daughters who were sleeping in the bedroom next to the master bedroom. The children were brought to the neighbor's house who had made the 911 call. Once the children were safe, the husband agreed to be questioned by detectives.

The initial responding detective arrived back at the scene to brief the others that were processing the crime scene. The responding detective went over his actions upon arrival, finding the victim in bed, feeling a pulse, and removing the gun from her hand. In his statement the detective recorded that the gun was "clutched" in her hand. Without any further questioning the detective was asked to return to his office and prepare a written report on his actions.

During his initial questioning, the husband provided a statement to detectives and explained that his wife was currently experiencing some stress and being treated for depression and was even prescribed Prozac. She had a recent history of mental issues but seemed like things were going much better lately. He also described his activity earlier that night by noting he came home from work, changed clothes, and then went to a small night club where he worked on weekends as a DJ. He went to meet with some friends and to check on his equipment to make sure everything was secure. He only stayed for a little while and then returned to find his wife in bed having shot herself. He saw the envelopes on the bed, and he believed he opened them and read the contents. He then dropped them to the floor and went next door to ask his neighbor to call 911 and get some help for his wife. He provided the police with a list of names to confirm his whereabouts at the nightclub and was then allowed to leave to take care of his children.

Awhile later the ME (medical examiner's) investigator having already collected the victim's body, arrived to view the scene and was briefed on the possible suicide notes and the initial detective's actions upon entering the scene. Detectives then stated that the victim was found with the gun held "tightly" in her hand.

Appendix 253

The ME investigator later prepared his own written report noting the circumstances as related by the detectives concerning the scene and notes, but then adding the gun was in her hand in a *"death grip."*

A forensic autopsy was conducted the following day, and the ME concluded based on the injury, the initial scene examination, the notes, and the presence of the weapon in her hand, the manner of death was determined to be suicide. One of the factors was finding the gun in her hand in a "death grip." This has a special meaning, and it refers to cadaveric spasm which is basically an instantaneous rigor mortis or stiffening of the body after death. What is so important about this phenomenon is this cannot be simulated, and it cannot be reproduced, so if the gun was found in her hand in a "death grip," then the gun had to have been in her hand at the time of death. At autopsy the victim was also found to be about six weeks pregnant.

Following the autopsy, the remains were released to a funeral home where the husband immediately had his wife cremated. This action took place even before he contacted his in-laws to report her death. This action is only significant because the husband and wife had been married for about 10 years, they had also grown up in the same small town, and the husband was well acquainted with his in-laws including his wife's siblings. Yet there was no effort to contact them to report her death before she was cremated.

In most agencies when the ME reports the manner of death as suicide, the police generally suspend any further investigative action. However, the responding agency in this case had a different protocol that required a full investigation of every reported death. Therefore, the letters were sent to the criminal laboratory for fingerprint and handwriting analysis and the gun sent to firearms for their analysis. Based on her reported mental health issues, detectives interviewed the victim's mental health counselors and psychiatrists. A canvas interview was also conducted of the neighbors and the husband's coworkers. the other witnesses that were at the night club were all located and interviewed to establish and verify his alibi.

The police were also able to locate several other customers who confirmed the husband's presence at the club as he stated. The wife's mental health counselors were interviewed and confirmed that she was initially seen for "depression," but her issues or problems turned out to be more marriage related. She felt her husband was neglecting her, was too controlling and was not helping around the house. She was also upset that she was not allowed to have her own money or leave the house without his permission. She had no access to a vehicle and was responsible only for taking care of the house and the children and to have sex with him whenever he wanted it. She had also expressed concern that her husband was involved in something unusual, because he was getting calls in the middle of the night and having to leave.

254   Appendix

According to her counselor, she had confronted him once with suspicions of infidelity and the husband "confessed" that he was part of a special government unit, and he was called out from time to time to do unsavory things. He insisted he did not want to worry his wife so he couldn't tell her of his secret missions. The counselor was certain that this was a lie, but the wife seemed to be a little naive and wanted to believe the story, probably because she did not want to face the fact he may be engaging in an extra marital affair. The counselor also provided that the wife only came to counseling on the insistence of her husband because of her "*depression*" and was initially prescribed "Prozac" to help with her depression complaint

The wife's family was clearly insistent during the initial investigation that the wife would not have committed suicide and provided some derogatory background information on the husband as evidence of their suspicions. The detectives investigating the case were also suspicious of the death and many believed the husband was somehow responsible. Especially after they learned the husband had collected $150,000 from a life insurance policy on the wife. However, when the laboratory analysis of the evidence confirmed the notes were written by the victim, that her fingerprints were found on the letters, combined with her reported history of depression, mental health issues, and no other solid evidence, the case was closed as a suicide some six months later. One last unexplained factor was her toxicology report that revealed that there was no alcohol or Prozac in her system at the time of her death. Medical personnel estimated that she had not been taking Prozac for at least two weeks.

In November 1991, the husband was contacted by the police agency and notified that the case was completed and was going to be closed as a suicide. The husband asked for the return of all the evidence police collected during the investigation as he intended to file a wrongful death lawsuit against the pharmaceutical company that manufactured Prozac, stating his believe his wife took her own life because she was taking the drug. All the evidence collected during the scene examination was eventually released to the husband and the case was closed.

Three months later, a witness came forward to the police with new information alleging the wife's death might not have been a suicide and implied she might have been murdered by the husband. The witness then provided detailed information that was either not known at the time of the initial investigation or was never corroborated. The witness provided the following information:

1. At the time of his wife's death, the husband was involved in an extra marital affair with another woman and they frequented the same club where the husband worked as a DJ.

Appendix 255

2. The husband and his mistress were so open in their relationship, that other customers at the bar actually thought the two were married.
3. The husband collected $150,000 in life insurance, immediately bought a new vehicle, a boat, and new DJ equipment.
4. Within two weeks of the wife's death, the husband moved this "girl-friend" into his house along with her two kids.
5. After the police closed their investigation the husband and other woman were married.
6. Prior to moving into the house, the husband had placed a help wanted ad in the local newspaper looking for a *"live-in nanny."* He made his girlfriend fill out an application and then "hired her." He then paid her $300.00 a month for being a *nanny*. This was done in case he was ever challenged for moving her into the house.
7. The witness was in the club the night of the wife's death and was sitting at the same table with the husband and girlfriend. The husband made a big announcement that he asked his wife for a divorce, and he would soon be single. Then after a while he stated he was concerned for her because she had taken the news badly. He left to make a phone call (This was before cell phones were available). At the same time the witness said she also got up to make a phone call at the bank of pay phones in the club lobby, the only place to make phone calls at the night club. But the husband was not there. The witness made her call and then returned to the table. About 20 minutes later the husband came into the club, red-faced and was out of breath. He stated that he had talked to his wife, and she was not doing well. He was concerned for her safety, so he left to go home. The witness noted that when he left to make a phone call, he was wearing a purple nylon jacket, but when he returned from the phone call about 20 minutes later, he wasn't wearing the jacket.
8. Lastly, the witness provided the name of another witness who had spoken to the girlfriend at the club later that same night and upon his arrival the girlfriend told him the "wife had committed suicide." But this was before the 911 call was ever received.

Based on this new information, a new detective not associated with the first investigation reopened the case to further investigate. During the first review of the crime scene photos the detective noted a purple jacket on the doorknob of the master bedroom. This photo was later shown to the witness

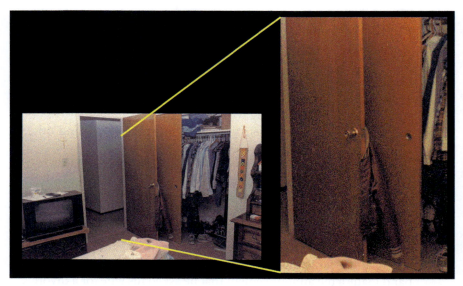

Figure A.1 The purple jacket on the master bedroom doorknob was identified by witnesses as the jacket worn by the husband when he left to make the phone call and was not worn when he returned.

who identified it as the jacket worn by the husband when he left the club to make his call but was not wearing it when he returned. See Figure A.1.

In other scene photographs, the detective noted the vial of Prozac was on a shelf on a dresser in the master bedroom. The vial seemed out of place because other medicines were located in the medicine cabinet in the bathroom. Also observed below the vial of medicine, was a double page newspaper article from the local paper, about people committing suicide while prescribed Prozac. See Figure A.2.

After familiarizing with the case, the first investigative step was communicating with the family of the deceased woman. This was to advise them the case was being reopened but also was seeking information on the victim for a victimology assessment, and some general background info on her husband. The family's reaction was almost overwhelming in their approval to reopen the case. Apparently, they had repeatedly attempted to provide additional information concerning the husband's past and their suspicion that he had murdered his wife. Their information was found in the case file, but most of the information and potential leads were never followed up. After receipt of the lab reports, the decision was made to close the case as a suicide.

In a lengthy and detailed .interview, the family was able to provide the following information concerning the husband and his wife. This included.

Appendix

Figure A.2 This figure depicted the vial of Prozac that was in plain sight on the dresser of the master bedroom. Just below the shelf is the newspaper article about Prozac suicides.

1. The wife thought she was pregnant again and had stopped taking Prozac a few weeks before. She was waiting for an opportunity to tell her husband she was going to have another child.
2. She was excited for the new child and was looking forward to another baby in the family. As a stay-at-home mom, she was very attentive to her other daughters and to her house.
3. The husband had a spotted career prior to his enlistment and was known in their small town as a thief and petty criminal.
4. The husband was always claiming he was finding things – like several pairs of new pants that just happened to be his size as well as tools and other such items that suddenly appeared at his apartment that he claimed he "found."
5. Every apartment he lived in he made a burglary complaint and filed an insurance claim for missing stolen property. (A later review of

the police reports noted each incident was in a different police jurisdiction and each report was very similar to the other reports.)

6. He was arrested for burglary in his hometown for breaking into a business and attempted to steal some property. This was not discovered during the initial investigation.
7. That he was an assistant Boy Scout leader in their small town and had volunteered to help out selling Christmas trees as a way of fund raising., In the three years he was involved in the Christmas tree sales they experienced break-ins and theft of some trees. This had never happened before and had never happened since he left. The family had received information that the husband and his brother had rented a truck and took the stolen trees to another spot and sold them and kept the money. The police could not make a case based on the information.
8. The family was very concerned about another incident that took place out of state when the couple and one child was living in a mobile home. The wife woke up one morning to a fire in the living room. The mobile home was filled with smoke, but she managed to get outside and alert neighbors who came over and managed to put the fire out as the fire department was arriving. The wife discovered that her husband and 2-year-old child were not in the residence at the time with no explanation where they were. The firemen cleared the smoke and discovered that both smoke detectors that were hard wired into the trailer had been disconnected. Shortly after the fire department arrived the husband drove up. He explained he had taken their child out for a ride to help her fall asleep. At the time of this fire, the husband had a $100,000 insurance policy on his wife.
9. The husband was also considered a person of interest in the disappearance and suspected murder of a teenaged female who was a resident of a "youth camp" for problem kids and where he worked..

The detective continued to locate numerous witnesses that were not found during the initial investigation and who provided additional background information on the husband. The detective discovered that the husband had changed the story about the night his wife died depending on who he was talking to. He told the police and friends that he had gone to the club and returned to find her dead. He told other female friends that he went to the store to buy ice cream for his kids and his wife shot herself in the few minutes he was away. This also happened when questioning witnesses that were present for the mobile home fire. He told the fire department and police that he had taken his child out for a drive because she was not sleeping.

Appendix 259

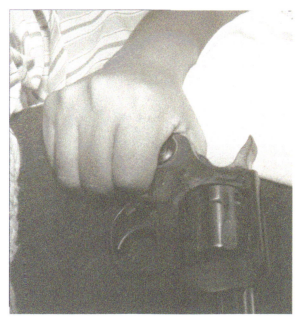

Figure A.3 This figure depicts the gun placed in the deceased hand during a reenactment. The pistol is in her hand as found by the first responding detective.

He told his boss and coworkers that he had helped extinguish the fire and rescued his wife.

One of the most important witnesses was the first responding detective because he was the only one that had observed the wife in bed after her injury. During a reenactment the detective placed the pistol in the hands of a female who was posing as the victim while lying down in a bed. The detective was asked to put the gun in the female's hand as he remembered seeing the gun in the deceased's hand. See Figure A.3.

However, the detective observed that all four fingers of the right hand were wrapped around the butt of the pistol. The new detective confirmed that this was how he observed the pistol in her hand. If that were so, then how was the victim able to put thew weapon up to her head and pull the trigger? See Figure A.4.

He was then asked about removing the gun from the wife's hand and he stated that he simply picked up her wrist and the gun fell into his hand. If this was the case then cadaveric spasm was not possible, as the rigor mortis would require effort to remove the fingers from the weapon. The new detective stated that no one had ever asked him about how the weapon was in her hand

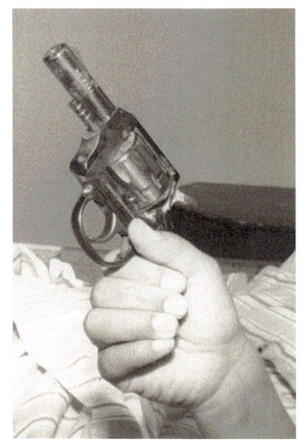

Figure A.4 With all four fingers around the butt of the pistol the wife would not be able to pull the trigger.

or about how he removed the pistol. The presence of what the ME attributed to cadaveric spasm was totally eliminated as a possibility.

The detective was eventually able to develop sufficient probable cause to obtain a search warrant for the husband's residence and was able to recover all of the evidence that was originally collected during the crime scene examination and returned to the husband when the case was closed.

Examining the evidence, the detective asked for additional forensic examinations. At this time DNA was still in its infant stage so the DNA extraction and analysis was a long process. The detective requested the crime lab examine the envelop flaps that had sealed each of the envelopes and search for the husband DNA. After a long wait for the analysis, the crime lab was able to find the husband's DNA on an envelope flap that sealed the envelope.

Appendix 261

This was important because the letter that was inside that particular envelope was addressed to the wife's sister and the opening sentence said that the husband was not aware of this letter and asked the sister not to tell him.

The letters themselves were consistent with what a normal suicide note might say, but a forensic psychiatrist noted that after reviewing the wife's results from taking the Minnesota Multiphasic Personality Inventory, more commonly known as the MMPI, is a psychological test that measures personality traits and psychopathology. The results indicated that she would be the type of person to write these letters and then leave them to be found by her husband. Her intention was for her husband to find them and pay attention to her. Although she wrote the notes, the psychiatrist believed she lacked the "energy" to actually follow through and commit suicide.

The reinvestigation took over a year to accumulate the necessary evidence, but the husband was eventually indicted for his wife's murder and later tried. In an unusual twist of circumstances, it was the defense arguing the wife's death was a suicide and the prosecution was arguing the death was a homicide. After a three-week trial the husband was convicted of murder and aggravated arson and attempted murder for the mobile home fire several years earlier.

Summary

In this case, the husband clearly murdered his wife and then staged the scene to appear as a suicide, the difference was the police response, and initially treating the death as a possible homicide and collected evidence, thoroughly documented the scene, and continued with a good preliminary investigation. The initial investigation lasted over eight months until the leads were exhausted and the initial forensic examinations were completed but did not provide enough evidence to counter to what the husband was claiming. Again, because of all of the work accomplished during the eight months of active investigation, when the case was reopened there was a tremendous amount of information and evidence available unlike many other cases.

Index

51% rule of suicide, 84, 105, 129, 135, 162
911 emergency notification system, 5, 10, 25, 26, 32–33, 140, 199, 205, 214, 218, 224, 251, 252, 255

A

Ability to commit suicide, 144–146
Acceptance, process of, 19
Accidental "chemsex", 168
Accidental deaths, 2–3, 8, 20, 61, 71, 102, 108, 242
   accidental falls, 203–208
   accidental fires, 208–213
   circumstances of, 221–222
      antemortem behaviors and events, 222–231
      limiting physical abilities, 222
   by coincidence, 199, 206, 212, 214, 234
   by drowning, 213–216
   firearm accidental deaths, 216–219
   leading cause of, 197
   meaning of, 197
   multiple "accidents", 231–235
   preliminary investigation of, 199–200
   preventable, 199
   responding to, 197–199
   themes used to stage a homicide, 198
   vehicle accidents, 200–203
   victimology and, 221–222
Accidental falls, 203–208
Accidental fires, 208–213
Accidental hanging, 102–103
Accusatory notes, 164
Actual suicide, 44, 179, 195
Adams, Evie, 174
Ad hoc staged scenes, 40–41
Adolescents, 117–119
   maturity and life experiences, 117–118
   subjective criteria for, 118

   suicides due to
      being a burden for their families, 119
      bullying, 117–118
Algor mortis, 85
Anger, as cause of suicide, 18, 20
Anorectal eroticism, 103
Anoxia, gratification achieved through, 102
Antemortem (before death events), 75
   activities of the victim, 28–32
   suicidal behaviors, 108, 134
Armed robbery, 28, 244
Asphyxia, death caused due to, 101–102, 204
Asphyxiophilia, 102
Attended deaths, 82
Autoerotic deaths, 102–103
Autoeroticism, 102
Autoerotic misadventures, 55, 102–103
Autopsy, 45, 47, 55, 81–83, 131, 143, 229
   to correlate an injury to objects producing the injury, 100
   for determining
      cause of death, 79, 83–84
      death caused by drug overdose, 103–104
      manner of death, 79, 83–84
      time of death, 84–86
   failure to request or conduct for, 238
   gunshot wounds, 87
   hanging and asphyxia, 101
   hanging injuries, 101–102
   identification and documenting of all injuries, 86
   important information and evidence obtained through, 82
   incised wounds, 95–96
   information made available by ME at the time of, 80–81
   location of injury, 87–89, 97
   psychological, 152–154
      outlines for, 154–155

263

Index

requirement to conduct, 79
shape of wounds, 97–98
for sharp force injuries, 93–95
stab wounds, 96
toxicology analysis for determining cause
of death, 104
types of
clinical, 81
forensic, 81, 104, 253
wound orientation, 98–100

B

Banzai charges, 180
Beck, Simone, 164–165
Believe nothing and verify everything,
concept of, 136
Bleeding from injuries, 95
Body cooling, as way to determine time of
death, 85
Bullying, suicides due to, 117–118
Burned bridges, concept of, 71–72
Bushido, ideals of, 180

C

Cafeteria evidence, 135, 241
Canter, David, 170–171
Canvass interviews, 24, 26, 121, 125–126
Carbon monoxide inhalation, 149
Cardiac tamponade, 88, 102
Cause and manner of death, 9–10, 83
Center for Disease Control (CDC), 12, 197,
213
Chancellor, A. S., 7, 32, 34, 39–40, 44, 49–50,
52, 54–55, 59, 129, 141, 150, 198,
202–203, 206, 216
Chesire Hospital (United Kingdom), 166
Child abduction, 108
Child injury, 108
Chubbuck, Christine, 54, 183
Clinical autopsies, 81
Cognitive bias, 27, 157, 241
Combined DNA Index System (CODIS), 248
Committing suicide, documented methods
of, 149
Common investigative mistakes
by assuming a suicide posture, 237
complacency and routine cases, 236

by conducting an incomplete
investigation, 241–242
by developing tunnel vision, 241
failure to
believe or listen to the family,
237–238
conduct victimology assessment, 239
consider motive, intent, and ability
(MIA) when considering
suicide, 241
follow logical leads, 243–245
fully exploit digital evidence, 245
interview significant witnesses, 240
look for also and validate risk
factors, 239
obtain toxicological samples, 238
properly document police activity,
242–243
request or conduct an autopsy, 238
seek corroborating evidence,
240–241
send evidence to the lab, 247–248
improper scene documentation, 237
interviews with next of kin and family,
239–240
investigation stopped too early, 245
lack of supervisory oversight, 248–249
by misunderstanding forensic analysis,
246–247
overdependence on forensic evidence,
245–246
Complacency and routine cases, concept of,
236, 237
Complex suicides, 35, 45, 142–144
Confirmation bias, 135, 139, 168, 241
Crime scene
arrival of detectives to, 66–69
CSI response to, 69–71
from detective's perspective, 74–75
determination of the time of
death, 75–76
documentation of, 24, 25–26, 73–74
examination of, *see* examination of
crime scene
first responders role, 64–66
photography of, 26
release of the body, 76
responding to reported deaths, 59–64
search beyond the, 77

Index   265

Crime scene staging, 39–40
  ad hoc staged scenes, 40–41
  as an effort to protect the family, 55
  behavioral evidence for, 75
  case study of, 34, 45–47, 51–53
  categories of, 39
  concept of, 39, 56
  done with criminal intent, 39
  efforts to misdirect a police investigation,
    40, 44, 50
  as effort to divert attention, 40
  false information provided by
    witnesses, 39
  information in relation to, 7
  motives behind, 43–44
  as need for the offender's self-
    preservation, 40
  original motive, 43
  premeditated staged scenes, 41–43
  primary staging, 40
  in relation to sex offenses or sexual
    homicides, 50
  secondary staging, 50–54
  staging motive, 43
  for suicides that are staged to resemble
    homicides, 44–49
  tertiary or incidental scene alterations,
    54–56, 62
Crime scene technicians, 70, 74–75
  professional disagreement with
    detectives, 71
Crime, theory of, 135–137
Criminal conduct, covering up of, 44
Criminal negligence, resulting in the
    death, 71
Cyber bullying, 118

D

"Date-rape" drug, 168
Death grip, 253
Death investigations
  basic investigative concept in, 3
  detective's role in, 2
  by establishing and maintaining a good
    working relationship with the
    deceased's family, 19–22
Defensive wounds, 47, 93, 95, 190
Depression, 12–13, 19, 39, 116, 148, 252–254

Detective(s)
  arrival to a death scene, 66–69
  basic questions that a detective should be
    asking themselves, 66
  crime scene perspectives, 74–75
  decisions based upon their gut
    feeling, 136
  filing of a search warrant, 77–78
  goal of, 2
    disproving various hypotheses, 136
  job training, 1
  professional disagreement with crime
    scene technicians, 71
  role in death investigations, 2, 133
  service training classes, 248
Diffusion of responsibility, psychological
    phenomenon of, 165
Distance determination, between the
    weapon and the injury site, 89–91
DNA analysis, 125, 246–247
Domestic violence, 2, 4, 11, 40, 61, 71, 86,
    113–114, 188–191, 240
Dramatic performance, suicide as, 181–184
Drowning, accidental deaths by, 213–216
Drug overdose, death caused by, 103–104,
    197
Drug-related deaths, 156, 168
Duty, virtue of, 194
Dwyer, Budd, 183
Dwyer, Robert, 54, 183

E

Electronic communications, 147
Episodic grief, 19
Equivocal deaths, 10–11, 28, 159
  suicide notes and, 168–169
e-Suicide notes, 162
Evidence
  cafeteria evidence, 241
  collection of, 24, 134–135
  destruction of, 25
  failure to
    seek corroborating evidence, 240–241
    send evidence to the lab, 247–248
  false evidence, 56
  forensic, 21, 172, 240
  hearsay, 171
  photographs of crime scene, 26

266 Index

physical, 26, 240
of prior suicide attempts, 93
testimonial, 240
Exaggeration, concept of, 213
Examination of crime scene, 24, 221, 237, 251
case study of, 33
completion of, 77–78
concept of, 70–71
to determine
cause of death, 71
time of death, 74–75
documentation of scene for
photography, 73–74
sketching, 74
written notes for, 74
movement of things inside a crime
scene, 71–72
Explanatory notes, 163
Extra marital affair, 54, 127, 145, 204, 211–212, 223, 254

F

Facebook, 117, 164–165
False evidence, 56
willingness of the offender to produce, 56
FBI Behavioral Science Unit, 7, 107
Final Exit (Derek Humphry, 1997), 80, 196
Fingerprint, analysis of, 147
Firearms
accidental deaths, 216–219
homicidal and suicidal events
involving, 87
suicides by, 41
First responders, duties of
in a violent crime, 64
Forensic autopsies, 81, 104–105, 253
Forensic evidence, 21, 240
loss of, 172
overdependence on, 245–246
Forensic examination, in homicide
investigations, 91
Forensic linguistics, 147, 172–175
Forensic pathologists, 81–82, 86
Forensic pathology, 81
Forensic techniques, used for collecting
evidence, 73
Forensic technology, 1
Foster, Vince, 14–15

G

Gamma-hydroxybutyrate (GHB),
see "date-rape" drug
Geberth, Vernon, 3–4, 13, 26–27, 135, 237
Gilfoyle, Paula, 169–170
Goebbels, Joseph, 192
Graham, G. D., 7, 32, 34, 39–40, 44, 49–50, 52, 54–55, 59, 129, 141, 150, 198, 202–203, 206, 216
Grief, stages of
acceptance, 19
anger, 18, 20
bargaining, 18
denial, 17–18
depression, 19
Gunshot injuries, 87, 238
correlating the weapon with, 91–92
distance between firearm and injury, 89–91
pattern of, 91–92
self-inflicted, 88
suicide events, 87

H

Handwriting, analysis of, 37, 147, 175
Hanging injuries, 101–102
death caused by, 101
inverted "V" pattern injury, 102
Hazelwood, Roy, 43, 107, 239
Hearsay evidence, 171
Heroic glory, definition of, 194–195
Hesitation wounds, 93–98
High-risk victim, 126–127
Hilton, David, 165
Homicidal ligature strangulation, 101–102
Homicides, 1–2, 6, 25, 67
categories of, 28
negligent homicide, 2
premeditated, 34
reasons for treating every death case
as, 3–7
suicides staged to resemble, 150–152, 251–261

I

Impulsivity, to suicidal acts, 160
Incised wounds, 94, 95–96, 100, 189–190
Incomplete investigation, conduct of, 241–242

Index

"In custody" hanging deaths, in jails, 101
Industrial accidents, 198
Instagram, 117, 165
Instructional notes, 164
Intention, to commit suicide, 141–142
 evidence of irrational thought, 186
 minimal evidence of, 186–187
 primary indicators of, 185
 psychological intent, 154
 secondary indicators of, 185–186
Interfamilial conflicts, 125, 198
Interpersonal conflicts, 71, 125
Interviews
 failure to interview significant
  witnesses, 240
 with next of kin and family, 239–240
Inverted "V" pattern injury, 102
Investigation stopped too early,
 consequences of, 245
Investigative plan (IP), 135, 137–139

J

Japanese Kamikaze pilots, 180
Jewish rebels, mass suicide of, 179
Job training, for detectives, 1
Judicial hangings, as a form of execution, 101
Justice
 definition of, 192–194
 obstruction of, 55

K

Kennedy, John F., 181
Kübler-Ross, E., 17

L

Lacerations, 95
Last communications, *see* suicide notes
Latent investigation for suicides
 after the preliminary investigation,
  131–133
 based on the 51% rule of suicide, 135
 case study, 131–133
 collection of evidence, 134–135
 general suicide investigative concepts,
  148–150
 homicide investigative considerations,
  139–140

importance of, 133–134
investigative plan (IP), 137–139
of recent changes to wills or insurance,
 147–148
scientific method, 136–137
suicide investigative considerations
 intent, 141–142
 motive, 140–141
of suicide notes, 147
of suicides staged to resemble homicides,
 150–152
and theory of the crime, 135–136
use of psychological autopsy for, 152–156
Lester, D., 181
Life crisis, 82
Life insurance policy, 5, 20, 44, 223, 233, 254
Lines of Langer, 97
Live streaming, of a suicide, 165–166
Livor mortis, 85
Logical leads, failure to follow, 243–245
Low-risk victim, 127–128

M

Mass suicides, 179–180
McVey, Timothy, 195
Medical Examiner (ME), 9, 79, 80–81, 204
Mental health, victim's state of, 12–13
Mental illness, 153, 160
Mercy, concept of, 191–192
Military suicides, 180–181
Minnesota Multiphasic Personality
 Inventory (MMPI), 261
Mode of dying, 80
Money laundering, 49
Motive, Intent, and Ability (M.I.A.), 140, 241
Motive, Opportunity, and the Means
 (M.O.M.), to commit the
 homicide, 139–140
Motive, to commit suicide, 140–141
Murder-suicide, 187–191
Myths, related to homicide/suicide, 88

N

National Center for Health Statistics, US, 197
National Safety Council, US, 203
Natural death, 4, 6, 71, 172
Negligent homicide, 2
"New media" note-leavers, 162

Index

New Religious Movements (NRM), 180
Ngo Dien Diem, 181
Non-fatal injuries, 93

O

Occam's Razor, concept of, 139
Online dating, 115–116
Online harassment, 118–119
Organized assassins, 179

P

Peer pressure, 115–116
Personal conflicts, 28, 43, 198, 238
Peterson, Drew, 213–214
Photography, of crime scene, 26, 73–74, 252
Physiological changes, after death, 75
Planned complex suicide, 142–143
Police activity, failure to properly document,
242–243
Police assistance, call for, 3
Police investigation, 6, 8, 10, 16, 38–40, 42,
44, 49–50, 56, 59, 86, 122, 143,
150, 155, 172, 189, 195, 198, 202,
208, 243
Pornography, 49, 103
Port, Stephen, 168–169
Poser program, for recreating the event of
crime, 229–230
Postmortem (after death events), 75
Postmortem interval (PMI), 84–86
Precipitating events, 146–147
occurring shortly before the homicide or
suicidal act, 36–37
Preliminary investigation for suicides, 24
51% rule for, 84, 105, 135
911 call reporting the incident, 25
antemortem activities of the
victim, 28–32
behavioral actions of the deceased or
others, 27
case study, 31, 33, 34, 35
of circumstances relating to the intent of
the victim to end their life, 36
components of, 26–27
to determine time of death, 75–76
explanation of events, 32
changes in, 33–36

high-risk factors that should be
considered for, 36
indications of deception found within
911 calls, 25
informational or testimonial, 26
physical evidence, 26
of precipitating event, 36–37
problem of mind set and assumptions,
27
scene documentation, 25–26
seven mistakes in, 27
of staged scene, 34
suicide notes, 37
on who would benefit from the
death, 37–38
Premeditated staged scenes, 41–43
Prior police reports, 26
Prior suicide attempts, evidence of, 93
Proof of suicide, 166
Psychache, 148
Psychiatric problems, 103
Psychological autopsy, 152–154, 159
court acceptance of findings of, 156
outlines for, 154–155
performed by mental health
professionals, 157
topics for, 155
value to the investigation, 155–156
Psychological pain, 148
Psychological state, of deceased, 155
Public suicide, 53–54

R

Reactions, to reported suicides, 27–28
Rejection, concept of, 188
Removal of the body, without contaminating
the crime scene, 76–77
Reported deaths
police complacency towards, 59
responding to, 59–64
case study, 60, 61
initial police responses, 61
Responding to a death scene
concept of, 24
with a preconceived idea, 3–4
Rigor mortis, 66, 75, 85, 204, 253, 259
Risk factors, for suicide, 119–120
assessment of, 126

Index

269

S

Sacred suicides, 179–180, 181
Sadomasochism, 103
Scene alterations, 54–56
  case study, 55
Search warrant, filing of, 77–78
Selbstmord (murder of oneself), 11
Self-immolation, public suicide by, 53, 100, 149, 181–182
Self-inflicted stabbings, 97
Self-inflicted suicides, 186
Self-inflict injuries, 33, 42, 66, 84, 86, 88, 100, 124, 186
  concept of, 100
Self-murder, *see* suicide
Self-preservation, notion of, 44
Self-punishment, 18
September 11, 2001 terroristic act, 182–183
Setting oneself on fire, *see* self-immolation, public suicide by
Sex offenses, 50, 104, 107
  victim of, 113
Sexting, 117
Sexual homicides, 28, 50
Shallow stab wounds, 93
Shape of wounds, determination of, 97–98
Sharp force suicide wounds, 93–96
Shneidman, E. S., 148, 153–154, 159
Shoplifting, 115
Sicarii (Jewish rebels), 179
Simple suicides, 142
Sketching, of crime scene, 74
Social media and bystander apathy, towards person attempting suicide, 164–165
Stab wounds, 96
  case study on, 99
  wound orientation in, 98–100
Stack, S., 181
Staged scenes, *see* crime scene staging
Standard of proof, 161–162
Statistical reports, of fatal suicide methods, 82
Stranger offenders, 127
Substance misuse, 162, 154
Suicidal ideation, 116, 120, 159, 161–162
Suicide, 3–4, 6, 8
  accidental death, 20
  actual suicide, 44

case study, 14–15, 32
criminal investigations related to, 14
death due to the use of firearms, 41
defined, 11
and "denial" stage of grief, 15, 17–18
due to
  anger, 18
  bargaining, 18
  depression, 19
emotions and reactions, 17
as a form of political protest, 53
as intentional self-destructive act, 17
investigations of, 11–17
live streaming of, 165–166
methods of, 13
motivational factors for, 11–12, 28
myths associated with, 15
risk factors, 11
routine cases, 14–15, 20, 28
staged to resemble homicides, 150–152, 251–261
stages of grief, 17
and victim's state of mental health, 12
Vince Foster case, 14–15
Suicide by Cop (SbC), 184–185
Suicide notes, 26, 37, 55, 147, 159
  absence of, 160
  accusatory, 164
  authenticity of, 169, 172–175
    forensic linguistic analysis to determine, 172
  authentic *versus* simulated notes, 173
  and equivocal deaths, 168–169
  e-suicide notes, 162
  as evidence during death investigations, 169–172
  evolution of, 166
  explanatory, 163
  factors influencing availability of, 161
  format of, 162–164
  general categories of, 160–162
  importance of, 160
  instructional, 164
  interpretation of, 166–168
  investigative considerations, 175
  left via social media, 164
  purposes of leaving multiple notes, 163
  themes of, 163
  verification of handwriting, 169

270 Index

Superficial incised wounds, 93
Supervisory oversight, lack of, 248–249
Swallowing caustic liquid, death caused
by, 100

T

Teenagers, 113–114
exchange of intimate photos with
strangers, 115
peer pressure, 115
risk factors and antemortem
behaviors, 114
social media/internet use, 116
subjective criteria for, 114–117
suicide attempts, 116
Tentative wounds, 93
Testimonial evidence, 240, 242
Testimonial of witnesses, 26, 240
Text messages, 49, 76, 134, 147, 160, 162,
172, 205
Thích Quảng Đức (Vietnamese Mahayana
Buddhist monk), 53, 181
TikTok, 117, 165
Time of death, determination of, 75–76
case study on, 76, 86
by measuring body's temperature, 85
postmortem interval (PMI), for, 84–86
by studying physiological changes in the
body after death, 85
Toxicological samples, failure to obtain, 238
Toxicology analysis, determination of cause
of death through, 104
Traffic accidents, 200–203
Tunnel vision, 27, 135, 137, 139, 241

U

Undetermined manner of death, 10
Unplanned complex suicide, 142–143
Use of firearms, suicide deaths involving, 41
US national crime statistics, 7

V

Vehicle accidents, 200–203
Verbal and behavioral indicators, of those
contemplating suicide, 30

Victim of a crime, 44, 113, 116, 126
Victimology
and accidental deaths, 221–222
of adolescents, 117–119
assessment, 82, 107–109, 120, 135, 152,
185, 223
centered on the child's caregiver, 108
employment history, 121
factual information, 109–110, 113
failure to conduct, 239
investigative use of, 123
of moderate or medium risk, 127
of physical attributes of the
victim, 123
of risk, 126
subjective criteria, 110–113
case study, 122–123
concept of, 107–109
domestic issues, 125–126
gathering information for, 120–121
high-risk victim, 126–127
importance and necessity of, 107
information concerning the victim's
living conditions, 110, 111
initiation of, 131
investigative uses of, 122–125
low-risk victim, 127–128
motive for self-harm, 126
personality characteristics, 110
and emotional maturity, 112
risk factors, concept of, 119–120
of teenagers, 113–114
Victim profile, formation of, 159
Victim's complaint, validity of, 107–108
Violent crime investigations, 25, 62, 109
first responders' actual duties in, 64–66

W

Witnesses
failure to interview, 240
reports, 80
testimony, 26, 240
Workplace violence, 192
Wound orientation, in stabbing
injuries, 98–100
Written notes, for crime scene
documentation, 74

9781032447735